Winning Alternatives to the Billable Hour

Strategies That Work

Second Edition

James A. Calloway
Mark A. Robertson
EDITORS

Foreword by Robert E. Hirshon,
*President of the
American Bar Association*

formerly
Win-Win Billing Strategies
edited by Richard C. Reed

LAW PRACTICE MANAGEMENT SECTION
FINANCE TECHNOLOGY MANAGEMENT MARKETING

Defending Liberty
Pursuing Justice

Commitment to Quality: The Law Practice Management Section is committed to quality in our publications. Our authors are experienced practitioners in their fields. Prior to publication, the contents of all our books are rigorously reviewed by experts to ensure the highest quality product and presentation. Because we are committed to serving our readers' needs, we welcome your feedback on how we can improve future editions of this book. We invite you to fill out and return the comment card at the back of this book.

Cover design by Jim Colao.

Form Fee Agreement reprinted with permission from Holland & Hart.
Fixed Fee for First-Year Services to Emerging Businesses exhibit reprinted with permission from Davis Wright Tremaine.
Form Fee Agreement for Estate Planning Representation reprinted with permission from Neal A. Kennedy.
Sample Fee Proposal for Real Estate Development reprinted with permission from Quarles & Brady, LLP.

Nothing contained in this book is to be considered as the rendering of legal advice for specific cases, and readers are responsible for obtaining such advice from their own legal counsel. This book and any forms and agreements herein are intended for educational and informational purposes only.

The products and services mentioned in this publication are under or may be under trademark or service mark protection. Product and service names and terms are used throughout only in an editorial fashion, to the benefit of the product manufacturer or service provider, with no intention of infringement. Use of a product or service name or term in this publication should not be regarded as affecting the validity of any trademark or service mark.

The Law Practice Management Section, American Bar Association, offers an educational program for lawyers in practice. Books and other materials are published in furtherance of that program. Authors and editors of publications may express their own legal interpretations and opinions, which are not necessarily those of either the American Bar Association or the Law Practice Management Section unless adopted pursuant to the bylaws of the Association. The opinions expressed do not reflect in any way a position of the Section or the American Bar Association.

© 2002 American Bar Association. All rights reserved.
Printed in the United States of America.

06 05 04 03 02   5 4 3 2 1

Library of Congress Cataloging-in-Publication Data

Winning alternatives to the billable hour : strategies that work / James A. Calloway, Mark A. Robertson, editors.— 2nd ed.
    p. cm.
    Rev. ed. of: Win-win billing strategies. c1992.
    Includes index.
    ISBN 1-59031-117-5
    1. Lawyers—Fees—United States. 2. Lawyers—United States—Accounting I. Calloway, James A. II. Robertson, Mark A. III. Win-win billing strategies.
    KF316 .W52 2002
    340'.068'1—dc21   2002011977

Discounts are available for books ordered in bulk. Special consideration is given to state bars, CLE programs, and other bar-related organizations. Inquire at Book Publishing, American Bar Association, 750 N. Lake Shore Drive, Chicago, Illinois 60611.

Contents

Foreword by the President of the ABA vii

Preamble ix

Acknowledgments xi

Introduction xiii

Chapter 1: The Search for the Meaning of Value 1
    Lawyers and Clients: Perception Is Reality 1
    Client Perceptions of Value 2
    What Is Value? 3
    Conclusion 5

Chapter 2: The Changing Legal Profession 7
    Technology Within the Law Office 8
    Clients' Understandings and Beliefs About Technology 9
    Consumer Attitudes in General 11
    The Only Constant Is Change 12
    Demographics 13
    Profit Squeeze and Income Compression 14
    The Legal Market as a Maturing Marketplace 15
    The Future of the Profession 20
    Impact of These Trends 21

Chapter 3: Ethical Rules and Practices 23
    The Basic Rule 23
    The Golden Rule 25
    Gray Areas 26

Chapter 4: Pricing Legal Services 31
    Historical Influences on Pricing Legal Services 31
    The Value Curve 37
    Hourly Billing Is Cost-Driven 50
    Variations of Hourly Rates 51

Chapter 5: Pricing Legal Services for the Solo and Small-Firm Lawyer 55
    The Value Curve 56
    Market Factors for the Main Street Lawyer 61
    Dealing with Unsophisticated Clients 61
    Pricing Structure as the Basis of an Office System 64
    I Cannot Do It at That Rate and Make Any Money 65
    Conclusion 66

Chapter 6: Foundations on Which to Build a Billing Method 67
    Self-Assessment Checklist 67
    Determining Cost 70
    Retrospective Analysis of Cost as a Guide 70
    Cost of Service Versus Value to the Client 71
    Knowing Costs Through Detailed Cost Accounting......................... 72
    Exercise in Cost Accounting... 75
    Determining Cost to Produce a Package of Services 77
    Task-Based Analysis 78
    Examining Closed Files to Create Minisystems or Predict Fees...... 80
    Recurring Variables or Uncertainties 81
    Examining Profitability as It Relates to Billing 82
    Conclusion 83

Chapter 7: Billing as Part of the Communication Process 85
    The Role of Effective Communication in the Billing Process.......... 85
    Elements of the Communication Process 87
    Know What You Want to Communicate 91
    A Model for Delivery of Legal Services 95
    Satisfaction and Price 99
    How to Prepare and Price Your Service Package 101
    A Few More Words on Communicating Value............................... 103
    Conclusion 103

Chapter 8: Technology and Billing 105
    Technology and the Billing and Collection Process 105
    Technology in Fee-Setting and Budgets 112
    Substantive Systems and Document Assembly 113
    Knowledge Management Tools 115
    Transaction Fees: Sharing the Costs (and Benefits) of Technology 116
    Collaborative Technologies 116
    Conclusion 117

Chapter 9: Developing the Case Plan or Transaction Plan 119
    Why Should I Bother with a Plan?.. 119
    Elements of the Case/Transaction Plan 121

Preparing in Advance 122
Setting Client Goals and Expectations 122
Determining Billing Methods 124

Chapter 10: Alternative Methods of Billing 125
Fixed or Flat Fee 125
Contingent Fee 127
Hourly Rate 128
Blended Hourly Rate 130
Fixed or Flat Fee Plus Hourly Rate 132
Hourly Rate Plus a Contingency 133
Percentage Fee 135
Task-Based Fee 136
Retrospective Fee Based Upon Value 137
Unit Fee 139
Relative-Value Method 140
Lodestar Method 141
Statutory or Other Scheduled Fee System 142
Availability-Only Retainer 143
Retainer as a Deposit Against Future Services 145

Chapter 11: Implementing Value-Based Billing 147
Value Billing and Profitability 148
Strategies for Profitable Value Billing 149
Position on the Value Curve 151
Change: How to Bring It About 153
Case Study: Could This Happen in Your Office? 155
Arguments in Favor of Changing Billing Methods 156
Impediments to Change 161
Concerns of Corporate Counsel 162
Conclusion 164

Chapter 12: Legal Representation Agreements 165
Matters to Address in All Legal Representation Agreements 165
Caveat 168

Chapter 13: Evaluating Results of the Use of Alternative Billing Methods 169
Review of Closed Files 169
Client Audits 170
Performance Evaluation 172
Profitability Analysis 172
Quality of Life and Quality of Work Product 172
Conclusion 174

Appendix: Fee Letters, Agreements, and Other Resources 175

Index 275

About the Editors 285

About the Diskette 287

Foreword

Fundamentally, this book is about relationships. It is about the relationships between lawyers and clients, which is without question the most important social contract of our profession.

Although there are many nuances to the lawyer-client relationship, the *economic* component is especially significant. How fee-for-service is constructed and executed can either help or hinder the overall health and vitality of the lawyer-client bond. As it does in most of life, money complicates. Whether this is a healthy complication or an unhealthy one depends in large part on the predefined structure in which money is tallied and collected.

This book will explore various constructions of this economic relationship. But before we begin, it may be helpful to first speak to the principles that we hope underpin a billing mechanism. That is, if we could create the perfect billing method, how would we describe it?

First of all, the perfect billing approach would *reward* lawyers for due diligence, talent, creativity, experience, efficient processes, and technological aptitude. The system would give lawyers and firms real incentives to develop a deep and strategic understanding of a client's long-term needs, to consider cost/benefit ratios of the client, and to have an overriding focus on the *quality* of the work. A perfect billing system would pay close attention to the *value* and *results* of the services rendered.

The perfect billing mechanism would *penalize* other behaviors, such as "busy work." It would discourage inefficiency, redundancy (i.e., re-creating the wheel), and technological apathy. It would care less about time spent and more about work product produced.

Keep these ideals in mind as you read this book and use them to judge each system. In practice, of course, no billing strategy is perfect, but the alternatives detailed in this book do a better job in serving the above ideals than does the prevailing system of today's legal marketplace. The billable hour, such as it is, encourages too many of the wrong principles and suppresses too many of the right ones.

It has been said that the billable hour is the "third rail" of the American legal profession—the issue that many consider to be "too hot to handle." But the ABA Law Practice Management Section has been undeterred and has been a national leader in the promotion and education of alternative billing strategies since the mid-1980s. They deserve our applause and gratitude because concerns about work-life balance, the disillusionment of lawyers, and the distrust of their clients will only increase if we do not figure out a better system to judge and bill for our work.

Thank you for taking the first step.

Robert E. Hirshon
President
American Bar Association
August 2002

Preamble

With apologies to Stephen Hawking, this preamble could be described as "A Brief History of Time." Going back to the nineteenth century, Abraham Lincoln is reported to have said, "A lawyer's time is his stock in trade," meaning that legal work involves selling the time of lawyers to consumers. This theme was reiterated by twentieth-century writers on law office management, including Dwight McCarthy (1927), Reginald Heber Smith (1942), and Lewis Powell (1969), before his appointment to the Supreme Court. In a series of "Salvation for the Solo Practitioner" programs in the mid-1970s, J. Harris Morgan reminded lawyers of the importance of timekeeping to law firm profitability.

With the advent of personal computers and timekeeping and billing software, it was possible for lawyers to keep records of time spent on a client matter, and translate these records into a bill based on the number of hours invested in the matter. It is not that lawyers could not keep time records or create hourly bills before computers, it is rather that technology put hourly billing into the hands of all lawyers. Hourly billing created the illusion that the hours a lawyer spent on a case multiplied by an accepted hourly rate would produce a bill for the services that equated with the value of the services in the eyes of the client.

Ironically, as hourly billing was gaining acceptance in many areas of law practice, it was drawing criticism from both commentators and clients. These critics questioned the merit of charges for services arrived at by multiplying hours times rate and the value of services to consumers. In the late 1980s, a task force of the ABA Law Practice Management Section investigated both the trends in hourly billing and the increasing calls for alternative approaches to billing.

In 1989, the Task Force on Alternative Billing Methods produced the first book in what was to become a billing trilogy. *Beyond the Billable Hour: An Anthology of Alternative Billing Methods* was a collection of thought-provoking articles on a variety of aspects of billing, including criticism of hourly billing systems. The immense popularity of *Beyond the Billable Hour* demonstrated that its message resonated with both lawyers and clients, and led to a second book in 1992, *Win-Win Billing Strategies: Alternatives That Satisfy Your Clients and You*. Where its predecessor had asked questions, *Win-Win* offered answers, by describing alternatives to hourly billing that lawyers could use in their offices. Like *Beyond the Billable Hour*, *Win-Win* proved to be extremely popular.

Both books were edited by Task Force Chair Richard C. Reed, of Seattle, Washington, a former chair of the Law Practice Management Section. In the years following *Win-Win*, Reed collected anecdotal reports from law firms that were experimenting with alternative billing strategies, some of them taken from the pages of the two books and others merely inspired by them. In 1996, these collected "tales from the front" emerged as the final book in the trilogy, *Billing Innovations: New Win-Win Ways to End Hourly Billing*.

It is now 2002, six years after the last billing book. Law firms continue to experiment with alternative billing methods, but hourly billing has shown great resilience, client lamentations notwithstanding. In 2001, ABA President Robert Hirshon, citing a number of deleterious effects caused by hourly billing, including pressure on lawyers to work longer hours, created the ABA Commission on Billable Hours to look at the question of hourly billing anew. Still committed to reform of billing practices, the Law Practice Management Section heeded President Hirshon's call to address billing issues by beginning work on an updated book on the subject.

Mark Robertson and Jim Calloway undertook the role that Dick Reed had performed for many years, to serve as both intellectual and editorial leaders of the billing project. Robertson and Calloway recognized that they could not simply produce (like a movie sequel) *Even More Win-Win Billing Strategies*. They needed to assemble a book that provides real answers to lawyers practicing in the twenty-first century.

Certainly, the legal profession has changed since the early 1990s, and by all accounts it will continue to change in the decades ahead. Lawyers dwell in a marketplace that is more competitive than ever, and the competitors are not just other lawyers. Technology has evolved by light years since the publication of the last billing book. Clients have become even more demanding and questioning about the professional services they receive. Lawyers, in order to survive in today's practice environment and thrive in the future, must be able to deliver their services efficiently, generate a reasonable profit for their work, and convey a sense of the value of their services to clients.

As you read the pages of this book, try to reflect on the long history of time and billing in the legal profession, from Lincoln to the present day. Think about how billing practices have evolved over time, as well as what billing principles are immutable. Look at your own practice to consider how you can better communicate value to your clients not only through the quality of your work, but also through the nexus between the work itself and your charges for it. Listen to the advice offered in these pages, which incorporates not only the lessons of history, but also new and creative ideas that look to the future. Above all, do not be afraid to implement these ideas in your practice, for both you and your clients.

Gary A. Munneke
Professor of Law
Pace University School of Law
White Plains, New York
Past Chair, ABA Law Practice Management Section
    and LPM Publishing

Acknowledgments

Sir Isaac Newton stated about the process of the scientific discovery, "If I have seen further, it is by standing on the shoulders of giants."

That observation is well applied to the book you hold in your hands. Leaders and forward-thinkers of the ABA Law Practice Management Section recognized long before many others the illogical and contradictory nature of attorney billing based solely on an hourly basis. This book is another link in the chain of a series of works on this topic.

The creation of the Task Force on Alternative Billing Methods by the ABA Law Practice Management Section in 1987 ultimately resulted in three prior publications on this subject: *Beyond the Billable Hour: An Anthology of Alternative Billing Methods*, published in 1989; *Win-Win Billing Strategies: Alternatives That Satisfy Your Clients and You*, published in 1992; and *Billing Innovations: New Win-Win Ways to End Hourly Billing*, published in 1996. To all of the many individuals who contributed, we owe a great deal of thanks—none more than Richard C. Reed, chair of the task force, who contributed greatly to all three publications as editor and author. Dick Reed has built the foundation upon which everything written in this book rests. A very special thanks and acknowledgment to the other contributors of *Win-Win Billing Strategies*:

Robert J. Arndt	Demetrios (Jim) Dimitriou
Luther S. Avery	Randall A. Hove
Ward C. Bower	Jon Klemens
Ezra Tom Clark, Jr.	James W. McRae
William C. Cobb	Peter D. Zeughauser
Milton W. Zwicker	

We greatly appreciate the prior work and assistance of these individuals.

This book, *Winning Alternatives to the Billable Hour*, also builds on the prior work of many others. Numerous members of the ABA Law Practice Management Section contributed their time, their wisdom, and examples of their agreements and office forms to this work and prior works on this subject. A special thanks goes to Beverly Loder, Director of LPM Publishing; Reid Trautz of the District of Columbia Bar Association, who served as the volunteer project manager; and to Tim Johnson, LPM Publishing Book Production Manager. People who have not been through the publishing process cannot imagine the ups and downs, roadblocks, problems, and new issues that crop up. Bev, Reid, and Tim served as unpaid therapists and counselors, coaches, cheerleaders, copy editors, and (where warranted) strong motivators throughout this process, and for that we truly thank them.

No comprehensive treatment of any aspect of the attorney billing process could fail to acknowledge J. Harris Morgan and his book, *How to Draft Bills Clients Rush to Pay*, published by the ABA Law Practice Management Section. His observations about billing and its importance as a critical communication in furtherance of the attorney-client relationship instead of merely a mechanical, mathematical task are still instructive for all of us today.

Finally, Mark Robertson would like to gratefully acknowledge and thank his wife, Susan, and sons, Matthew and David, for their support and understanding, allowing him to work on this book even during what should have been "their" time. Jim Calloway would like to thank his wife, Terri, for proofreading as well as tolerance, and his 6-year-old son, Tanner, who thinks he contributed greatly to this book, since all the work was done at home and he heard far too many times, "No, Daddy is working on his book."

Introduction

"A gunfighter doesn't charge by the bullet."
—Poster in well-known criminal defense lawyer's office

This book examines alternative billing methods for lawyers—whether practicing in large or small firms, or as solo practitioners. The "alternative" label is telling. We are discussing an alternative to what? Well, hourly billing by lawyers, of course. That very label suggests we are considering an exception to the rule. Is hourly billing truly "the rule"? If so, why?

As most of you know, many legal services provided by lawyers are not billed on an hourly basis at all. Many cases are handled on a contingency-fee basis. These often include plaintiffs' personal injury claims, workers' compensation claims, and collection cases. Many other cases are handled on a percentage-fee basis. Examples include probate cases, corporate mergers, initial public offerings of stock, and professional service contracts for athletes, authors, and entertainers. Many consumer matters—such as uncontested bankruptcies, real estate closings, drafting of simple wills, and the like—are handled on a flat-fee basis.

So why is hourly billing considered the norm while all these other forms of determining lawyers' fees are "alternative"?

Is it because lawyers have always done it that way? No, hourly billing is a relatively recent method of determining fees. One doesn't picture Abraham Lincoln filling out time sheets and filing them next to his *Blackstone's Commentaries*, nor does one imagine, in the precomputer and precalculator days, a lawyer meticulously recording time by tenths of an hour to calculate the amount to bill for services.

Is it because hourly billing is popular among clients? Well, that is certainly not true for most individual consumers. Imagine that your local bakery or appliance store set prices in the same way lawyers often set legal fees: "Well, the price for this loaf of bread really depends upon a lot of factors—how much our supplier decides to charge for flour, how much time it takes to ship it here, and how long it takes me to prepare and bake a loaf; also, certain government officials can change the price by their rulings. But if you will agree to pay, then we will deliver you a loaf of bread and tell you the price when we are finished." Imagine that type of pricing system for an airline ticket!

Hourly fees became popular because they are easily determined—they are clear, unambiguous, and perceived by many to be objective and definite. Technology and accounting systems made it possible to track time and easily multiply the time by a rate to arrive at a fee.

Before hourly billing took hold, one can imagine some insurance company or corporate executive examining bills for legal services and questioning why one matter cost twice as much as another matter when the matters were exactly the same. The response would have been that one took a lot more time than the other, and the rejoinder would have been that there should be time records to review. After all, the business paid most of its employees by the hour; so the concept of objective and unambiguous hourly billing made sense. Also, once there were more than a few lawyers in the firm, the firm needed some measurement of productivity. So, in one fell swoop, hourly billing met both the needs of business clients for some objective measurement of the cost of their legal services, and the needs of law firms to manage and quantify lawyer production and value.

Frankly, hourly billing has worked very well for many years, and its use will continue in many situations. Business clients have become acclimated to receiving these types of bills. In many consumer cases, there is a certain fairness in the method. The divorce client who insists on calling his or her lawyer every few days (or nights) is appropriately charged more than a less time-consuming client.

Advances in technology clearly change the status quo. From the first IBM typewriter with memory to the latest computer network, the modern tools of the trade allow law offices to track time and produce documents more quickly and easily. Also, the time involved for other tasks is reduced. When a law firm reduces the time required to produce documents and complete tasks, and yet adheres to an hourly billing method, the result is a drop in the fees charged for a particular task. This is by now no surprise to the lawyers reading this book.

The question that must be asked is whether the value of legal services has decreased just because the methods of production have improved. Is a "Last Will and Testament" that bore a value of $350 in the marketplace now reduced in value because the lawyer invested effort, energy, and expense in creating a document-drafting system that substantially reduces the preparation time for this important document? We believe that the value of the will to the consumer is based upon the lawyer's analysis of the client's circumstances and the resulting quality and appropriateness of the document, not upon the mechanics of the document's creation.

In fact, the actual time a lawyer contributes to a task can be almost meaningless in relation to the value of the product. A narrow and specialized medical malpractice case might require dozens of hours of research, consultation with experts, and careful drafting just to prepare interrogatories. After the lawyer has prepared and tried four or five of these types of cases, preparation of the interrogatories may take only an hour or two, as the lawyer can customize the prior work product according to the specific facts of a case. Due to the increased experience of the lawyer, however, would anyone doubt that the interrogatories in the fifth case were superior to those propounded in the first case, even though they took less time to draft?

Experience improves a lawyer's work product and abilities. As experience allows a lawyer to perform tasks more efficiently and quickly, the traditional response has been to raise the lawyer's hourly billing rate, with the result that associates charge one rate, and junior and senior partners another. Yet, as many lawyers have come to realize, upward hourly rate adjustments are not always possible. Experience may not always be rewarded with higher rates. If the medical malpractice lawyer in the previous paragraph charged $1,800 for preparation of the first interrogatories (12 hours at $150 per hour), can he raise his hourly rate to $900 per hour for the two hours it took him to do the interrogatories in the fifth case?

Technology allows for the easy re-use of a lawyer's prior work product, whether through forms or document assembly systems. Technology also allows for faster and more efficient performance of tasks. Should technology be used only to reduce the fees charged to clients based upon the reduced time required to perform a task, or should the benefit of these efficiencies be shared between the lawyer and client?

If the implementation of technology means only that lawyers receive less compensation because they invest less time on tasks, then a logical conclusion would be to avoid improving practices through the use of technology. We all know that proper implementation of technology also improves work product, eliminating typographical errors and freeing trained staff from mind-numbing repetitive work to concentrate on more important tasks. But should this be done if it penalizes lawyers whose fees are determined only by the hours spent on tasks?

Clients expect their lawyers to use the best and latest practice methods. They have a right to expect it. Systems developed to save time and resources, along with proper use of technology, save money for law firms and clients alike. Compare the cost and efficiency of using a fax machine to send a document across the country or around the globe with using the mail or a courier service. Now compare the cost of sending an e-mail attachment of that same document with sending a long-distance fax.

So, we should use technology to deliver the best possible products to our clients, but at what cost to our livelihoods? The paradox: the focus of most technology in law practice is to decrease the time it takes to accomplish a task; but the more productive you become using technology, the less income you make if you bill only by the hour! The value of the legal services to clients has not changed (or if it has, it has gone up, because the service is more immediate), so why should the charge for such legal services be less?

It seems that the benefits of technology and systems designed to work more efficiently should accrue to both clients and lawyers—especially when the lawyers must invest money, effort, and time into harnessing technology and establishing systems.

Many forces inhibit the implementation of alternative billing practices, from both clients' and lawyers' points of view. In fact, the adoption of many of these practices has been much slower than predicted by many who were examining the concepts more than a decade ago. But there can be no doubt that these changes are coming. Insurance companies in particular have been initiating new fee-setting arrangements with their counsel that would have been improbable a decade ago. It is also noteworthy that many consider insurance defense practice less lucrative than it was some years ago. How many of those lawyers would have been better prepared to deal with proposals of new fee arrangements if they had an understanding of the concepts contained in this book?

Reading this book may not change your law practice or your billing practices overnight. But challenges to "hourly only" billing practices will continue. Maybe the challenge will occur in the form of your best client proposing a restructuring of the fee arrangement. Do you now have the tools in hand to analyze all the implications of such a proposal? Maybe the challenge will occur when a new lawyer fresh out of law school opens a practice down the street from you, charging an extremely low price for certain routine legal work that you now perform. You may believe it is impossible to handle such matters competently at such a rate, while the new lawyer views these services as only filling in a few blanks in a form and printing the document. Maybe the challenge will occur when a judge or agency limits the fees that can be charged for a certain service.

No one should have a better understanding of how much it costs to produce services than the lawyer who depends on billing for those services to make his or her livelihood. It is imperative that the lawyer be prepared to cope with future challenges, whether from those outside the law firm or from systemic changes in the manner that legal services are provided. The purpose of this book is to inform, stimulate thinking, and provide tools for the lawyer to deal with the inevitable challenges and future business decisions that will occur in this area.

Hourly billing is not an inherently evil practice. In fact, certain types of tasks—such as those that are time-intensive and outside the control of the law firm—are still best billed on an hourly basis. But economic pressures and challenges will continue to build. Is a complaint filed in court devalued because a firm's expertise and technology allow assembly of the complaint in a shortened time frame? Are raising billing rates and/or hiring more associates a law firm's only paths to increased profitability? We think not.

Whether you call it alternative billing, value billing, fixed-fee billing, or task-based billing, the time has come to examine how to charge fairly for legal services, so the outcome can be "win-win" for everyone.

This book is designed to be used by all lawyers—whether practicing in large or small firms, or as solo practitioners. Reading the book sequentially will provide a solid foundation for understanding the subject of alternative billing.

The first five chapters provide the theoretical underpinnings of law firm billing and client value, with examples and practical tools and tips thrown in for good measure. Chapters 6 through 9 offer the framework for implementing alternative billing methods, with specific tools for implementation covered in Chapters 11 and 12. A list of alternative billing methods is found in Chapter 10. The final chapter covers evaluating the systems that have been developed and making adjustments. The Appendix has useful examples and forms from lawyers who have implemented alternative billing methods.

If you are a solo practitioner or small firm lawyer, your needs may be a bit different. Your clientele may differ and you clearly do not have to deal with as many other lawyers internally, such as associates and practice group heads. We suggest the following road map for you to study these concepts. Read the first three chapters for the basic thoughts and understanding. Then read the first eleven pages of Chapter 4, "Pricing Legal Services," to understand the basics of the Cobb Value Curve. Then move to Chapter 5, "Pricing Legal Services for the Solo and Small Firm Lawyer." From there you will want to read Chapter 7, "Billing as a Part of the Communications Process," and Chapter 8, "Technology and Billing." You then may want to read Chapter 11, "Implementing Value-Based Billing," and Chapter 12, "Legal Representation Agreements," before determining what other chapters you may wish to peruse. The remaining chapters and the Appendix do have very useful and important information.

CHAPTER ONE

The Search for the Meaning of Value

Value is an elusive quality, but discussing billing methods is impossible without considering the "value" received by the client. This book is intended to be practical. But implementation of the concepts espoused depends upon a number of individual factors and considerations. In making these decisions in your law practice, some familiarity with the underlying theoretical and conceptual issues is required.

In *Marketing Warfare*, Al Ries and Jack Trout assert, "There are no facts in a human mind. There are only perceptions. The perception is the reality." From a client's standpoint, the value of legal services is the client's perception that there has been a benefit. Value may be a positive, in the sense of acquiring a desired result, but it may also be a negative, in the sense of avoiding a detriment or risk, such as in the successful defense of a civil or criminal case. When the price of the services reflects the client's perception of value, the client will be satisfied.

LAWYERS AND CLIENTS: PERCEPTION IS REALITY

One of the keys to understanding value is recognizing that lawyers' and clients' perceptions and points of view frequently differ. Lawyers are trained to make calculations on probable outcomes and risks. They may not consciously calculate the odds in a mathematical fashion for all client matters, and they may resist reducing complex situations to stated probabilities or percentages. But, in many situations, clients and lawyers can communicate only in terms of possibilities when trying to make appropriate decisions.

Lawyers frequently deal with dozens of these judgments every day and in every matter. Will the jury believe a certain witness? Will the judge view the case as analogous to precedent A or precedent B? Will the taxing authorities oppose or accept a certain proposed tax treatment? What amount of damages would a jury award for a certain injury in a certain region of the country? What sentence would the judge impose for a certain offense? What type of zoning change serves the client's proposed use and is also most likely to be approved by the authorities? Will a certain document be admitted into evidence or excluded? (As an aside, we note that wrestling with these matters contributes to the reason why so many cases settle. The attractiveness of an agreed-upon settlement—with its absolutely certain outcome—increases as risks and benefits are analyzed.)

If a lawyer is pinned down and forced to assess the odds of winning or losing a matter, the client and lawyer may view those odds very differently. For example, if the lawyer says there is a 60 percent chance of success, the client may perceive and relate this as, "Our lawyer said we will probably win." The lawyer, on the other hand, views this as a toss-up, with only a slight advantage to the client. Stating that the odds are 90 to 10 in a client's favor usually leaves the client with the idea that victory is assured, while the lawyer understands that if ten of these cases with these exact facts are tried, one will be lost.

A lawyer may therefore counsel that paying $100,000 to settle a 1-in-10 chance of losing $1 million is a rational decision, especially considering the attorneys' fees that will be incurred on the way to the court date. The client may be aghast at the prospect of paying $100,000 to settle a sure winner, especially when the attorneys' fees already incurred are considered.

The possibility of a "disconnect" between the lawyer's perception and the client's perception is a critical concern in all aspects of the attorney-client relationship, including setting fees and billing.

CLIENT PERCEPTIONS OF VALUE

Clients perceive value in a variety of ways. When spending money adds to the value of what a person has, the dollar outlay is an investment, not an expense. For example, a developer-client may invest in raw land, hoping to have it rezoned as a residential subdivision. The developer pays for planning and engineering services to lay out the tract, for a lawyer whose expertise results in appropriate rezoning, and for streets and utilities to be installed. Each of these investments adds value to the developer's land. They are clear and, in a sense, tangible.

Individuals would prefer to achieve a result or to conserve existing assets. Businesses would prefer to invest capital in assets upon which there will be a return. Thus, both individuals and businesses would prefer not to pay legal expenses unless there is a benefit. For example, an individual client may wish to have an estate plan that will provide for family needs with minimum tax impacts, or a business client may want to collect a past-due account. When the client's objectives are reached, value has been achieved.

But perceptions are affected by many factors. A client's prejudices, experiences, cultural background, social and economic status, religious background, or education may affect the client's perception of a legal matter. A client sued for divorce who does not want the divorce may not fully appreciate the valuable advice and counsel of the lawyer. The same is true for a businessperson who is sued over a course of conduct that he or she deems proper.

WHAT IS VALUE?

Lawyers tend to take for granted the many ways they bring value to their clients and the transactions in which they are involved. After a transaction becomes somewhat routine, a lawyer may underestimate the experience—and therefore the value—he or she brings to bear on a legal need.

The following examples relating to how clients perceive value, while not exhaustive, should stimulate the lawyer's thinking and provide a reference source for the future if the lawyer is challenged regarding his or her value.

- Avoiding exposure to risk (or possible ruin), such as losing all assets or going to jail, is value. Thus, lawyers can provide value in the form of enabling a successful corporate reorganization or a not-guilty verdict in a criminal case.
- Sometimes a brilliant idea or insight can produce great value, even though it occurs in a small amount of time. A simple solution to a complex and seemingly unsolvable problem occasionally results from restructuring the problem posed, a burst of brilliance, or the deep experience of the counseling lawyer.
- The ongoing process of supporting a client's needs can represent value. Routine handling of a client's ongoing needs in a complex society gives the client peace of mind and frees the client to pursue other ends, whether personal or financial. Representation by a strong, competent, loyal, well-established, and highly regarded lawyer can bring stability and credibility to the client's life.
- Wisdom is an elusive concept. But maturity of judgment, a steady hand, and a restraint on impulsive actions clearly represent immense

value. The lawyer's ability to persuade against unsound courses of action, or in favor of taking preventive action, may be of great benefit to the client.

- The lawyer's acceptance of responsibility can produce value. In high-risk transactions, having a competent lawyer act with knowledge of the risks involved and with a willingness to put his or her reputation on the line may in itself constitute value.
- The ability to communicate can be a source of value when used to help clients understand what is occurring or what is planned. To many clients, legal matters are a mystery. The lawyer's ability to speak in terms that clients can understand helps dispel the mystery.
- Timely performance is value. Clients have time schedules and appreciate services that are timely. Providing prompt service demonstrates that the lawyer gives priority to the client.
- High-level, specialized expertise and skill create value. Some matters require unique skills and experience. In those situations, clients will seek lawyers who provide highly valued specialized services.
- Exclusivity or unavailability to others can be value. The traditional retainer to ensure availability shows that clients recognize the importance of having a lawyer or law firm available in the event they need legal services. The lawyer can serve as the client's anchor when the need for legal services arises, even if those needs arise only occasionally. Long-standing relationships are usually the foundation for successful law practice.
- A timely follow-up to see that there are no "loose ends" can be an important source of value. Most clients want the transaction completed and the matter terminated, and they become restive when most, but not all, of the necessary steps are taken.
- A straightforward approach can be an appreciated value. Lawyers provide value when they do only what is needed. This may include advising a client that nothing need be done, telling the client how to proceed without the involvement or expense of the lawyer, or finding a simple solution. Simple solutions are, by their very nature, often underrated and undervalued. But providing a reasonably acceptable solution, even though deluxe alternatives might be available, is a true mark of professionalism and value when the client needs only a reasonably acceptable product.
- Guaranteeing satisfaction is certainly value. Clients stick with a lawyer when they know that lawyer will "make it right" in terms of what is done or what is charged.

Dependability, integrity, evenness of performance, reliability of product, personal and professional stability, and many other factors constitute value. A lawyer should never underestimate his or her value, whether as a recent entrant in the legal marketplace or as a seasoned veteran.

CONCLUSION

All the benefits named in this chapter, when viewed from the standpoint of the client's perceptions, are elements of value that create the basis for determining what the client will be willing to pay. As we shall see, two other factors affect value and the client's perception of value. The first is supply and demand. The second is communication—the ability of the lawyer and client to understand each other throughout their relationship. The lawyer must understand the client's problems and needs and take appropriate actions; but in today's marketplace, it is not enough to merely provide value. It is incumbent upon the successful lawyer to deliver value, to communicate to the client the value that has been delivered, and to endeavor to ensure that the client's perception of the value received is in line with the perception of the lawyer.

CHAPTER TWO

The Changing Legal Profession

In the rapidly changing world of law practice, the rate of change continues to accelerate. In fact, the world of law practice has undoubtedly changed since this book was written. The past two decades have seen remarkable and significant changes in the legal profession. There have also been many changes in attitudes about the law and lawyers in society. The key is to adapt to change and to create change in the way law is practiced and law firms are managed. These changes have an effect on how lawyers bill for their services.

Coping with change is now a constant circumstance for the lawyer. Change is a frightening process, perhaps doubly so for the legal profession, which relies upon tradition and adherence to precedents. The rearview mirror has seemed a comfortable way to view our world. Many of us are uncomfortable with the changes we are witnessing and experiencing in our practices and with the profession as a whole.

But we must fearlessly discuss and examine these changes if we are going to be equipped to deal with them. We will all cope with changes outside our control. But we should also be alert for opportunities to shape our own future and to direct positive change for our own benefit. Many of the changes discussed in the latter parts of this chapter are only indirectly related to alternative billing. But if implementing alternative billing was as simple as announcing that henceforth flat fees will be charged instead of hourly fees, it would have already been broadly implemented and you, the reader, would not have bothered to pick up an entire book on the subject.

The economy is changing, becoming more global and less inefficient. Whole sectors and industries diminish, while an explosion of new services and ideas occurs. The wise lawyer will still want to draw on as many sources as possible for information. The recent history of changes in the legal profession is therefore a productive ground for study and reflection.

TECHNOLOGY WITHIN THE LAW OFFICE

No one can ignore the fact that law office technology has greatly changed the practice of law within the last two decades. Fax machines, computers on lawyers' desks, automated document-drafting procedures, computerized legal research, handheld computers, Internet access, and dozens of other changes have affected both the way lawyers work and the nature of legal work within substantive practice areas. For a simple example, consider whether limits on the number of interrogatories allowed in litigation would have become necessary if lawyers still operated in an environment where it was necessary to engage a lawyer to draft—and pay a legal secretary to type—each individual question. Now, with some advance planning, a few quick keystrokes can yield hundreds of "canned" interrogatories.

Law office technology has revolutionized the practice of law, and, as with most revolutions, there has been some degree of bloodshed. The implementation of technology within law offices is perhaps the greatest present force for change that affects lawyers' business operations and opportunities for alternative billing methods.

Lawyers have long used checklists, forms, brief banks, and other methods of reusing work products while enhancing and developing improved documents. It is probably fair to say that at present, no law office can function reasonably without computers, for both word processing and reuse of prior work products. By developing smart systems to expedite document production, lawyers reduce costs of production. This can yield benefits for law firms or clients or both.

But, as every lawyer holding this book has no doubt already determined, if the only method of charging clients for legal work is the hourly rate, then every advance in saving lawyer time brings a corresponding decrease in lawyer income. If the sole method of law firm compensation is based on lawyers billing by the hour, and technology continues to reduce the time required by lawyers to do the same work, the result has to be less income. This has been referenced by some commentators as the "productivity paradox."

In a traditional law firm structure with hourly billing practices, where an experienced partner can do a certain task in far less time than a new associate, a "balance" in income has been achieved by the partner having a higher hourly billing rate. But as technological sophistication increases, it is unlikely that one can raise the billing rate high enough to cover future contingencies. One can easily foresee a future where law firms must invest huge amounts of time and money into certain processes, with the end result being that the actual tasks take only seconds. For example, it is no longer science fiction to envision a future where the lawyer first says to her computer, "Start with will form 6, insert Mr. Toffler's personal data, incorporate special tax treatments using variables red and green, and show it being executed here today instead of in his home state," and then reaches for the completed documents as they instantly appear.

Sophisticated clients expect their law firms to have modern office technology. It is difficult to imagine these clients giving their business to firms that do not have fax and e-mail capabilities, Internet access, and the ability to deliver, receive, and handle digital documents. Staying current with the latest in law office technology costs money. Training staff to use the latest technology costs money. Compensating well-trained staff so they stay with the firm costs money. Adding and training new staff costs money. Computers, Internet access, Web pages, virtual private networks, and legal-specific software all cost money. Paying for necessary technology can be challenging if the lawyer bills only by the hour.

There is a very positive side to implementing law office technology improvements. These tools can free lawyers and their staffs from many mundane, repetitive tasks. Efficiency can be increased. Given the complexity of the law today and the length of many legal documents, having technology to assist with document preparation and other tasks is an absolute necessity. E-mail saves time and money for law firms as well as clients.

Another positive aspect of technology is the potential superior service that can be rendered to clients. For example, not only can digital legal research be done more quickly than the traditional method of reviewing books in a library, but it can also be done more extensively. A couple of hours of traditional book research might have allowed a lawyer to read a dozen recent opinions and a few more oft-cited landmark opinions. A skilled digital researcher can easily examine many more cases, and online publishing increases the likelihood that more obscure sources of law can be obtained.

CLIENTS' UNDERSTANDINGS AND BELIEFS ABOUT TECHNOLOGY

The prevalence of technology in society affects the ideas and attitudes of our clients. Only those living as hermits over the last several years would have missed all the media coverage about the rise of the Internet, the boom and bust of the dot-com businesses, Microsoft and its legal battles, and the many ways technology affects our lives. Nearly everyone believes he or she understands something about technology. People are familiar with the impact of computers and the Internet, regardless of whether they use these tools themselves.

Let's discuss how this applies to drafting fairly routine legal documents, by way of example. In an earlier age, one of the bundle of values that the lawyer provided to the client was the mechanical ability to produce documents. Not everyone owned or could use a typewriter. In the minds of both lawyer and client, this value was often overshadowed by the knowledge, education, and experience the lawyer provided in producing legal documents. Then many clients, particularly consumer clients, lacked the knowledge and literacy required to prepare documents.

Today, computers and printers are pervasive. Many consumers own them, and those who do not usually can obtain access to them, usually at a school or library. Physically preparing and printing a document presents few challenges. There is no mystery. Many who have gone to get a bank loan have watched a bank employee quickly prepare and print loan documents. Everyone understands that legal documents are rarely written "from scratch," but instead are compiled from forms and prior work products.

In fact, others may not appreciate how much time lawyers *do* spend drafting language for unique situations. Lawyers are trained to identify potential pitfalls that must be avoided. We appreciate the evolving nature of the law and how court decisions and legislative enactments alter legal strategies and the language contained in documents we prepare. We understand how adding a single, unique component to a transaction may create the need for different provisions in several of the documents drafted. Those who do not regularly prepare such documents do not. Business clients in particular may use many computer-generated forms for office paperwork. These can be generated quickly because they are used for essentially the same transaction, with only the name, address, quantity, and price being changed. Such clients often see paperwork only as a means to an end, and, absent trouble, attach no value to the document itself.

Sophisticated clients who expect their law firms to have modern technology often have themselves reaped huge benefits from technology upgrades, usually directly related to their paperwork production and reduction. Consequently, lawyers are increasingly confronted with clients and potential clients who believe their legal matters are very routine and involve "just filling out forms" by the lawyers. Sometimes these clients seek to save money by preparing the documents themselves. In other situations, they discount the value lawyers bring to transactions and, mentally, the legal fees that should be charged for "just filling out forms."

In other words, the ease with which documents can be physically prepared has caused many to devalue the expertise, ability, and time necessary for drafting sound legal documents.

These aspects of technological revolution present a dilemma for lawyers. As we develop more effective methods of harnessing technology for speedy document preparation and document assembly, charging an hourly rate for the final steps that generate a document unfairly overlooks the investment the firm made in designing its systems and effectively using its tools. But a switch to charging a fixed fee per document can generate a negative reaction if the client believes this is merely an increase in the fees the lawyer is charging just to fill out a form.

This issue emphasizes the need for good communication between the lawyer and client about the varied complexities of a legal matter and the value of the lawyer's advice. If the client believes that all he or she has received is a document prepared by using a computer to fill in the blanks, the lawyer's service will be seen as negligible and minimal.

CONSUMER ATTITUDES IN GENERAL

A half-century ago, people and their attitudes were significantly different from those of today. Most clients greatly appreciated lawyers who took them by the hand and managed important legal matters. Many clients were uneducated and unaccustomed to dealing with documents and legal matters. Legal services may have tended toward directing courses of action, as opposed to offering advice.

The twenty-first-century consumer of legal services is usually better educated and more independent. We all prize independence and control over our own lives. The consumer of today wants explanations, information, and options. This consumer does not want to be told what to do, either by government officials or by lawyers.

This attitude affects many aspects of the attorney-client relationship. For example, an innovative lawyer does not direct a course of action, but outlines the facts and the law and empowers the client with options and choices, thus allowing the client to reach a decision. The fact that a decision may be clear to the lawyer at an early stage does not mean that the time invested in explaining options to the client is wasted. It is, after all, the client's matter and the client must comprehend the situation. This attitude also means that clients are much more likely to question a lawyer's fee or the method by which the fee is determined.

Consumers can now go to retailers like Home Depot™ to get the materials and information necessary to do fairly major home repairs and improvements on their own. Pro se representation on matters like divorce cases is on the rise nationwide, and not always because individuals cannot afford lawyers. Often litigants want to retain as much control as possible and resist "turning over" their cases to lawyers. There will be increasing pressure on the courts to adopt procedures that better accommodate those who exercise their constitutional rights to self-representation.

Another result of changed consumer attitudes is a trend toward unbundling of legal services, a concept that merits a book on its own. In fact, the ABA's Law Practice Management Section has published such a book: *Unbundling Legal Services: A Guide to Delivering Services à la Carte* (American Bar Association, 2001), by Forrest S. Mosten. Simply put, unbundling means assisting clients with some portions of legal services, while either allowing them to do other portions themselves or facilitating that process.

In an earlier day, a client might not have considered undertaking any part of legal representation. Filing one's own documents at a court clerk's official office might have seemed a daunting task. Now everyone has seen advertisements for "do-it-yourself" divorce kits at a nominal fee.

A client today might find it illogical to pay for someone from the lawyer's office to file copies of a document in dozens of different counties. The client might assert that she has several employees at her business who could do that, or a teenage son with a driver's license who could use some after-school work. The lawyer may honestly believe that putting such an important final step in the hands of an untrained individual is a foolish way to save a few dollars and may not result in any net cost savings, as the law office would still need to check the returned documents carefully to ensure the job was done correctly. Discussion of these types of issues may seem repetitive and unnecessary to the lawyer, but they help form an important part of clients' understandings of various processes.

The busy pace of modern life means that today's consumer is likely more "time challenged" than his or her forebears. A desire for convenience and flexibility is another consumer attitude that affects the delivery of legal services. We will see more law firms that cater to the individual consumer market, employing "innovative" ideas such as expanded and convenient office hours, "one-stop shopping," integration with other professionals, and rapid production of legal documents while the client waits. In fact, only lawyers view these practices as innovative, as they have already been widely adopted by other providers of consumer goods and services.

THE ONLY CONSTANT IS CHANGE

Observers who note major changes in the legal industry over the last few decades often cite the following factors:

- Introduction of office automation and computer systems
  By now, virtually every law office operates with many computerized systems, including word processing, time and billing systems, e-mail, and facsimile. Many offices also use case management software and document management software.
- Advent of paralegals and increasing use of nonlawyers in production of legal services
- Abolition of minimum-fee schedules, as a result of the U.S. Supreme Court's decision in *Goldfarb v. Virginia State Bar*, 421 U.S. 773 (1975)

- Permissibility of lawyer advertising, as a result of the U.S. Supreme Court's decision in *Bates & O'Steen v. State Bar of Arizona*, 433 U.S. 350 (1977)
  This decision prompted some law firms to pursue a host of other marketing activities, including the production of newsletters and brochures, presentation of seminars, and formation of law firm networks.
- Advent of legal clinics, as a result of the two cases cited above
- Growth of the Internet and its tendency to render borders and legal jurisdictions less relevant in the minds of many "netizens"
- Growth of corporate and government law departments
- Development of prepaid legal services plans and legal insurance programs
- Dramatic growth of major law firms, including geographical expansion regionally, nationally, and internationally
- Deteriorating image of lawyers and general "demystification" of the profession

As important as all these factors are, let us consider in some detail three areas of dramatic change in the profession and their likely impact on the profession in the future: demographic changes, profit squeeze and income compression, and the legal market as a maturing marketplace.

DEMOGRAPHICS

The ABA estimates that there are 1,049,000 lawyers in the United States, up from approximately 858,000 in 1995 and approximately 350,000 in 1970. With a total population estimate of 285 million, this translates to having one lawyer for every 272 persons now, versus one lawyer for every 572 persons in 1970. This includes adults and children. Although not all these lawyers are engaged in private practice (approximately two-thirds are), this rate of increase in the number of lawyers is dramatic. International Bar Association records suggest that between one-half and two-thirds of the lawyers in the world are in the United States.

Law school enrollment dropped slightly over the last decade, but remained at approximately 125,000 from 1997 to 2000. Law schools in the United States produce between 38,000 and 40,000 new law graduates each year, with 38,157 law degrees awarded during 2000, according to the ABA Section of Legal Education and Admissions to the Bar. This number is not expected to change markedly. There are still approximately four applicants for every seat in U.S. law schools, and rates of admission have remained steady in recent years.

Furthermore, U.S. law schools are unlikely to close their doors or limit enrollment artificially. All but a handful of law schools in the United States are affiliated with—and very profitable for—major universities. Tuition and fees for law school approximate those of other areas of graduate education, while costs are much lower. The profession itself is unlikely to limit its growth or numbers by stricter bar admission standards, as bar examiners are unlikely to expose themselves to the type of discrimination lawsuits they encountered in the late 1960s and early 1970s. As a result, marketplace economic factors will determine who will make a living as a lawyer and who will not. Because of the tremendous influx of new lawyers, the average age of a lawyer in the United States is now under forty. Also notable in the changing demographics of the profession is the fact that 30 percent of licensed lawyers are female. Because approximately 47 percent of law students are female, that percentage is likely to increase.

Demographic changes in the country as a whole will affect the legal profession as well. Lawyers will serve a more diverse population. Dealing with different cultures, languages, and belief systems will present a series of new challenges. Approximately one-fifth of current law school enrollment is described as belonging to a minority group.

PROFIT SQUEEZE AND INCOME COMPRESSION

Against the backdrop of an ever-increasing population of lawyers, we must measure the nationwide market for legal services. The impact of these statistics is frightening. When adjusted for inflation, the gross domestic product of legal services is actually in decline (see Exhibit 2-1).

One does not have to be a statistician to ascertain a systemic problem for the legal profession in general, and individual lawyers in particular, as the demographic information is combined with the economic trends. If the growth in the number of practicing lawyers equates to growth in the gross income of the legal profession, then lawyer income would remain flat. More lawyers alone, combined with a static gross national product, would suggest fewer dollars per lawyer. With the actual number of lawyers increasing and gross income declining (at least in real, inflation-adjusted dollars), the projections are sobering indeed.

We have all heard the old aphorism equating statistics to lies. In truth, the situation may not be quite as terrible as these statistics indicate. Anecdotal evidence suggests that many who hold law degrees and licenses to practice law are, in fact, involved in other endeavors in other sectors of the economy.

But, there still can be no other conclusion after reviewing the statistics than that success in the legal marketplace is not guaranteed. A greater assurance of success depends upon efficient client service models, superior legal services, and pricing/billing structures that reflect the value clients receive for the legal services provided.

Exhibit 2-1

Gross Domestic Product of Legal Services
(In billions of dollars)

Year	Dollars	Real (1996) Dollars
1990	82.7	108.8
1995	101.1	105.1
1997	108.5	103.8
1998	116.5	107.1

Source: U.S. Census Bureau, *Statistical Abstract of the United States: 2001.*

THE LEGAL MARKET AS A MATURING MARKETPLACE

All successful marketplaces for goods or services—if they have any economic value—emerge as "embryonic" marketplaces, in which initial demand exceeds supply. Over time, suppliers increase production capacity, and new suppliers enter the marketplace until the balance of supply and demand shifts. This results in a shift toward a "buyer's market." Once this "oversupply" occurs, supplier behavior is characterized by price competition, market segmentation, differentiation of the good or service, and geographic growth and expansion.

In many respects, the marketplace for legal services in the United States has reached a significant level of maturity. Interestingly enough, ours is not the first profession or service industry to mature. Maturation has already occurred for brokerage houses and financial institutions. Many of the identifiable effects of the maturing marketplace in these other service industries are evident in the legal profession today.

CONSOLIDATION

Industry consolidation—characterized by a growth of service providers, and much of it occurring by way of merger—led to the formation of the large accounting firms, as well as the large brokerage houses. Consolidation is also occurring in the banking and financial services industries.

In the legal profession, there are now global law firms with more than 3,000 lawyers. Much of the dramatic growth in these large law firms has been driven by merger. Such growth is likely to continue. Leading accounting firms and brokerage houses account for between 5 and 10 percent of market shares in their professions and industries. The megafirms account for only a fraction of a percent of the fee receipts of law firms. By that measure, there is room for continued growth in the market share, and therefore in the size, of law firms.

The traditional argument against such growth has been that conflict-of-interest considerations in the legal profession will prevent it. As a matter of fact, experience in another jurisdiction, Australia, indicates that conflict-of-interest rules comparable to those in the United States need not inhibit the growth of law firms. The market share of a number of Australian firms, if projected into the U.S. marketplace, would result in law firms of 10,000 or more lawyers.

Although there has been a trend toward consolidation, the opposite trend can be detected as well, as some law firm practice groups have left their firms to establish smaller, specialized boutique firms. There have been several highly publicized firm dissolutions and anecdotal examples of firms forgoing usual hiring practices and even paying associates to leave.

It seems unlikely that the legal marketplace will consolidate to the extent that a "Big Five" (or even a "Big Twenty") set of law firms will result. Tens of thousands of law firms are—and likely will remain—independent entrepreneurial entities. The trends of consolidation may play out in other ways. For example, there has been a detectable consolidation and limiting of practice areas. Specialization, although not approved formally in many jurisdictions, is certainly a fact of life. So, consolidation in the legal marketplace may be expressed more as certain groups of lawyers dominating certain markets rather than as the traditional formation of ever-larger monoliths. Certainly the Internet provides the opportunity for less hierarchical business models and the possibility of alliances rather than permanent partnerships.

BRAND NAMES

PriceWaterhouse Coopers, Merrill Lynch, and the like are household names. Although law firms such as Cravath, Swaine & Moore; Baker & McKenzie; Skadden, Arps, Slate, Meagher & Flom; and Wilson Sonsini Goodrich & Rosati are not yet household names, they are the equivalent of household names in sophisticated business circles. The emergence of the legal press during the 1980s and its maturing in the 1990s, combined with the focus of the business press on the profession, opened the doors to this previously discreet profession. Large law firms are disproportionately the focus of reporters, so they are gaining brand-name recognition.

PRICE COMPETITION

We see price competition in the form of discount brokerage houses and banking services. Clearly, price competition in retail outlets has been extremely aggressive with the emergence of Wal-Mart™ and similar retailers. The Internet has facilitated the emergence of price-cutters like Amazon.com™, contributed to the possible destruction of small independent travel agents through direct airline ticket sales, and brought together buyers and sellers directly in venues like eBay™.

In the legal profession, price competition emerged at the low end of the marketplace in the late 1970s, with the advent of legal clinics. Price competition has accelerated, as virtually every community now has advertising for routine legal services in telephone directories, local shopper guides, and television listing publications, with the advertisements focusing on price.

We are now seeing price competition at the upper end of the marketplace. Client-induced price competition in the field of insurance defense has resulted in firms doing work at hourly rates that are half—and sometimes one-third—of what rates would be for comparably experienced litigators using similar skills for different clients and with different fact situations.

Price competition is also beginning in corporate services, as sophisticated clients cede transactional legal work by soliciting bids from a number of law firms in "beauty contests" or through Internet postings. The clients ask how the transaction will be approached, how it will be staffed, what the rates will be, and what estimated total fees will be. Retention decisions are then made largely upon the basis of price.

BACKWARD INTEGRATION

Maturing service marketplaces are also characterized by movement of the customer into the supplier's marketplace. Strategic planners refer to this as backward integration. In the accounting profession, backward integration occurs when corporate accounting staffs handle the work once performed by outside accounting firms.

In the legal profession, backward integration is represented by the 70,000-plus lawyers employed as in-house counsel in U.S. corporate law departments. There is no doubt that increasingly, in-house counsel handle more legal matters that were formerly handled by private law firms.

CLIENT SOPHISTICATION

Backward integration results in a more sophisticated client, represented by a trained, skilled, and experienced general counsel, rather than a lay business executive. In such an environment, clients can determine the quality of service provided by different law firms, and choose and use law firms differently. Depending upon the matter, these sophisticated clients select among several outside counsel, based upon the counsel's specialty or reputation, rather than relying upon a full-service law firm to meet all the corporation's legal needs.

MARKETING

In mature service industries, service providers spend much more out-of-pocket on marketing, business development, advertising, and promotion than in embryonic marketplaces. For example, according to some estimates, accounting firms and brokerage houses spend from 3 to 10 percent of revenues on marketing, promotion, and business development.

Surveys show that the typical law firm traditionally spends much less in this area, even using a liberal definition of what constitutes a marketing or business development expense. But law firms are placing more emphasis on marketing, with many law firms now staffing full-time marketing and public-relations specialists. Although marketing is necessary, it is just another law firm operation that requires an investment of staff time and money. It may be successful and bear rewards for the firm, but it does not constitute the production of billable legal services.

INCURSION BY OTHER SERVICE PROVIDERS

Marketplaces mature partly because existing service providers increase their productive capacity, and also because new providers enter the marketplace. Those who have made significant incursions into the traditionally quasi-monopolistic domain of the legal profession include accounting firms, consulting firms, and financial institutions.

Accounting firms not only practice more tax law than do law firms in the United States, they also are entering other areas of business law practice, including insolvency, workouts, and reorganizations. Although the effects of the Enron and WorldCom matters and the government's efforts to separate auditing from other services within accounting firms have not been determined, even if accounting firms are forced to separate auditing from other functions, accounting professionals will continue to compete with law firms in providing management and tax advisory services. Interestingly enough, management advisory service divisions of some major accounting firms have targeted the legal marketplace. Based upon what they have learned, those firms have chosen to expand into the fastest-growing and most profitable areas of business-related (as opposed to litigation-related) services. In Europe, where there are fewer restrictions on interdisciplinary practices, three of the largest "law firms" are parts of Big Five accounting firms.

Labor and environmental consulting firms are hiring qualified labor and environmental lawyers to practice law on behalf of their clients. Financial institutions, such as banks and insurance companies, also employ lawyers to practice estate planning and estate administration.

Many lawyers view this trend as an improper and possibly illegal endeavor—the unauthorized practice of law. Traditional remedies for combating these incursions, such as suits in equity seeking injunctions against the unauthorized practice of law, or even criminal prosecutions, are often thought to be less viable against large, well-financed, professional providers delivering high-quality products. Also, one must bear in mind that traditional proscriptions against the unauthorized practice of law were based upon the desire to protect clients from shoddy or improper services, not to protect the "turf" of the organized bar.

Some attempts to contest these incursions have already backfired.

The Texas Unauthorized Practice of Law Committee was most aggressive in pursuing unauthorized-practice-of-law allegations against companies for distributing "self-help" books and specialized document assembly software in Texas. On January 22, 1999, U.S. District Court Judge Barefoot Sanders ruled that the software package Quicken Family Lawyer™, a publication of Parsons Technology, did constitute the unauthorized practice of law. (The committee was pursuing similar claims against Nolo Press at the time.) There was an outcry among many who believed this ruling was both anticonsumer and an abridgement of free speech (see Unauthorized Practice of Law Committee v. Parsons Technology, Inc. No. Civ.A.3:97:CV-2859H, 1999 WL 47235).

Before the end of 1999, a bill had been passed into law by the Texas legislature negating this decision. The enacted language provided that "the 'practice of law' does not include the design, creation, publication, distribution, display, or sale, including publication, distribution, display, or sale by means of an Internet web site, of written materials, books, forms, computer software, or similar products if the products clearly and conspicuously state that the products are not a substitute for the advice of an attorney." (Tex. Gov't Code Ann. § 81.101 Vernon 2000).

To the extent state laws prohibit other providers from entering viable markets, one can anticipate more challenges in both courts and legislatures. Although there are very good policy reasons behind many aspects of rules regarding the unauthorized practice of law, lawyers should expect that these rules will be carefully examined, and that they must be justified to be upheld.

"FREE AGENCY"

As if the newly mature marketplace in the legal profession is not volatile enough, the situation is intensified by the "free agency" of lawyers, arising in part from the unenforceability of covenants not to compete. Basically, lawyers are free to leave their firms at any time and take their clients with them. The law firms can do little to keep them. Considering the way the courts have construed these provisions, anything even remotely resembling a covenant not to compete (such as a "forfeiture for competition" clause) may not be enforceable.

BARGAINING POWER OF BUYERS

In the newly mature marketplace, sophisticated clients are buying legal services differently. As already mentioned, they are selecting outside counsel transactionally, rather than institutionally. This spreads out the work. Many corporate clients spread work intentionally, letting it be known that the work is being spread; they use their ability to compare billing rates and total fees for comparable matters to induce fee competition.

By spreading work, these clients also lower their costs to switch firms. A number of outside law firms become familiar enough with a client's business to shorten the learning curve otherwise associated with moving work from one law firm to another. This has introduced a new element of competition into the profession.

THE FUTURE OF THE PROFESSION

The ABA Law Practice Management Section was instrumental in arranging a series of "Seize the Future" conferences in 1997 and 1999. These conferences—which featured speakers such as management guru Dr. Tom Peters and lawyer-futurists William Cobb, Charles F. Robinson, and Roberta Katz—allowed many influential and thoughtful lawyers the opportunity to explore the future of lawyering and the practice of law. The major point of this chapter was also a theme of the "Seize the Future" conferences: the only certainty in our future is change. There is no avoiding the change and no possibility of turning back. Change is happening at a rapid pace all around us.

Vexing issues about the structure of the bar and our organized systems for delivery of legal services, such as multijurisdictional practice and multidisciplinary practice, will continue to generate concern and may ultimately provide new models for the delivery of legal services. But while regulators and lawyer organizations debate the merits of these new models, others will embrace them and implement them without waiting for official approval.

Independent-minded individuals will continue to explore self-help products, pro se representation, and alternative dispute resolution. The expense and delays of litigation will cause many to view it as "a sport for the rich." Pro se representation is one facet of disintermediation, which may be summarized as "out with the middleman." The Internet will accelerate disintermediation in many ways that are not limited to the legal profession. Two examples have been noted: eBay, an online auction house that allows buyers and sellers to interact directly, and Amazon.com, where the local bookseller is bypassed in favor of cost savings.

Unconventional approaches may have the best chance of great success. A law firm of people who all think alike will be ill-prepared to deal with the

> ### *Looking to the Future*
>
> The future of the legal profession may be quite uncertain, but it is still interesting and exciting. For more information on seizing your future, your attention is directed to the following resources:
>
> 1. The Web site of the ABA Law Practice Management Section, at www.abanet.org/lpm.
> 2. The book *Seize the Future: Forecasting and Influencing the Future of the Legal Profession* (American Bar Association, 2000), by Gary M. Munneke, which was based on the ABA's 1999 "Seize the Future" conference. (This book is available from the ABA Law Practice Management Section.)
> 3. Well-known futurist Charles F. Robinson's Web site, The Future of Law Practice, at www.rclaw.com/future.html.
> 4. The ABA's e-lawyering Web site, at www.elawyering.org.
> 5. The latest book by British academic and consultant Richard Susskind, *Transforming the Law: Essays on Technology, Justice and the Legal Marketplace* (Oxford University Press, 2001), which supersedes his groundbreaking *The Future of Law*. (This book is available from Amazon.com.)

challenges of the future. A multicultural group with varying points of view has a greater chance of success. As one conference speaker suggested, "Hire the guy with the purple hair."

Fee competition will intensify as sophisticated clients continue to treat an ever-increasing portion of legal business as a commodity for firms to bid on. In the fully mature marketplace—where arguably every client is sophisticated, where there is a choice of suppliers in every segment of the market, and where price competition is such that there is not much difference among law firms—differentiation based upon value (price, scope of services, client/industry experience, and geographic orientation) will become increasingly difficult.

IMPACT OF THESE TRENDS

Successful law firms will learn to control costs, increase lawyer productivity, and reap some of the benefits of these advances (while sharing some of them with clients) through innovative pricing. A law firm can hardly benefit from reducing its costs through automation if doing so turns a five-hour lawyer job into a two-hour job and the firm bills clients on an hourly basis. (On the other hand, continuing to bill for five hours for a task other law firms can do in two may result in a total loss of the client's business.) To price such services profitably while remaining price-competitive in the market, the firm must raise the economic consciousness of its partners.

Some firms will extend value to clients by sharing risk with them, enabling "value billing" dependent upon results and client acceptance of such a concept. Some of the methods of value billing discussed in later chapters will apply to situations that involve increased risk sharing.

This is the challenge for progressive law firms for the future: to confront the inevitability of change. Billing is but one area where lawyers will be challenged to change. Unless lawyers adopt innovative pricing, escalating costs threaten to overtake revenues. The lawyers will then be unable to reap the benefits of their investments in productivity, quality, and service.

Chapter Three

Ethical Rules and Practices

Special rules and restrictions apply to lawyers and the fees they may charge. Even the most innovative billing method must comply with those ethical rules and practices. Each lawyer must make certain that the fees charged and the methods of billing comply with the applicable requirements.

THE BASIC RULE

Although each jurisdiction's ethical rules and court decisions vary, the ABA Model Rules of Professional Conduct, as amended in 2002, set forth the basic ground rules governing all fees. Model Rule 1.5, dealing with attorneys' fees, states, "A lawyer shall not make an agreement for, charge, or collect an unreasonable fee. . . . " *Model Rules of Professional Conduct* R. 1.5(a) (2002). The rule sets forth eight factors to consider in determining the reasonableness of a fee:

1. The time and labor required, the novelty and difficulty of the questions involved, and the skill requisite to perform the legal services properly
2. The likelihood, if apparent to the client, that the acceptance of the assignment will preclude other employment by the lawyer
3. The fee customarily charged in the locality for similar legal services
4. The amount involved and results obtained
5. The time limitation imposed by the client or by the circumstances
6. The nature and length of the professional relationship with the client

7. The experience, reputation, and ability of the lawyer or lawyers performing the services
8. Whether the fee is fixed or contingent

Model Rule 1.5 recommends that the fee agreement be in writing unless the lawyer regularly represents the client. If the fee is contingent, then the agreement *must* be in writing, signed by the client, and must set forth (1) the method by which the fee is determined, including the percentage accruing to the lawyer if the matter is settled, tried, or appealed; (2) the litigation expenses to be deducted; and (3) whether the deduction is made before or after the contingent fee is calculated. Also, upon conclusion of the matter, the lawyer charging a contingent fee must provide a written statement of the outcome. If there is a recovery, the lawyer must also provide an accounting, establishing the basis for the remittance to the client.

Model Rule 1.5 further provides that contingent-fee agreements are not permitted in criminal matters or in domestic relations matters involving the securing of a dissolution, support, or property settlement in lieu of support. The comments to Model Rule 1.5 provide that contingent fees, like any other fees, are subject to a reasonableness standard.

Finally, the rule addresses the question of fee-splitting between lawyers. Lawyers who are not members of the same firm may not split fees unless the following criteria are met:

1. The division is in proportion to the services performed, or each lawyer assumes joint responsibility for the representation;
2. The client agrees to the arrangement, including the share each lawyer will receive, and the agreement is confirmed in writing; and
3. The total fee is reasonable.

The comments to Model Rule 1.5 state that a lawyer may require an advance payment of a fee, subject to remitting any unearned fee balance to the client. Whether the lawyer should place such fees into a trust account to be withdrawn as earned is governed by Model Rule 1.15 and is discussed later in this chapter.

Rule 1.5 goes on to provide that the lawyer may accept property, including an ownership interest in an enterprise. However, the lawyer may not accept an interest in the subject matter of the litigation or have a proprietary interest in the cause of action, except to the extent a lien is granted by law securing the lawyer's fees or as permitted in contingency-fee matters. A lawyer entering a business transaction with a client should review Model Rule 1.8(a), which governs such conduct.

Because fees are an area of great concern to lawyers, courts, legislators, clients, and the public, each jurisdiction develops its own particular version of acceptable conduct and standards regarding fees. To confuse matters more, ethics opinions explaining what is acceptable or required vary from jurisdiction to jurisdiction. Even jurisdictions that have adopted the ABA Model Rules often modify Rule 1.5, or the rule is later modified by court decision, the legislature, or local ethics opinions.

Some jurisdictions mandate arbitration of fee disputes. Others make it available, and still others are silent on the subject or apply it only to certain types of cases, matters, or substantive areas of law.

Some jurisdictions have specific requirements, conditions, or provisions for certain types of fee agreements, such as contingency-fee agreements. Some limit the requirements to specific types of cases, or prohibit certain types of fee agreements in particular kinds of cases, and some set maximum fees or caps that lawyers may not exceed.

Familiarity with local ethical rules may bring comfort to some law firms. But for a law firm that expands across state lines, jurisdictional variations on the acceptability of fee agreements compromise the firm's ability to fashion standard fee agreements that can be used throughout the various jurisdictions.

THE GOLDEN RULE

It is important to consider that even if a fee agreement is signed by a sophisticated client and sets a fee that is within the "going rates," it may not be acceptable. The underlying principle is that the fees charged must be *reasonable*. Although the eight factors listed above provide a guide for determining reasonableness, a court may consider other factors when reviewing the fee. The bottom line is that the overall fee charged must be reasonable when measured against the benefits received by the client, even if this standard appears to involve a certain amount of hindsight.

To illustrate, imagine that you have a written contract with a knowledgeable client, which sets a fixed, reasonable, hourly rate. The agreement results in a fee of $50,000 over a dispute involving an issue worth only $25,000. You would have difficulty in sustaining the fee in the face of client objection. If your fee is "the going rate" in your community but nevertheless unreasonable, you will have difficulty obtaining approval of the fee by the court over a client's objection. In spite of contract terms, time expended, client sophistication, or any of the other factors you may consider in justifying or rationalizing the fee, it all comes down to one question: Is the fee reasonable?

Clearly, then, a lawyer does not have complete freedom to enter a contract with a client for any amount of fees. A client who is satisfied with the representation and outcome may gladly pay the fee, no matter what the amount. But if the client disputes the fee or a court must approve the fee, the potential for second-guessing arises. Bluntly put, Model Rule 1.5 strips the lawyer of unfettered freedom to set fees and gives the court the authority to set them at a level the court thinks appropriate. If a judge believes a lawyer is "gouging" the client, there will be ample rationalization in the factors listed in the rule to support a fee reduction. On the other hand, most fees can be supported by the factors contained in the rule, if the court is inclined to do so.

GRAY AREAS

Although each jurisdiction may have its own peculiar rules, court opinions, procedures, and legislative enactments governing fee agreements between lawyers and their clients, there are some controversial areas where ethicists disagree. These are currently in a state of flux.

TRUST ACCOUNTS FOR PREPAID FEES

One such area deals with the question of whether lawyers who receive fees from clients in advance for work to be done in the future should put those prepaid fees into a trust account. For example, imagine a client pays you a fixed fee to form a corporation or to defend a criminal charge. Should you put the funds you receive into a trust account to be withdrawn as the work is completed? What if the fee received is a payment on account of fees and the agreement is that you will bill against the deposited fee as the work is done—should you deposit that fee into a trust account? What if the initial fee you receive is not refundable (or only partially refundable) and you are to bill against the fees on deposit—should you deposit the entire fee into a trust account, or only the portion above the amount that is not refundable? Or should you put the entire amount into a trust account and take money out as you earn the fees?

Some jurisdictions have addressed one or more of these questions. *See, e.g.*, Cal. Standing Comm. on Prof'l Responsibility & Conduct, Formal Op. 1990-121; San Francisco Bar Ass'n Ethics Op. 1980-1. Articles have also been written on this subject. *See, e.g.*, Shank, *Are Advance Fee Payments Clients' Funds?*, 55 Cal. St. B.J. 370 (1980); Dimitriou, *Should Prepaid Fees Be Put in a Trust Account?*, 6 Cal. Law. 20 (1983); Brichman & Cunningham, *Non-refundable Retainers: Impermissible under Fiduciary Statutory and Contract Law*, 57 Fordham L. Rev. 149 (1988); Brichman, *The Advance Fee Payment Dilemma: Should Payments Be Deposited to the Client Trust Account or to the General Office Account?*, 10 Cardozo L. Rev. 647 (1989). *See also* Jay G. Foonberg, *The ABA Guide to Lawyer Trust Accounts* (American Bar Association, 1996) (comprehensive treatise on trust accounting published by ABA Law Practice Management Section).

These writers do not speak with a single voice. How a particular jurisdiction would answer these questions is beyond the scope of this chapter.

FEE AGREEMENTS IN WRITING

Opinions also differ on the need for a fee agreement to be in writing. Model Rule 1.5 requires a written fee agreement only in contingent-fee matters; the effort by the ABA Ethics 2000 Commission to require all fee arrangements over $500 to be in writing failed to pass in the ABA House of Delegates in February 2002 when it was presented. However, the comments to the rule suggest that, in an effort to reduce the possibility of client misunderstanding, the fee agreement be reduced to writing when the lawyer has not regularly represented the client. (The rule itself provides that in such circumstances, the fee arrangement shall be "communicated to the client.")

As with the ABA rule, jurisdictions differ about whether a written fee agreement need be used only in contingent-fee matters. Some jurisdictions require that all fee agreements be in writing, and some only if the fee is expected to be over a certain dollar minimum. Some require a written agreement only in certain types of contingent-fee matters, and others have no special requirements relating to contingent fees. To understand the requirements in various jurisdictions, lawyers must review local rules, court opinions, ethics opinions, and laws.

We acknowledge the differing opinions among scholars concerning which fee agreements should be in writing; yet, in our opinion, sound business practice dictates written fee agreements in almost every situation. Written fee agreements allow lawyers the opportunity to formalize their representations and financial arrangements. Experienced lawyers note that many potential fee disputes have been silenced by reference to written (and signed) fee agreements.

MANDATORY ARBITRATION

Could your fee agreement include a provision for mandatory arbitration of any fee or malpractice dispute? At least one ethics opinion and one appellate court opinion indicate that such a provision—as it related to malpractice—may not be permissible. However, both suggest that such an arbitration provision would be permitted if it were clearly worded and put the client on notice concerning the detriments of the provision (for example, loss of the right to a jury trial and the right to select a judicial forum). Various jurisdictions have passed laws that establish procedures for arbitration concerning attorneys' fees and that impose limits on contractual provisions. There is currently very little guidance in this area, but much interest.

BUSINESS INTERESTS RECEIVED IN PAYMENT

Lawyers also find themselves in difficulty concerning fees when as payment, they accept property (such as an ownership interest in an enterprise or other property where reasonable people can differ regarding value). Accepting "a piece of the deal" of a new business may seem logical to both the lawyer and the entrepreneur, as a way to accomplish legal goals while preserving limited cash. Care should be taken to review Model Rule 1.8(a), which provides that a lawyer should take certain steps to protect the client when entering a business transaction with that client.

But this can create a problem if the client later objects and attempts to apply an after-the-fact analysis. The client may never object to the lawyer's fractional interest in a business enterprise that becomes worthless. But if an enterprise succeeds spectacularly, then the lawyer risks defending a client's claim that the resulting fee is unreasonable.

Furthermore, a practical effect of accepting an interest in a business enterprise or other asset in lieu of fees is that the lawyer and client become "business partners," thus creating the potential for a future conflict of interest between the lawyer and the client. Model Rule 1.7 addresses conflicts between a lawyer's own interests and the client's interests: "a lawyer shall not represent a client if the representation . . . will be materially limited . . . by a personal interest of the lawyer [unless] the lawyer reasonably believes that the lawyer will be able to provide competent and diligent representation [and the] client gives informed consent, confirmed in writing." *Model Rules of Prof'l Conduct* R. 1.7 (2002). Model Rule 1.8(i) (as amended in 2002), dealing with conflicts of interest, may come into play because neither of the two exceptions to this rule would apply; namely, (1) a lien authorized by law to secure fees or expenses, or (2) a contract for contingent fees in a civil case. That rule sets forth the ground rules that must be followed by a lawyer who accepts fees from a client in the form of property or property interests belonging to a client, or who takes a security interest in property for payment of fees. The ABA Ethics 2000 Commission added a significant amount of commentary to Model Rule 1.8, addressing issues of business transactions between client and lawyer. (The comments were adopted by the ABA House of Delegates in February 2002.)

Does a fee arrangement that depends upon closing a transaction violate Model Rule 2.1, which requires the lawyer to exercise independent professional judgment? One court found that a lawyer aided and abetted a violation of Securities and Exchange Commission Rule 10b-5 by failing to act when the lawyer (who was also a shareholder, officer, and director of the business) stood to profit "handsomely" from the transaction. *SEC v. Nat'l Student Mktg. Corp.*, 457 F. Supp. 682 (D.D.C. 1978).

Each jurisdiction has created its own version of acceptable conduct for the lawyer in all these circumstances. Although the Model Rules will help you focus on the issues that must be addressed, you must also refer to the rules and opinions of your own jurisdiction for guidance on appropriate and safe conduct in these circumstances.

CONFLICTS

As touched upon earlier, it is important to consider not only the underlying fairness of the fee, but also the conflict-of-interest issue, both when determining the amount of the fee and whenever the fee is being paid by someone or some entity other than the client, such as a friend, an insurance company, or an employer. *See Model Rules of Prof'l Conduct* R. 1.8(f), R. 5.4(c) (2002). The conflict issue is also present and must be considered every time you have more than one client in the same matter.

FEE-SHARING

Beyond the conflict issue are other important questions. These include the ethics of fee-sharing among lawyers who are not members of the same firm. (See the discussion above concerning Model Rule 1.5.) Even more thorny is the issue of fee-splitting with nonlawyers. *See Model Rules of Prof'l Conduct* R. 5.4(a) (2002). Such fees may take the form of staff incentive bonuses, finders' fees, rental agreements based upon a percentage of gross fees, and other direct or indirect payments to a nonlawyer of a portion of the fees that the lawyer has earned or collected.

It behooves a lawyer to run each fee agreement through an ethics check, just as lawyers run each new client through a conflicts check. This is particularly true whenever the agreement concerns an unfamiliar or unusual area of practice, more than one client, or legal services in more than one jurisdiction.

CHAPTER FOUR

Pricing Legal Services

Many lawyers may look at alternative billing methods as a means of either making more money or doing less work in the billing process. In fact, appropriate use of these methods could ultimately result in one or both of those goals, and will encourage everyone to focus on value provided to the client. Though many hours must be invested in the transition from hourly to alternative billing methods, and in fine-tuning alternative billing methods in the future, it is a positive investment in the future of the practice.

Whatever billing method you use, it is critical to know the cost of producing legal services. Cost, however, should not be the sole basis for setting the price to charge the client. Price can be defined as the amount of money that a well-informed client (the purchaser) is willing to pay for the value of the services of the lawyer (the seller). A useful technique is to consider where the firm falls on the "value curve," which depicts clients' views of the value of various types of services. Many factors, both theoretical and practical, contribute to the pricing of legal services. Lawyers must understand these factors to succeed in the current legal environment.

HISTORICAL INFLUENCES ON PRICING LEGAL SERVICES

How do our clients value our services? How should we price those services both to reflect value to the client and to be profitable? After a certain time, the old English custom of slipping money into the barrister's robe was no longer an acceptable method of compensating the barrister, with the client—and only the client—determining the price to pay for services. The practice of law, we have been told, is both a profession and a

> **A Special Note for Solo and Small-Firm Lawyers**
>
> Many of you, particularly those who represent mainly individual consumer clients, may believe this chapter is directed to, or more appropriate for, lawyers in larger firms. Though we believe this chapter to be valuable—perhaps the most valuable in the book—it may be that you will want to review only the first eleven pages of this chapter and then skip ahead to Chapter 5, Pricing Legal Services for the Solo and Small-Firm Lawyer.

business. In attempting to be more businesslike, lawyers increasingly used hours spent on matters as a measure of the value of those services.

Until the late 1970s, most lawyers gave little thought to the pricing of their services. This lack of concern stemmed in part from the prosperity that many lawyers enjoyed and the lack of competition. Studies in an earlier time period showed that clients valued effort, sometimes over the results obtained. This lulled lawyers into believing that value to the client was measured by effort. The lawyer's perception was that the greater the effort, the more the clients would benefit, and the more the clients would pay.

PRICING BEFORE AND AFTER *BATES*

To understand why the concept of pricing is new and sometimes difficult for lawyers to understand, it is helpful to review the nature of the legal profession before the landmark U.S. Supreme Court decision in *Bates & O'Steen v. State Bar of Arizona*, 433 U.S. 350 (1977), which enabled lawyers to market legal services.

For many years, lawyers would analyze the file (often at the end of the representation) and establish a fee based upon the value to the client. Establishing the fee was often as much art as science, and was a skill a lawyer needed to survive. Gradually, minimum-fee schedules were established by bar associations or common practice in the area. Then, roughly forty years ago, experts using surveys of the legal profession found that lawyers who recorded their time earned more than those who did not. Lawyers knew how much it cost to provide the services based upon the time spent, and could therefore set the fees appropriately. In the same general time period, because of possible antitrust violations, lawyers stopped using the traditional minimum-fee schedules. *Goldfarb v. Virginia State Bar*, 421 U.S. 773 (1975).

With the abolition of minimum-fee schedules and the experts and consultants telling lawyers that timekeeping was good, hourly billing rapidly evolved as a billing method of choice—particularly as law firms started to grow; it was an easy measure of "value" of associates and increasing leverage for partners.

Lawyers had been advised to keep time records to know the *cost* of providing services. No one said that billing solely on time was always appropriate, but the profession moved in the direction of multiplying time by an hourly rate to set fees. The time-rate method became predominant. The time spent on a matter moved from a measure of a lawyer's *cost* to a measure of a lawyer's *value*—hence hourly based bills. With the development of computerized record keeping and computerized billing, time became the dominant basis for charging, and the transformation from value-based billing to time-based billing was complete. This was the case even though most computerized systems provided an opportunity for the billing lawyer to exercise judgment, based upon the value of the services to the client, by "writing up" or "writing down" the initially calculated fee.

Detailed time records appealed to lawyers, clients, and the courts because they appeared to provide a tangible, objective means for setting fees. Contemporaneous time recording enabled the lawyer to produce a detailed transcript of the services provided. If effort was the major objective, time records could demonstrate—with detailed descriptions—all the efforts that had been undertaken. The courts had some tangible evidence upon which to base a fee award. The semiautomatic business process of billing according to the hours spent, multiplied by an hourly rate, reduced the need for lawyers and judges to exercise discretion.

During the 1970s and 1980s, the demand for legal services often exceeded the supply, so the amount billed was largely price-insensitive. This enabled lawyers to increase their hourly rates at periodic intervals to meet their increased overhead expenses, without attention to finding efficiencies in the delivery of legal services. In addition, more and more hours were logged by more and more timekeepers. The legal profession expanded as more and more graduates entered the profession.

Gradually, however, the market shifted from a seller's market to a buyer's market. Inflation and operating costs drove up legal fees due to rates and increased efforts by lawyers on matters they perceived to be important to value. Clients became critical of the escalating legal costs and the lack of law firm sensitivity to efficiency, and began exploring ways to reduce outside counsels' fees through fee and billing requirements, legal fee audits, and consolidation of work in fewer (and often less expensive) firms. Spiraling associate salaries and downward fee pressure from clients forced many firms to examine their hourly rate billing systems for many types of legal work.

In the midst of the increasing supply of lawyers, some requirements for traditional services shrank as businesses brought work in-house or demand declined. Because marketing and client development were permitted after the *Bates* decision, many lawyers became more aggressive and competitive in these new market conditions. Newly established law firms would often market and advertise, offering lower prices without a good understanding of their costs to produce legal services.

CONSTRAINTS ON THE MARKETPLACE

In classic economic terms, when supply exceeds demand, price declines. There are, however, some constraints on the free operation of the marketplace for the legal profession, both positive and negative. Some would argue that prices for legal services are inflated by the monopolistic effects of requiring licensure of lawyers as professionals for delivery of certain services. Several provisions of our ethical rules (discussed in Chapter 3) impose artificial constraints on the operation of the market. For example, no contingent fees are permitted in criminal and matrimonial matters, and every fee, regardless of the billing method, must be "reasonable."

Not all fees result from an agreement between a lawyer and client, nor are the parties absolutely free to contract. In a fee-shifting case or when a court approves a fee, factors other than the market may affect price. Here are three illustrations:

1. The fee is set by an out-of-date or uninformed judge who does not understand the current economics of law practice, the current market for legal services, or the value to the client.
2. In fee awards, the court strikes a balance between the prevailing party and the losing party who must pay the fee.
3. In a bankruptcy case, there is balancing between the lawyer and the creditors, whose recovery will be affected by the amount of the fee awarded.

The operation of the marketplace is also affected by the client's perception of value. For the client's perception to be accurate, the client should be educated and informed about what he or she needs to purchase and is purchasing. Some clients are unsophisticated and uneducated about the legal process, so they need the protection of the ethical constraints. However, some clients are highly sophisticated purchasers of legal services and, in a buyer's market, can exert extreme pressure on price because of the leveraging that results from having high volumes of work to assign to outside counsel. Along the continuum of unsophisticated to sophisticated purchasers of legal service, perceptions of value may differ.

Historically, most lawyers and law firms determined price on a subjective or rule-of-thumb basis, taking into account some or all of the following factors: inflation, costs, and the desired level of profit or income. With a declining amount of law work available and an increased number of lawyers, combined with increased and more direct competition through marketing, clients saw other providers as alternatives to their traditional legal counsel, thereby forcing lawyers to be less casual about billing methods. To remain competitive for the future, more careful internal study is warranted for fee pricing.

THE MODERN FOCUS ON VALUE

Tying attorneys' fees to hourly billing tends to force lawyers to perceive all matters as being of equal importance. But all matters are not of equal importance and value. Lawyers perceive value as a function of the hourly rate and effort; clients do not. If a lawyer enables a client to acquire a $200 million company for $10 million less than the client expected, the lawyer's fee of $30,000 easily seems appropriate. On the other hand, if the client's perception is that the lawyer was merely to draft the paperwork for the deal that had already been negotiated between the companies, this fee may seem extreme. The difference is in the perception of value. With the hourly billing approach, the lawyer need not get involved in understanding the client's value system and business, because hourly billing "should be" an accepted practice. How much ribbing would the lawyer get from some of the hourly martyrs in the firm who would ask, "Couldn't you have used more associates, billed more hours, and developed a higher fee?" A classic situation comes to mind, in which a partner asks why the firm needs to invest in a litigation system when it would just make the lawyers more efficient, reducing the fees and, therefore, the firm's profit. Lawyers who base price upon hourly billing rates cannot meet the following challenge: Reduce the client's legal fees *and* maintain quality *and* increase firm profitability.

In today's legal marketplace, the trend should be away from cost-based billing represented by hourly billing and toward billing methods that recognize that the client's perception of value should be a primary consideration. Client demand drives pricing strategy and affects internal law firm responses regarding the manner in which services are provided.

In the business world, pricing is a profit-planning exercise where management searches for alternative pricing policies and evaluates the profit consequences of various alternatives before reaching a pricing decision. Some lawyers know a great deal about profits and how to produce them, while many do not. Today, all lawyers must understand the relationships among the value of services in the market, the internal costs of production, the fees set, and the effect of alternative billing methods on profitability.

Given the client-driven market, lawyers must understand and respond to clients' desires for predictability and value if they are to succeed in the marketplace. A lawyer should know enough about the practice and obtain enough accurate information from the client to answer the following questions:

- Should I take this case for the fee available?
- How much money will I make/lose if I take this case?
- Are the fees established by my competition too high or too low for my particular practice?
- Can I be more effective in choosing the tasks to be performed and in delegating work to less expensive lawyers and staff?

- Can I be more efficient, provide the same quality of service, and still make some money?
- Should I stop handling this type of case altogether?
- If I decide to take this case as a loss leader, just how much is my loss likely to be, and what must I do to leverage the credibility gained into higher-profit cases in the future?
- Is my overhead unreasonably high, or is it low enough that I can compete and provide high-quality services in this type of work while still making some profit?
- What kind of cases, clients, and work produce the most/least net profit?
- Is the nature of my practice changing from year to year? If so, is it changing toward more net profit or less net profit?
- Is one type of fee arrangement more profitable than another?

These questions are natural and appropriate for your self-interest. However, you should answer them with an overriding concern for the value of your services to the client. How are you to know the client's perception of value? That is the fundamental threshold for each new case or matter—understanding each client's objectives. If you do not know your client's objectives, you will find it impossible to be confident that your services will meet those objectives and hence conform to the client's perception of value. You may also find you have trouble getting paid.

Ideally, your talents and skills should exactly match the client's needs or requirements. As a practical matter, this is difficult to achieve in many situations because lawyers are not all alike, and the needs of clients vary. Even a single client's needs or wants may vary from matter to matter. At times, a routine service requiring only minimal skills will suffice. If so, the services may be performed by a nonlawyer supervised by a lawyer. At other times, the client may need highly skilled services that can be provided only by a lawyer with specialized expertise.

As an analogy, consider the purchase of clothing. Some buyers want high quality; others are more concerned with price. Some are interested in prestige or the label. Some buyers are concerned about fad and fashion, while others are not. Likewise, when selecting a restaurant, some customers want fine dining where atmosphere and location are very important. Other customers prefer good food served in a simple eatery. Sometimes a customer wants a five-course meal, and at other times a bowl of soup, a cup of coffee, or a hamburger.

Regardless of how a price is determined, there are upper and lower limits to that price. The upper limit is usually apparent when the price is so high that hardly anyone wants or can afford to purchase the good or service. Few purchases also result when a price is so low that it raises concerns about quality and value. If the price is higher than the client's perception of value, the client will seek other solutions by altering the process, going outside the system, or seeking other lawyers to service his or her needs.

Clients have always determined value. But, as discussed in Chapter 2, in earlier times there was never the ability to choose so easily among competing providers. The shift from the supply-driven competitive legal market of the 1970s to the demand-driven market of today requires more sophisticated tools for pricing legal services. In the supply-driven market, the demand for legal services was growing faster than the supply of lawyers, and lawyers' billing rates were low because the rates were driven by lower costs of operation. There are several manifestations of the shift:

- Greater buyer influence on the scope and price of legal services purchased from law firms
- Greater sophistication in planning, directing, and controlling legal costs based upon the values added by the outside law firms
- Strong competition among law firms for available work
- Increased competition from other professionals to provide services that were once (or may still be) considered within the scope of traditional legal services

The value of a service is not tied to the tenure of the lawyer working on the matter or to the billing rates set by the firm during the budgeting process. In a demand-driven market, value is determined by the client, not the law firm. Value is what the client perceives the lawyer adds to the client's business or legal affairs.

THE VALUE CURVE

The price of a service or the billing rate for the service must reflect the value perceived by the client. A law firm can no longer set its billing rates and price its work in a vacuum; it must have an intimate working knowledge of the client's business and value system.

Herbert Maslow, an eminent industrial psychologist, once said, "If the only tool you have is a hammer, everything begins to look like a nail." In the legal profession, we need alternative tools for pricing services. William C. Cobb of Cobb Consulting of Houston, Texas, has developed and popularized the "value curve" as such a tool. It supplements the hourly rate or cost-based billing and can identify areas where the client's perception of value is not tied to the hours a lawyer spends on the matter.

The value curve (and competitive position profile), which is illustrated in Exhibit 4-1, shows the relative value of services versus the volume of the work

Exhibit 4-1

Value Curve
(Competitive Position Profile)

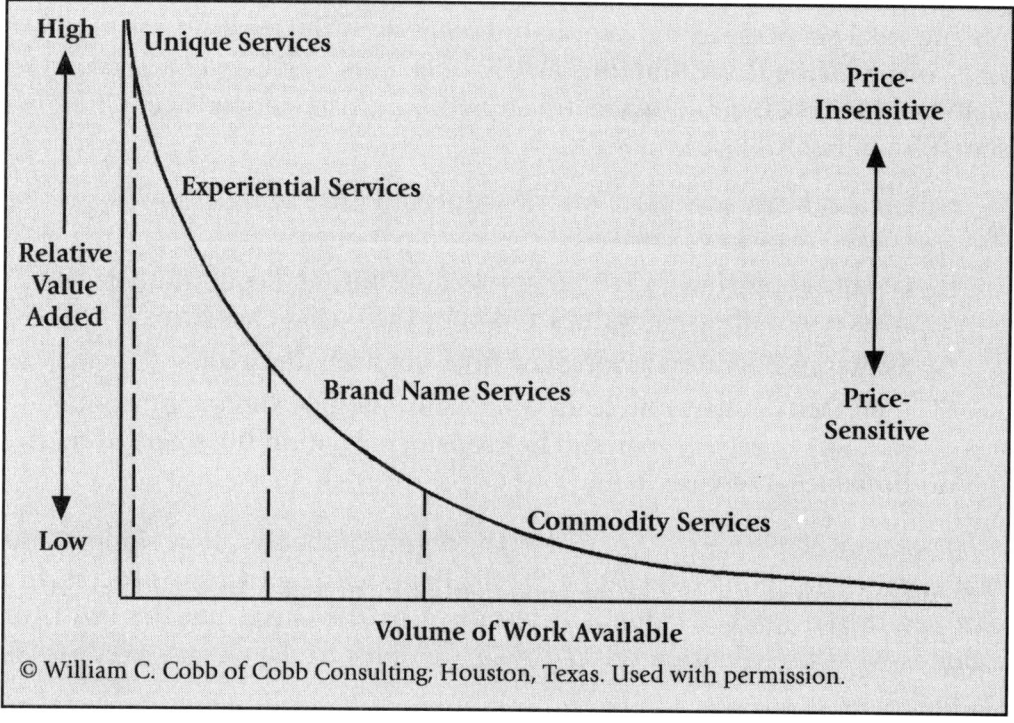

© William C. Cobb of Cobb Consulting; Houston, Texas. Used with permission.

available to a law firm. The greater the volume of available work (horizontal axis), the more lawyers there are who can capably perform the work. The more lawyers there are to perform the work, the more price-sensitive the service. In other words, when customers (clients) can shop around, they will look for a low price. The curve may be compared to a product life cycle. The longer a profitable product is around in the market, the more producers will enter the market to produce price competition. For example, look what has happened to the personal computer. Prices started in the range of $3,000 to $4,000 and have come down, with the increased number of producers in the market, to as low as $400 to $600. Legal services will not escape the laws of economics.

The vertical axis of Exhibit 4-1 shows the relative value of the service. The greater the perceived value to the client, the higher the position on the line. Value may be added by the client's perception of the lawyer's worth, availability, timeliness, prestige, and other factors discussed in Chapter 1. As the value moves from high to low, the client becomes more sensitive to price.

INTERPRETING THE CURVE

For clarity, the value curve is segmented into four classifications of work:

1. *Unique*: This is a nuclear event to the client. Less than 4 percent of the work in a market is unique work.
2. *Experiential*: This is a high-impact or high-risk matter for the client. Such important work will go to the lawyer the client feels will personally handle it. The client will find a limited number of lawyers qualified to perform the work. About 16 percent of the work available in a market is experiential.
3. *Brand Name*: This work is more routine but still important to the client. It will go to the firm or group of lawyers who have established a brand name with the client. Size is an important factor here, but reputation for a niche is just as important. About 20 percent of the work available in a market is brand name.
4. *Commodity*: In the view of clients, this is work that practically any good lawyer can perform. The majority of the work available in a market, about 60 percent, is commodity work and is very price-sensitive.

Although these classifications appear precisely defined in Exhibit 4-1, there is in fact a transition range from one classification to another. The curve may differ slightly with different industries and different types of work, but the principle is the same. Note how quickly the value of work tapers off in the market. Before the work gets to brand name, it is already becoming price-sensitive.

To get a quick feel for what these classifications mean, think of some calls a lawyer might receive from a significant business client about a legal problem:

- *Unique*: the CEO or chairman of the board calls
- *Experiential*: the general counsel or a top-level executive calls
- *Brand Name*: an assistant general counsel or mid-level executive calls
- *Commodity*: one of the department managers calls

An early example of a unique event was Wachtell Lipton's $20 million fee for representing Kraft, Inc., in the takeover by Philip Morris Companies. A lead Wachtell Lipton lawyer noted that this client was shopping for quality, not price. "If a client is willing to pay $20 million, that's between Wachtell and its client," he said. Quality is in the eye of the client, not the law firm, and is related to the value added by the law firm, not the law firm's billing rates. To continue the quote: "In a transaction of that size and of this complexity, who is to say what is an appropriate fee? One has to look at the value created and the responsibility assumed by the law firm."

APPLICATIONS OF THE VALUE CURVE

For the sake of perspective, the value curve can show the relative position of the legal service(s) in a specific competitive market. In each market, consider the relative value to the client of (1) the firm, (2) the legal service, (3) the legal task, or (4) the legal product. Here are some examples:

- A national market for legal services where most of the brand-name work would go to nationally recognized firms
- A regional market where the brand-name work would go to one of the regionally recognized firms
    The unique work would go to a few lawyers or law firms with an established reputation in a specific service crucial to the survival of the client's business.
- A local market for legal services where unique or experiential work might still go to an established regional or national lawyer or firm
- A segment of clients who have a homogeneous set of business needs (for example, the regional banks or real estate developers)
    A particular segment of clients (such as large banks) may classify all work (such as creditors' rights work) as high volume and low impact. Such a service would be perceived as a commodity to be either sent to the firm with the lowest billing rate or brought in-house.
- A client whose needs and perception of values vary depending upon the importance of the service to the client's profitability or survival
    A large developer might classify a $100 million loan as a brand-name service, while a small developer might classify that interim loan as a very high-value, or experiential, service.
- The matter where different tasks and legal products have different values to the client or to the judge to whom the firm is submitting a fee request

The lawyer must assess the value of legal services he or she delivers relative to other lawyers in the market. An objective assessment will show that clients place matters, services, and legal products at different points on the value curve.

When a law firm or individual lawyer adequately assesses the markets in which it competes for delivering legal services, the value curve provides additional insights. Billing rates for a lawyer are driven by operating costs. These costs include the cost of occupancy, employees, investments in technology, and, of course, the required draws of the partners or minimum distributions to the lawyer. When the average billing rates due to leverage are overlaid on the value curve, the value of services may not coincide with the value to the client.

For example, Exhibit 4-2 shows the range of billing rates for Firm 1, which are driven by overhead and lawyer tenure. Even at the lowest billing rate, such a

Exhibit 4-2

Position of Two Firms on the Value Curve

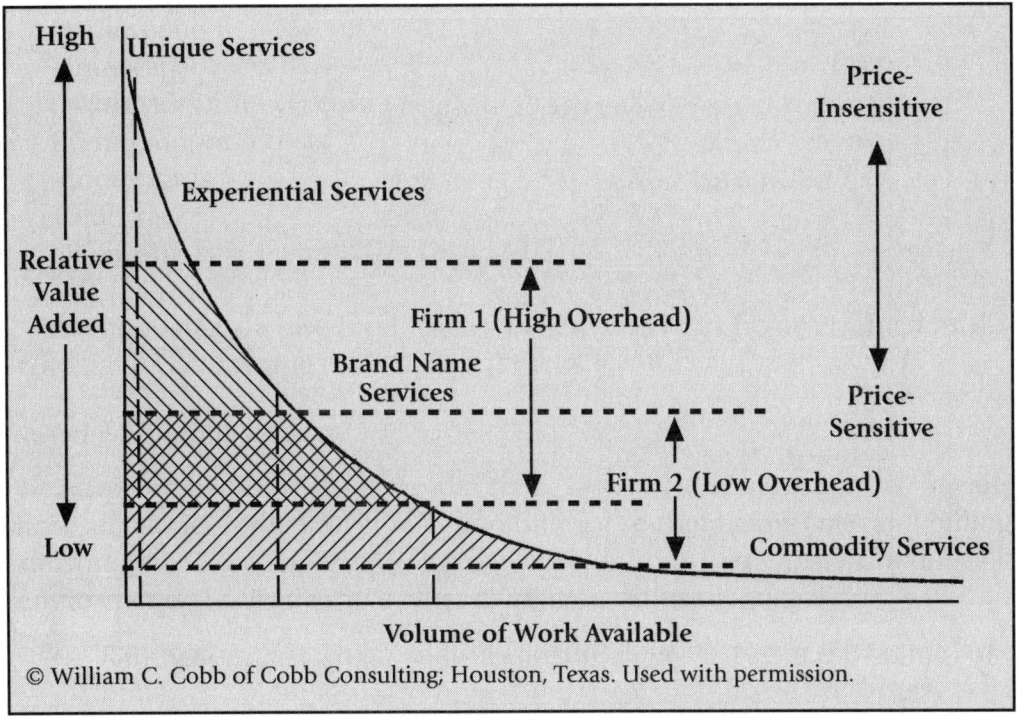

© William C. Cobb of Cobb Consulting; Houston, Texas. Used with permission.

high-overhead firm cannot do much commodity work without significant write-downs or effective use of substantive systems. Firms with particular structures and overhead cannot, in the context of a competitive market, be all things to all clients. The lower operating costs for Firm 2 mean that the range of billing rates will be lower. Of course, if a firm uses only hours as the key element in evaluating its performance, instead of return on the hour (realization), then any work along the curve will be acceptable.

The value curve is the tool to analyze the firm's competitive position within a market. That market could be a geographic market, a client segment market (such as large commercial loan departments), a client, or an area of practice (such as environmental).

IMPLICATIONS OF THE VALUE CURVE

Competitive Position

A lawyer must understand his or her relative competitive position by services—or bundles of services—offered. A lawyer can move up the curve by improving

Exhibit 4-3

Sample Points on the Value Curve

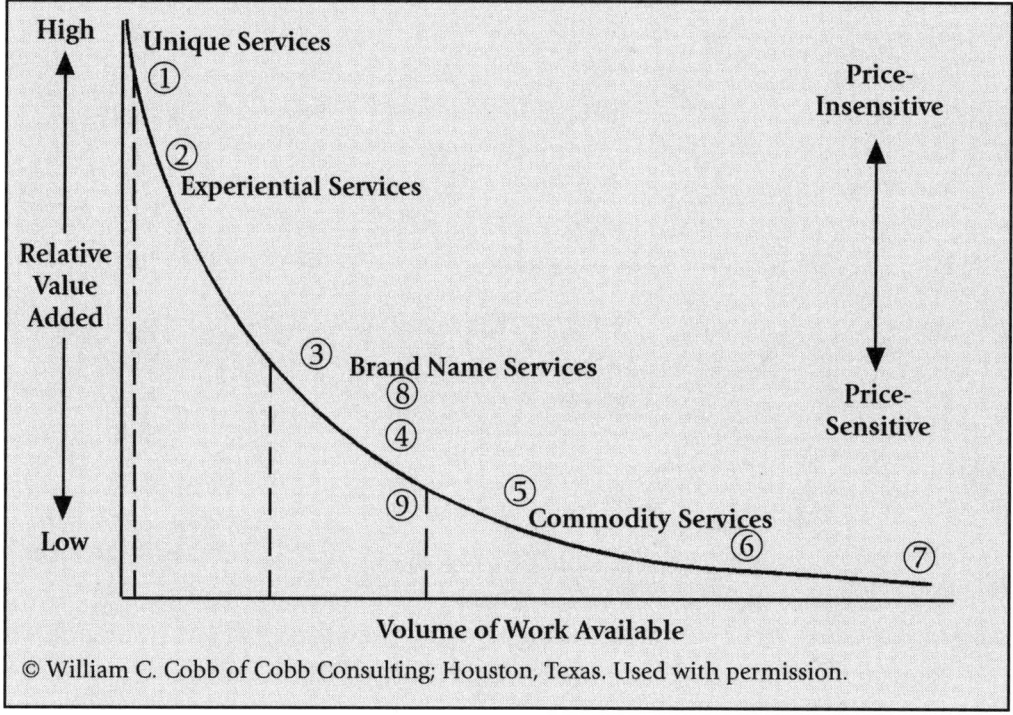

© William C. Cobb of Cobb Consulting; Houston, Texas. Used with permission.

intake procedures to focus on higher-value work. However, a very high-value service in the market in one month may move from point 1 to point 4 in Exhibit 4-3 as volume increases and as new competitors enter the market.

For example, in the early 1980s, there were very few top bankruptcy lawyers in the Southwest. Creditors' rights suits were rare. The best lawyers were hired at very high rates to defend the banks against potentially catastrophic losses. By the late 1980s, creditors' rights defense had become low-end brand-name or upper-end commodity work with the concomitant pressures on billing rates, delegation, and the use of substantive systems to lower professional hours.

To maintain their competitive position and stop the slippage of value as more competitors enter the market, firms add value to the services offered. Sources of added value include timeliness, quarterly client briefings, project management, project status reporting, and other additions to the standard bundle of services.

Price

Where a client locates a service on the value curve determines what the client is willing to pay in either billing rates or some other form of fee. If a client wants a particularly stellar lawyer to appear in court on an experiential matter, the lawyer may be able to charge 150 percent, 200 percent, or even 500 percent of his or her normal billing rate. If the task is a commodity project, the client may want a very low billing rate or fixed fee. If the work is in the brand-name range, the client may want the blended rate (the average billing rate per hour) for the work to be competitive.

The lawyer or firm must understand its relative competitive position as a provider of certain services. Within a firm, groups also may provide services to significant clients with specific ranges of value. The real estate group may offer services that range from point 2 to point 4 in Exhibit 4-3. The securities group may offer services that range from points 1 to 3. The litigation group may offer services that range from points 3 to 6. Therefore, the pricing approaches of these groups may vary, as may their structure and leverage.

The firm or lawyer must interview clients to determine their value systems. Individual employees of the clients may have different objectives, which also must be understood in the acceptance of any work. Always ask, "Who *is* the client?" One corporate officer may be trying to win quickly, another may be trying to postpone settlement, and still another may be trying to protect his or her corporate position by hiring the largest firm. Therefore, the added value of timeliness may be important to one and not another.

Realization is the percentage that a firm receives through collections on standard billing rates. If the standard billing rate for a lawyer is $150 per hour and the effective collected rate is $135 per hour, the total realization is 90 percent. Losing 1 percent of realization has the same effect on the bottom line as writing off 1 percent of the hours worked or giving a discount of 1 percent on standard billing rates. If the lawyer's fees are above the client's value curve (for example, point 8 in Exhibit 4-3), the lawyer will end up getting only the value the client perceives—point 4—and realization will therefore be less than 100 percent. If the lawyer's fees for the same project are normally at point 9 and the client has agreed in the engagement letter to pay the price reflected in point 4, realization will be greater than 100 percent. A 1 percent increase in realization produces the same increase to distributable income as a 1 percent increase in hours or standard rates.

Law Firm Structure

Firm structure and the leverage used by a firm must be driven by the types of services offered, *not by some arbitrary ratio*. A particular leverage ratio will not guarantee profitability. For example, a firm operating in a niche that is experiential and unique in the market may operate without much leverage and still maintain a high level of profitability. One of the reasons some New York firms are so profitable is that they are able to use leverage in the unique and experiential classifications of work.

If a firm is going to compete in the brand-name area, it must have some leverage to lower the average billing rates so they are competitive. Using only partner time in the brand-name area will quickly price the firm out of that market.

If a firm must compete in the commodity area, it must significantly leverage the work through delegation. The firm must also use substantive systems to minimize the number of professional hours used to create legal products.

The divergent mix of services and consequent leverage in a law firm appears most disruptive in a practice that includes general commercial litigation and insurance defense litigation. General commercial litigation may be in the range of points 2 to 4 in Exhibit 4-3. Because of the approach of insurers, typical insurance defense work is in the range of points 4 to 6. Commercial litigation is a high-overhead practice requiring top recruits at high salaries, litigation support, and investments in training and development. The insurance defense practice can manage on lower-cost associates and lower overhead. Internal conflicts develop because of the overhead, the use of delegation, the investments in support, and similar items. Assuming that high-priced associates are recruited by a firm, a new lawyer whose experience and billing rate increase with tenure must move in one of two directions:

1. The lawyer must move through the insurance group into the commercial group with its lower leverage and possibly higher overhead to realize his or her assigned billing rate.
2. He or she must become a manager of a highly leveraged operation and become an excellent manager of people and systems.

To continue doing the low-end work at senior-associate or new-partner rates will cause discounts and write-downs, which will lower realization on billing rates. The net collections for that partner will not be able to support his or her compensation and related overhead.

USING THE VALUE CURVE

The value curve can help clarify a variety of strategies. You can use the value curve for positioning your firm, for client management, for setting prices, and for project management.

External Positioning of the Firm

For a few significant clients, evaluate the work performed for them in the context of the value curve. In the opinion of the respective client teams, where do which services fall on the curve? Prepare a briefing memorandum on the work performed, which can be used to develop questions for client interviews.

Next, conduct client interviews to determine needs and the value systems of key client employees. In these interviews, learn what the employee perceives adds to, and detracts from, the value received. From those interviews, define the bundle of services the clients feel are most important and the value-adding elements of the bundle of services. For example, for a particular client, what adds value to the completion of an interim loan document for the construction of a building? Or what adds value to the client in managing and controlling legal cost in litigation?

By gaining this information over series of interviews, a firm or an individual lawyer can begin building a focused marketing program. Clients and referral sources can better understand the bundles of services offered by the firm or lawyer, and the values added by using the firm or lawyer.

Client Management and Intake

Establish briefing notebooks on clients, noting the key players, their value systems, and the bundles of services the firm provides. Every member of each client team should have a working knowledge of that client's notebook.

Based upon the analysis of where the firm or practice group can most effectively compete on the value curve—given operating overhead, structure, and mix of experience—begin restructuring the practice groups to conform to the structure required to compete effectively. In addition, redesign the firm's intake criteria and procedures to ensure that the focus is on the bundles of services that will provide the highest realization while minimizing the risk that the firm will be susceptible to economic cycles.

Using this book, redesign your intake procedures to include project planning and engagement letters that document the firm's understanding with the clients on cost, schedule, and performance.

Internal Determination of Pricing

The basic goal of using the value curve and alternative pricing is to increase the efficiency and effectiveness of the services provided. The short-term cost will be the loss of revenue hours, but there are a number of long-term payoffs:

- The lawyers anticipate client demand and have fewer crises to address each day.
- The clients have more predictability in fees, more involvement in establishing the scope of legal work, a reduction in legal costs resulting from lawyer efficiency, and faster response times.
- Quality improves through debriefing of current projects. Debriefings identify quality and efficiency improvements to be made in future projects and create checklists for anticipating the effort required on legal tasks and products. The result: improved quality with better training and less duplication of effort.
- Lawyers are no longer motivated to log hours into files or use too many associates. This approach moves the firm *away* from the hourly

criteria for personal performance. It moves the firm *toward* profitability of the client service team.

- Revenues increase through higher realization on rates. Higher realization reduces the time partners must spend in pure billable work. They are freed to spend that time to develop and secure client relationships, manage the practice, train others, improve quality assurance, and recharge their batteries.
- Growth slows because resources are used more efficiently. This relieves the demand for growth capital for recruiting, hiring, and training.

The keys to the success of alternative billing are excellent client relationships and project management. The client relationship is key because a billing lawyer must know the client's value system. With that value system in mind, the lawyer can determine which tasks are price-sensitive and which are not. A clear and concise representation agreement, which addresses the pricing approach used in a matter, helps build a strong client relationship.

Project Management

Project management concerns planning, directing, controlling, and organizing staff for a client matter. The following steps will help determine a pricing strategy for a client or bundle of services.

Begin by selecting significant clients of the firm with whom the firm has credibility and wants to cement long-term relationships. Significant clients offer at least some of the following attributes:

- Fee volume
- Profitability
- Prestige
- Access to new work that fits the firm's strategy

Next, select the key client employees who set the criteria for evaluating the law firm and are the referral source for legal work.

Through interviews and conferences with employees of key clients, determine the needs of those clients. Record the needs in terms of bundles of services the clients require, not in terms of the law firm's products. A bundle of services consists of the major services provided to a client and the important valuing criteria in each of those services. For example, a bundle of services may be a medium-sized asset-based new loan, or the workout of a medium-sized asset-based loan. Each bundle of services has specific phases of effort containing elements of work. Each element or group of elements of work must meet certain valuing criteria. A client's perception of value added may include twenty-four-hour turnaround, status reporting, a budget projecting anticipated effort and fees, and/or other criteria that satisfy the client's need to maintain control over legal costs.

Break the work of a particular service into phases of effort, each ending with major milestones the firm and client can identify. Milestones might include an initial conference, the completion of loan documentation, or a closing.

Within each phase, show the elements of work in sequence. The first product will be an outline of each major phase, with each element of work (task or product) listed in the subparagraphs or sub-subparagraphs. Debriefing from a similar, previous project will help identify the phases of work, milestones, and work elements. Seek and identify ways to eliminate excess hours and duplicated efforts on tasks.

Using the value curve as a tool, determine the value of each element to the client, based upon the client's value system and price sensitivity. Each element of work is a task or the development of a legal product. Assign each element of work an hourly rate, a blended rate, a fixed rate/price or flat fee, or a contingency fee:

- *Hourly Billing Rate*: Use this when you do not know the time or mix of professionals required for the element of work. The hourly rate is the rate that appears on the work-in-process billing memorandum. If the total fee on the billing memorandum is $10,000 and the total number of hours in the matter is 100 hours, then the weighted average billing rate, or hourly rate, would be $100 per hour.

- *Blended Billing Rate*: Use this when you do not know the time required for the element of work, but can anticipate the mix of professionals needed to accomplish the task. If a fixed rate quoted to the client is $135 per hour, the client is assured of that rate for the task. Internally, this is based upon assumptions about who will do the work. For example, the $200/hour partner anticipates contributing 25 percent of the time in the task, an associate at $125/hour will contribute 50 percent of the time, and a paralegal at $75/hour will contribute 25 percent of the time. Thus, the blended rate will be $131.25, providing a premium of $3.75 per hour. If the partner can manage the task more efficiently and get an additional 5 percent of the work to the associate, the blended rate in work-in-process will be $127.50, for another $3.75 premium. If the blended-rate tasks amount to 1,000 hours, the premium will be $7.50 times 1,000, or $7,500. The effective billing rate for each timekeeper will be 106 percent of the standard billing rate. (For example, the associate's effective billing rate will be $132.35 per hour.) If, across the firm, the blended billing rate can be used for up to 10,000 hours each month, with no increase of overhead, the premium will increase. That premium will also replace many hours of billable time and allow the partners time for improving service and client relationships.

- *Fixed or Flat Fee*: Use this when you can estimate the time and mix of professionals required for the effort. For example, the preparation of an employment agreement may be estimated for the client at a fee of $100. If the partner can create a system to produce the legal product for $75, each employment agreement prepared will produce a premium of $25. The effective billing rates of the professionals working on the agreement will be 133 percent of their standard billing rates.
- *Contingency Fee*: This is appropriate when you believe there is a bona fide cause of action and you can afford to make the investment in the matter or case. If given enough time for negotiations with the client, use a reverse contingency. For example, you and the client can agree that the probable legal expense will be $200,000, and that if you can dispose of the matter within ninety days, you get 50 percent of the difference between your fees and the $200,000. This is a simple example; lawyers throughout the country use variations of this approach.

Once you have identified each phase, milestone, and element, and have established the most appropriate pricing approach for each element, you can use the outline to budget the effort and assign appropriate professional resources. The firm may use these approaches in combinations, as shown in Chapter 10.

Next, develop a time-phased schedule showing the calendar time required for each phase and, within each phase, the calendar time of each element. Some firms use software such as Harvard Project Management™ and Timeline™ to create such schedules. The time-phased plan is the project plan. The project plan identifies the path of effort, showing the limitations on resources (time and experience), the calendar time of the effort, and the critical path. The critical path represents the series of elements of work that need the most management attention. The critical path minimizes slack time and drives the calendar dates of the milestones. The project plan provides notice of what must be done, which professionals (at which rates) should do the task, when the task must be accomplished, and how much time the task should take. Finally, the project plan establishes the cost, schedule, and performance outline for drafting the engagement letter.

The most efficient way to create a project plan is through a debriefing from a series of similar, completed matters. The billing memoranda can be pulled and, from that information, the lawyer can outline the elements of work and create the time-phased project plan. Lawyers are always surprised at the duplication of effort and inefficiency identified by the debriefing. A lawyer can almost always find efficiencies that can reduce fees or increase realization.

IMPORTANCE OF THE VALUE CURVE

The value curve helps a firm understand the market's value system, as well as the implications of the firm's mix of services on the firm's structure and economics. Use the value curve and the cost determination approach as reference points in reading the remaining chapters. Use these tools to explain pricing to clients. As you establish pricing strategies, these tools will give you a picture of the firm's practices and positioning strategies.

Legal services are subject to the operation of the market. In the long run, lawyers as sellers of legal services, and clients as purchasers, will seek other solutions if a price is higher than the client will pay for the value received. As stated earlier, these solutions involve altering the legal system, clients going outside the system, or clients seeking other lawyers willing to service their needs.

MULTIPLE VALUE CURVES

The value curve for a law firm does not actually consist of a single line, as discussed thus far. For each firm—and possibly for each lawyer or practice area in the firm—the work being done may be positioned at different points along the value curve. Even work in the same practice area may fit at different points along the value curve, due to factors such as client perception, responsibility assumed, and amount involved.

Except for a single-focus practice (often found in a small law office or a boutique law practice), a law office generally has separate value curves for each of its practice areas, as shown in Exhibit 4-4. The significance of this phenomenon is severalfold.

First, as noted earlier, not all clients of a law office perceive the value of their work in the same way. This suggests you should at least consider valuing (charging) for services in relation to the value provided to the client (as the client perceives it).

Also, if your law office provides the same client services in different areas of law, you might consider charging a different hourly rate (even possibly for the same lawyer) if the client perceives the value of the services differently. Similarly, different clients—oftentimes in the same area of law—may have substantially different views about the appropriateness of separately billing for ancillary services such as document creation, computer usage, word processing, or copying.

The differing cost and leverage patterns often found in different areas of law suggest that the law office should consider using different billing rates for lawyers having similar experience levels but working in different areas of law.

Differing supply and demand patterns usually exist within different areas of law, often at different times of the year and varying over time. Causes of these differences could include seasonal factors, competitive factors, new legislation, or unusual business, political, or natural events. This suggests that you should lower hourly rates in periods of low demand and high supply, and raise them in periods of high demand and low supply, to adjust for the way supply

Exhibit 4-4

Value Curve by Practice Area

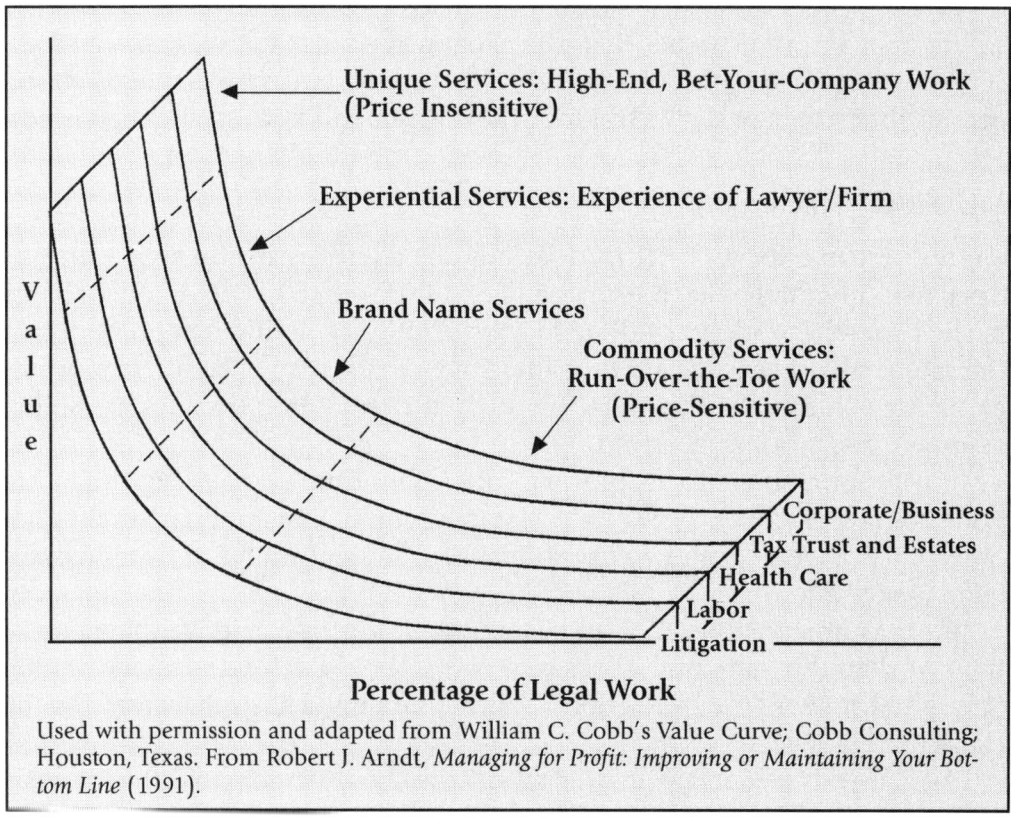

Used with permission and adapted from William C. Cobb's Value Curve; Cobb Consulting; Houston, Texas. From Robert J. Arndt, *Managing for Profit: Improving or Maintaining Your Bottom Line* (1991).

and demand patterns occur at different times in different areas of law (and, in many cases, for individual lawyers).

Although not directly related to billing practices, note that clients on different points on the value curve(s) may need and expect different levels of responsiveness. To maximize the clients' views of the value of the services provided, lawyers must continuously remind themselves of these differing needs and expectations, and they must continually monitor their clients' value systems.

HOURLY BILLING IS COST-DRIVEN

For many years, law offices have based hourly billing rates upon costs and desired profits. The techniques used to do this have varied from simple to complex. On the simple side, law offices have used the "rule of three":

$$\frac{\text{Compensation} \times 3}{\text{Chargeable Hours}} = \text{Billing Rate}$$

The rationale for this approach is that the multiple of 3 covers compensation, overhead, and a profit. Of course, this method has been tempered by market forces, and profit results have been dampened in many communities because overhead costs per lawyer exceed compensation costs of the lawyer.

This led to the slightly more complex method of estimating (budgeting) overhead expenses, compensation, and billable hours; deciding on desired profit levels; and setting billing rates (considering market forces) to produce the desired profits. The next level of complexity was to set hourly billing rates by budgeting, but to do so by practice group and, in large firms, by office. This gives rise to differing cost and leverage patterns and generates competitive pressures among different practice groups and offices.

Although these methods for determining hourly rates are affected by market forces, the underlying factor driving their initial determination is total cost. This approach is sound from an economic standpoint, and it probably will continue to be used for some time to guide the setting of hourly billing rates.

However, cost-based billing rates should be used only as a guide for determining how much to bill a client. This type of billing may promote inefficiency, ineffective use of staff, and poor delegation, and it may discourage the use of substantive systems, forms, and innovative technology. Generally, for the purposes of pricing legal services, cost plus hourly rates should be used as an internal project-costing system.

VARIATIONS OF HOURLY RATES

As suggested, hourly rates should probably vary because of different cost and leverage patterns. At this point, a few examples might help show how this works. Assume the following information about a law firm:

	Total	Partner	Associate
Compensation	$75,000		$75,000
Overhead	195,000	$120,000	75,000
Desired profit	200,000	125,000	75,000
Total cost and profit	$470,000	$245,000	$225,000
Estimated chargeable hours		1,700	1,800
Cost-based rate/hour		$145	$125

In terms of chargeable hours, these numbers may be fairly representative for two litigation lawyers. But change the assumption slightly and make the same calculations for two tax lawyers (with the same level of experience) who frequently have smaller projects and a lot of stop/start time, and who must do a lot of reading of new tax bulletins, thus resulting in lower chargeable hours. We want to produce the same profit for the partner:

	Partner	Associate
Total cost and profit	$245,000	$225,000
Estimated chargeable hours	1,500	1,600
Cost-based rate/hour	$163	$141

Each of these cases assumes a 1:1 associate/partner ratio. But assume a slightly different scenario for a partner working in family law and sharing an associate (half-time) with another partner. Then our picture would look like the following:

	Total	Partner	Associate
Compensation	$ 37,500		$ 37,500
Overhead	157,500	$120,000	37,500
Desired profit	200,000	162,500	37,500
Total cost and profit	$395,000	$282,500	$112,500
Estimated chargeable hours		1,500	800
Cost-based rate/hour		$188	$141

Although leverage and chargeable hours can affect hourly rates, differences in costs also should affect rates. Cost differences could occur at the practice group level or at the client level, due to different views of charging (for word processing, for example), different payment practices (such as slow pay), or different support needs (such as a "war room").

These examples suggest that the beginning point for setting hourly rates (that is, cost-based rates) should take into account differing chargeable hour, leverage, and cost patterns to produce similar profits for similarly experienced partners. Chapter 11 includes a discussion of the sensitivity of the bottom line to such changes.

MAJOR ISSUES REGARDING BILLING METHODS

Pause here to think about some of the concepts that have been advanced to this point. As you read further, consider the major issues confronting the legal profession in connection with billing methods, such as the following:

- Is the currently predominant method of hourly billing the best way to measure the value of legal services?
- How should value be measured?
- Is there any way by which value can be objectively measured?
- Who determines value—the lawyer or the client—even though the "test" is value to the client?
- Is the process truly a matter of value in the theoretical sense, or can it be accomplished on a workable, practical, day-to-day basis?
- Are there several different billing methods that can be used on a case-by-case basis or in the same client matter that will measure value to the mutual benefit of the lawyer and client?
- Is the ultimate issue how to use traditional and innovative billing methods in ways that fit individual situations? (If so, tailoring billing methods to fit different clients, phases, or matters may be the most precise approach.)
- How can lawyers be educated to understand and accept the concept of alternative billing methods, including the problem of lawyer egos and "value"? (Chapter 11 includes some possible approaches.)
- How can alternative billing methods be implemented and controlled in a law firm with many partners? (This problem is exacerbated when a firm grows into an institutional-style facility, with multiple departments and offices.)

CHAPTER FIVE

Pricing Legal Services for the Solo and Small-Firm Lawyer

The majority of lawyers in the United States practice in a solo or small-firm setting. These lawyers often face different challenges concerning pricing for their services. Yet, in many ways, a smaller-size practice—with its lack of bureaucracy and certain institutional traditions—allows lawyers to move more nimbly in adopting changes. For many of these practices, the analysis of pricing requires considerations not present in the larger law firm, while some of the factors important in the larger firm are either minimized or nonexistent.

Solo and small-firm lawyers are not homogeneous. Many small firms operate in the same manner as larger law firms and serve similar clients. This is particularly true for small firms that originally existed as practice groups of larger firms. When lawyers who spent their early years practicing in large-firm settings move to smaller-firm settings, they tend to continue practicing in the same way they always did.

But for many solo and small-firm lawyers, there is a significant difference between their practices and those of their large-firm brethren. This difference relates to who or what might be a typical client. Generally speaking, larger law firms spend most of their efforts representing businesses, and the bigger the business clients are, the better. This is not to say that law firms of all sizes do not represent individuals. But generally, corporate clients constitute the bedrock of a larger firm's clientele.

Many solo practitioners and small-firm lawyers spend a larger portion, if not all, of their time representing individual consumers of legal services and the local "mom-and-pop" businesses. Although many elements of the previous chapter on pricing relate to the ongoing matters handled on behalf of small-business clients in the same way as large-business clients, there are still unique differences. The smaller-business owner often has more in common with a consumer making any other type of purchasing decision than a large corporate client engaging in business-to-business negotiations with a large law firm.

Let us examine whether the lessons of the previous chapter hold true for small-town lawyers, suburban lawyers, and those in other practice settings who represent mainly consumers. Some of these lawyers consider themselves to be general practitioners, while others have highly specialized or limited practices focusing on areas such as consumer bankruptcy, criminal defense, or family law. Many lawyers in urban settings also have these types of practices. For easy reference and lack of a better term, we shall refer to these lawyers collectively as Main Street lawyers.

THE VALUE CURVE

The value curve as outlined in the previous chapter denotes rules of economics from which the Main Street lawyer is not exempt. In fact, examination of the value curve as it relates to general practitioners provides a convincing explanation for the financial squeeze that many such practitioners have noted over the last several years.

The value curve states that different types of services share common characteristics. Let us repeat these characteristics as they are stated in the previous chapter, but in reverse order. Here are the four classifications of legal work:

1. *Commodity*: In the view of clients, this is work that practically any good lawyer can perform. The majority of work available in a market, about 60 percent, is commodity work and is very price-sensitive.

2. *Brand Name*: This work is more routine but still important to the client. It goes to the firm or group of lawyers that has established a brand name with the client. Size is an important factor here, but reputation for a niche is just as important. About 20 percent of the work available in a market is brand name.

3. *Experiential*: This is a high-impact or high-risk matter for the client. Such important work goes to the lawyer whom the client believes will personally handle it. The client will find a limited number of lawyers qualified to perform the work. About 16 percent of the work available in a market is experiential.

4. *Unique*: This is a nuclear event to the client. Less than 4 percent of the work in a market is unique work.

Let us examine each of these classifications, starting with commodity work.

COMMODITY WORK

The majority of work in the legal marketplace is commodity work. Many associates in large law firms have workloads that consist of commodity work, and many Main Street lawyers find that their practices have far more than 60 percent commodity work, perhaps even approaching 100 percent. This should not be taken as a disparagement or belittlement. Nor does this fact suggest that these matters are unimportant. In fact, one can argue on several levels that a contested child custody determination is more important and profound than a dispute between two large corporations over a contract provision. Moreover, not all commodity work is easy or mundane. Many times a "simple" real estate transaction can involve quite complex title issues.

But most Main Street lawyers have experienced some puzzling disappointments in the legal marketplace—such as long-term clients going to new, wet-behind-the-ears lawyers for no apparent reason, clients who discuss matters in depth but then apparently take no action, local clients taking significant matters to firms in larger urban areas when local lawyers are more than competent to handle the work, or otherwise reasonable and responsible clients disputing legal fees. Accepting for a moment the legitimacy of the value curve and its definition of commodity matters may answer these nagging questions.

Understand that the predominant market variable of commodity legal services is that they are extremely price-sensitive. The lawyer's reputation and past services may well take a back seat to pricing factors in this sector. It is often difficult for Main Street lawyers to accept this premise. When through herculean efforts a lawyer rescues a family from the brink of disaster or obtains a financial settlement that changes a client's life, it is difficult to believe that a few years later the client will select another lawyer to draft a will based upon a price savings of $50. Yet the value curve suggests this may happen, and many lawyers have experienced that precise event.

One situation that is particularly hard for the Main Street lawyer to digest and accept is when a client goes to someone the lawyer views as providing inferior services. The new lawyer fresh out of law school may have a significantly lower hourly billing rate, but the experienced lawyer "knows" that due to experience, he or she can accomplish the task more quickly, with the total fee being the same—or perhaps even less.

The price-sensitive consumer may, on the other hand, focus on only one comparison. The experienced lawyer quotes an hourly rate of $165, while the rookie quotes an hourly rate of $90. This illustrates a pitfall of hourly rates in consumer commodity practice. The experienced lawyer may have a better work product and give superior advice. But the only information given to the client is that the services cost nearly twice as much.

If the project were quoted on a flat-fee basis, with both lawyers quoting a total fee of $450, then what would be the likely result? The experienced lawyer, with a past connection to the family, would probably be retained instead of the new lawyer in town. This may well be true even if the experienced lawyer's price is slightly higher. But lawyers must remain attuned to the fact that we have reached an era in the legal profession where there is extreme price sensitivity in these types of matters. With competition from do-it-yourself kits, Internet legal services, independent paralegals, and other nonlawyer service providers, the conflict is even greater. The price differential may be even more extreme.

Quality looms as an issue, too. With the new lawyer in town, there is an expectation that at least the services will be done correctly—the "practically any good lawyer" doing the commodity practice. Can the same be said of an untrained document preparer or an Internet document assembly service? Main Street lawyers can recount many problems resulting from the preparation and execution of do-it-yourself documents—such as documents that are incorrectly completed, never finished, or never filed. Increasingly, courts see divorce pleadings that were obtained from the Internet and that fail to comply with the jurisdiction's specific requirements. Also, although independent paralegals who provide services directly to consumers are licensed and recognized in a few states, many layperson document drafters do not have the training and experience to recognize pitfalls that may lurk behind completing form documents. Objectively, it may be that a lawyer's service is superior in many ways beyond the document itself (for example, a lawyer has potential liability for errors and a stringent code of ethics). But, in fairness, it must be said that an experienced paralegal can at times produce documents indistinguishable from those a lawyer prepares.

Among themselves, Main Street lawyers have long discounted the effects of incursions from other providers. They focus upon incidents of demonstrably shoddy work. They note the large fees they have earned through dealing with the problems resulting from documents drafted by laypersons. They can defend their fees; in fact, lawyers have a long history of firmly quoting fees to clients. A friendly, direct, and often-used statement is, "That's what I must charge to do a good job. If you don't want to pay that, you'll need to go elsewhere." The problem is, more and more consumers are accepting that invitation and seeking services entirely outside the community of lawyers. Experienced lawyers who doubt this should reflect on whether their offices receive calls from "price shoppers" more frequently than a few years or decades before.

Although it may be somewhat humbling to accept, the value curve helps us understand that nationally known lawyers—those who are often featured on television and have become household names (at least in legal circles)—can still name their price, on a "take it or leave it" basis, for unique and experiential matters. But things are now different for many legal services widely believed to be routine.

Consumers themselves use language that indicates they believe their work to be commodity work. ("I just want a simple will." "We do not have much." "This probably doesn't sound that important to you, but ...") There is certainly a tendency for many consumers to believe that a will is a will, no matter who drafts it, or that the conclusion of a probate case is preordained, no matter who handles it for them.

Lawyers armed with an appreciation of the price sensitivity of commodity work have the opportunity to craft an approach that is win-win for the lawyer and client. This does not mean engaging in a price war of reckless underbidding, which does not benefit the lawyer in the end. But it may mean highlighting other values the lawyer provides. This will be discussed in more detail later in this chapter.

BRAND-NAME WORK

Upon reflection, Main Street lawyers can recognize the brand-name market grouping, particularly if they practice in a small community. Certain lawyers may be recognized as preeminent within the legal community, and perhaps within the broader community as well. There may be one firm that has several lawyers, while the other lawyers in the community operate either as solos or duos. In a community with only one or two banks, for example, many people know which lawyer represents the bank and attends its board meetings. Similarly, although there may be many competent family practice lawyers in a community, there seem to be a few who often represent a party when the community's most wealthy or influential citizens experience a divorce or other legal problem. Other examples abound, from the second generation of lawyers representing the second or third generation of local business owners, to the affluent citizen who wants the best of everything, including the "best" lawyer in town.

This is one area where the ultimate truth of the value curve applies, but the application is a bit more indirect. When viewing the legal market from a national or global perspective, there might seem to be fewer brand-name service opportunities than the 20 percent projected. But within a given community, this percentage seems accurate. The prominent feature of this area of legal business is the client seeking the lawyer based upon reputation or perceived expertise. Lawyers hope that as they become more experienced, their practices will likewise mature by including an increasing number of these desirable attorney-client relationships.

With the exception of certain well-known areas like bankruptcy and personal injury practice, Main Street lawyers have traditionally avoided advertising and other marketing efforts targeted at the public. (Advertising is problematic in some ways, and readers are reminded that the ABA Law Practice Management Section has published several books dealing with marketing for lawyers.) But Main Street lawyers will do well to pay attention to the benefits of establishing a brand name. Developing a reputation and becoming known as the best and most educated in a certain area of the law, even a narrow one, is a positive approach with positive results. For example, though a lawyer perhaps cannot become renowned in all aspects of a criminal law practice, the lawyer might become *the* expert in administrative drivers' license suspensions or vehicle forfeitures. It might be surprising how readily other lawyers and clients will seek services and advice in a narrow area. Although such a narrow subspecialty might not be a source of extensive income, it does place the lawyer in a market niche where the price sensitivity of the consumers is not so strong. This provides the opening for a greater premium, at least on these matters.

EXPERIENTIAL AND UNIQUE WORK

For the purposes of this discussion, we can combine experiential work (high-impact or high-risk matters, composing about 16 percent of all legal work) and unique work (nuclear events or matters of the utmost importance, composing about 4 percent of all legal work).

This combined category embraces all the deadly serious, life-or-death needs for legal services. Hanging in the balance is the survival of the company, success or bankruptcy, the accomplishments of a lifetime, freedom of movement, or perhaps even one's very life. The client is focused. The stakes are enormous. It is understandable that the price of legal services recedes into the background and the ultimate outcome holds center stage. Does O.J. Simpson regret the large fees he paid to his criminal defense team? This does not mean that there are no ethical, practical, or moral restraints on the fee that can be charged. As noted in Chapter 3, the fee must always be reasonable. And the client's resources may be limited, even though motivation may be high.

It is useful, however, to understand the dynamics of this combined category. One familiar lawyer group often represents clients who have problems of this magnitude and, generally speaking, comprises those most free from dependence upon hourly billing—the criminal defense bar. For most individuals, a serious criminal charge is a nuclear event. Certainly the prospect of destruction of reputation, imprisonment, or the ultimate penalty—death—is exceedingly serious. The prospect of a criminal trial is so filled with tension, conflict, and drama that countless movies, television shows, and novels have been placed in this setting. There is no doubt these cases involve large stakes, and not just any lawyer will do. Members of the public generally understand that not all lawyers go to court and not all litigators handle criminal matters. So how have members of the criminal defense bar charged for their services?

Generally speaking, attorneys' fees for criminal defense lawyers are not based upon hourly rates. Instead, these fees are usually determined according to one of the so-called alternative billing methods—either a flat fee for the entire defense, or a separate fee for reaching clear landmarks (for example, one fee for a grand jury proceeding, another for a preliminary hearing, and another for the jury trial). In most instances, these fees are payable in advance. White-collar criminal defense cases are sometimes contracted on an hourly basis, but not often. Several factors have led to the use of a flat fee (or similar alternative billing method) in these cases, with assurance of payment being one. If a defense is unsuccessful, it may be difficult to obtain payment. Mailing billing statements to a prison cell is likely to be unsuccessful. There is an obligation among defense counsel to explore all avenues of defense, and therefore this should not be a situation in which the client and lawyer can make joint business decisions about the scope of the representation.

The point for the Main Street lawyer is that the value curve does predict the conclusion here. With nuclear events, there is little price sensitivity.

MARKET FACTORS FOR THE MAIN STREET LAWYER

Consumer clients represent the most price-sensitive area of legal practice. Though there are a variety of reasons for this, one factor cannot be ignored—the advertisements quoting fees for many "standard" or "uncontested" legal services. Few communities seem to be exempt from this circumstance.

These consumer areas are those of highest incursion by nonlawyer providers, who offer document drafting services for matters like bankruptcy and uncontested divorce. These also are areas of much confusion, because many of these clients seek simple solutions and "uncontested" fee structures when, in fact, they have a myriad of complicated problems.

Main Street lawyers cannot ignore the effect of these market forces and attitudes. These lawyers must be prepared to differentiate their services from others. The lawyers understand that the main differences are their professionalism and the high quality of their services. Clients must understand the value a lawyer provides. They are better served (and are more likely persuaded to hire the lawyer) when they are given concrete examples of that value. Among these examples are attorney-client confidentiality, the lawyer's familiarity with the case when the uncontested matter becomes contested, the lawyer's years of training and experience, the time savings the client achieves by having the lawyer provide the service rather than using the "do it yourself" approach, and the lawyer's ability to appear in court and speak on behalf of the client (as many clients have a great fear of public speaking).

Even in a price-sensitive area, the lawyer cannot—and should not—attempt to compete on price alone. The concept of value includes paying a bit more to receive superior services or superior results.

DEALING WITH UNSOPHISTICATED CLIENTS

In consumer-oriented practices, lawyers deal with a greater percentage of relatively unsophisticated clients. This does not imply that these clients are in any way graceless or ignorant. But they are often inexperienced in dealing with lawyers. Whether a matter concerns adoption or arrest, a will or a workers' compensation claim, the simple fact is that a consumer client may have no prior experience with the legal subject matter and had no prior need for a lawyer.

Therefore, some of the techniques discussed in the previous chapter on pricing simply do not apply in the same way in this situation. There can be no give-and-take discussion about various alternative billing methods when the client has little or no understanding of the process. There is little common ground for negotiation, and the fee is often presented to the client as a take-it-or-leave-it proposition. For consumer legal services, fees are often based upon market forces and lawyer experience, rather than negotiation with prospective clients. In fact, many Main Street lawyers have a long tradition of refusing to negotiate their fees. This is understandable, particularly with hourly rates: a lawyer charges a set fee per hour, and it seems unfair to charge a lower rate to one client just because that client pleads for one. Also, many offices have been organized to compute at one rate, and instituting various billing rates would increase administrative complexity in preparing bills.

Of course, most of us understand that Main Street lawyers might sometimes charge a discount rate, but generally that rate is reserved for business clients who have a regular volume of matters to be handled and who always pay their bills. Sometimes clients receive a "professional discount" if they are likely to refer clients to the lawyer in the future. In general, if there has been a discounted rate, it has been for "wholesale" or preferred customers, while the client coming in off the street with an initial need for a lawyer on a single matter would be considered a "retail" customer.

There have been ample ethical rules and community standards that have proscribed a fairly narrow range for an acceptable fee or rate. Unsophisticated clients are those who might most appreciate the simplicity and clarity of many fixed-fee arrangements.

Suppose a potential client makes an appointment with the lawyer about a relatively straightforward probate proceeding. The Main Street lawyer discusses handling the matter and discloses his or her billing rate. For many consumer clients, a statement of the lawyer's hourly rate—the cost per hour—is not sufficient information. Almost immediately, the next question is, "How many hours will it take?" or, "What will the total cost be?" This is when lawyers often give a most unsatisfactory answer: "It depends."

It is not surprising that this can be a source of frustration for the potential client. After all, most consumer purchasing experiences do not proceed like this. Throughout retail stores, price tags and signs abound. There, the price is stated in advance. Imagine buying a refrigerator after being told that the final price will be set only after you agree to make the purchase! Even a car dealer will make a firm offer. In fact, the Main Street lawyer has a fairly accurate mental understanding of what an average fee for this matter will total. But the estimate communicated to the client is often couched in broad terms, with many disclaimers. The lawyer cannot give an exact quote when the number of total hours to be expended is unknown to the lawyer, as well as the client.

Although some may view this reluctance as an attempt to conceal something from the consumer, in reality, the lawyer is exercising time-tested judgment. The experienced lawyer knows that if an average fee is mentioned, the client will focus on that number as "the fee." If the lawyer quotes an estimate of $2,000, the lawyer will view a final total billing of $2,165 to be right on target. But too many clients would respond with, "No, wait, you said $2,000." So the lawyer learns to express the estimate as a range, with plenty of room at the top end of the range to ensure that the total fee will almost certainly be less than the highest number mentioned. In this example, the lawyer, if pressed, would quote a range from a low of $2,000 to a high of $4,000 or $5,000.

Imagine how much more consumer-friendly and nonthreatening this transaction would be if the lawyer simply said, "This probate case can all be yours for the low price of $2,450." We are all consumers. We understand the attraction of simplicity. We understand the value of limiting the risk of a charge being much higher than anticipated. It is disingenuous to deny that we would prefer the certainty of the fixed fee if we were the client.

"Wait," many lawyers would cry, "there are many variables, and many contingencies." The extent of legal services required are often outside the lawyer's control. The lawyer understands that an unreasonable opposing counsel, a procrastinating opposing party, or a recalcitrant judge can increase the workload by several orders of magnitude. The lawyer does not want to bear that risk, and the hourly rate serves that purpose very well. Whether it is a necessary party who cannot be located for service of process or an unanticipated and complicated factual situation, if the matter becomes more burdensome, the lawyer invests more time and the lawyer should be paid more.

But the lawyer *does* know the variables—far better than the client. In many ways, lawyers do not want to get pinned down. Lawyers know they will treat a client fairly, but they also want to make sure they are not treated unfairly by working many extra hours without additional compensation.

In fact, though, in a matter involving contingencies that might dramatically change the work involved, the fee arrangement need not be based upon only one flat fee. The fee agreement may cover numerous contingencies: if event A happens, one fee will be charged; if B happens, then another fee. The most important thing is for the unsophisticated client to understand and comprehend fees quoted in this manner, without referring to an hourly billing rate. The client no longer must ask, "How many hours will it take?"

Where the sophisticated and experienced business client may need a jointly developed plan based upon the experiences of both the client and the lawyer, the consumer client needs information, explanation, and less uncertainty about the future. Written materials for the client to take home and review are extremely useful in these situations.

For many consumer cases, so-called alternative pricing is quite naturally a part of the case plan. (See Chapter 9 for more discussion of case and transaction plans.) A large law firm may invest in discussing costs or pricing structures with sophisticated clients, and those clients may choose à la carte from sets of possible services. Consumer clients, however, usually need their matters handled by one lawyer from beginning to end. They need understanding and reassurance. They need certainty and as much information as possible about the uncharted waters ahead. Hourly billing may be simple for the lawyer, but a consumer will appreciate the clarity and certainty of a fixed fee—even if that certainty is embodied in a road map with a dozen possible total fees, depending upon future variables.

PRICING STRUCTURE AS THE BASIS OF AN OFFICE SYSTEM

The pricing structure, when properly communicated to the client, can provide the basis of the attorney-client agreement and the case plan. The less familiarity the client has with the situation, the more detailed the disclosure should be.

In the probate case example, the consumer may indicate she will likely hire the Main Street lawyer and asks about the fees. In response, the lawyer produces not an intimidating document entitled "Attorney-Client Fee Agreement," but one called "Case Plan." This document appears in the form of a timeline, and may be more graphically designed than the standard legal document. The lawyer explains the anticipated chain of events—drafting and filing documents, sending notices, and so on. The document clearly notes the fees at each stage of the proceeding. The document or set of documents may also include many typical provisions and disclaimers. Much of this form can be preprinted, but because the client decides certain variables (such as sales of property within the probate), the form has blanks that are completed during the interview.

Of course, there may be unknowns and unknowables, in which case the lawyer makes a good-faith estimate *in writing*. Yet, the end result is a complete document detailing the entire course of the legal matter, the anticipated timing of events, a likely date of conclusion, an estimated fee, and the probable maximum fee.

Some lawyers object to attaching any estimate to an unpredictable fee. They may also disagree with giving clients time lines for completion of tasks, no matter how general. After all, probate cases sometimes drag on. But the message to the client should be that they do not "drag on" in this lawyer's office. The beauty of a case plan is that it is constructed to interlock with the lawyer's office procedures. The case plan provides a road map for the lawyer's staff, detailing tasks and anticipated timelines. The law firm's system provides not only for the drafting of required documents, but for important standardized client communications. Instead of receiving two-sentence transmittal letters, the client receives detailed status reports accompanying file-stamped copies, which refer to events outlined in the case plan. If contingencies occur and trigger a fee increase, the system generates a thoughtful explanation and discussion of what has transpired, to accompany the request for additional fees. The client has a reference guide throughout the matter to judge the lawyer's performance against predictions.

With this approach, the Main Street lawyer is highly motivated to improve, embellish, and streamline the system. Compared with other clients, the Main Street lawyer's clients may receive superior, regular, and more detailed communications, because the lawyer has judged that a few "extra" letters are less expensive to the firm than receiving numerous "extra" telephone calls from the client.

And what of the estimate of the unknowable fee, when the fee was underestimated due to an event that has now improbably occurred? Will the lawyer be judged by his or her own candor? ("Yes, I stated probably no more $2,000, and the charges are now $3,500. But, . . .") This is yet another aspect of the system that the lawyer should design and prepare in advance. When it becomes evident that an estimated charge may be exceeded, a letter of explanation can be sent to the client immediately, not when the final fees are requested. ("Please be advised that A and B have occurred, and the costs are exceeding our original estimate. You may contact me at no additional charge if you wish to discuss this.") This is not to say there will never be a time when a consumer manages to use a fee estimate against a lawyer, even if only for bargaining position to compromise the final fee. But the system functions to create understanding, predictability, and trust. A client is then predisposed to view a contingency as something that happened in his or her particular case, and not as the lawyer simply deciding to charge more.

The benefit for the Main Street lawyer is that the system encourages and rewards efficiency. Exploring advanced document assembly methods holds no downside. If the lawyer notes he or she typically receives a number of calls at a particular stage in the representation, for which the lawyer receives no additional compensation, then the lawyer is motivated to improve communications in that area proactively, perhaps by covering the area better in the initial interview or perhaps by adding to the language contained in a standard client communication during this time frame. The Main Street lawyer constantly hones and improves the system, while the clients benefit from an ever-evolving model of client service, explanation, and communication.

I CANNOT DO IT AT THAT RATE AND MAKE ANY MONEY

Often, the Main Street lawyer's initial reaction to decreasing fees in some consumer areas is steadfast insistence that lower fees make it impossible to turn a profit or deliver competent representation. It is absolutely true that an in-depth examination of office procedures and the tasks to be accomplished on behalf of clients may drive a lawyer to conclude that certain practice areas are unprofitable and should be dropped. It may also be true that to be a full-service law firm for consumer clients, a small firm in a small community may need to handle some matters that are only marginally profitable.

But a Main Street lawyer cannot "wish away" market forces, the impact of technology on the practice, or consumer attitudes. The simple fact is that many law offices have not arranged their operations for maximum efficiency. A lawyer may believe that a certain matter cannot be profitable, based upon the fact that it requires at least ten hours of lawyer time. But by fine-tuning and improving the system, the amount of lawyer time may be drastically reduced. The lawyer can use technology-based systems and/or support staff to move into a more profitable position. Some so-called routine legal services may be done for less and still be profitable. And the lawyer will then have more time available to work on other matters.

CONCLUSION

For the Main Street lawyer representing mainly consumer clients, the decision to embrace alterative billing is not as simple as changing from hourly fees to flat or fixed fees. Rather, it involves a potentially painful examination of office procedures, use of staff, and use of technology. It involves an understanding of consumer attitudes, even when the lawyer believes such attitudes are incorrect and unjustified. It often involves changing the lawyer's mind-set from a case-by-case approach to a system of processes focused on efficiency. The result should not be a "cookie-cutter" or "assembly line" style of practice, but rather a system where the lawyer has more time available for face-to-face client consultation and counseling.

In many ways, the search for the completely efficient, productive office system is like the quest for the Holy Grail. Improvements and refinements can—and should—continue. But the promise is not illusory. This quest can lead to an office where the clients are more informed and more certain about the fees they will pay, where more information about the progress of a matter flows regularly to the client, where the client is given realistic goals and expectations by which to measure the lawyer's delivery of services, where the lawyer is more confident that matters are being handled efficiently, and where the lawyer is rewarded for efficiency by increased profitability.

The journey may not be easy, but the rewards will be substantial.

CHAPTER SIX

Foundations on Which to Build a Billing Method

Which billing system is right for my practice? How can I change from an hourly based billing system to a value-based system? How do I determine whether my practice can make such a change? These questions must be asked and answered before a lawyer considers changing billing methods. This chapter presents checklists of some things to do and tools to use to determine the cost of producing your legal services and evaluating the billing method suitable for your practice.

Before starting any crossover from an hourly (cost-based) billing method to an alternative (value-based) method, you must know your own environment and practice, and engage in a detailed self-assessment process. Before you get deeply involved with the analysis in this chapter, you may wish to jump ahead to Chapter 10, which describes alternative billing methods. Then come back and thoughtfully go through the assessment described here, while considering which—if any—alternative billing arrangements work with your particular practice.

SELF-ASSESSMENT CHECKLIST

The considerations described in Chapters 4 and 5 regarding pricing legal services in your practice area and the effect of the value curve will strongly influence your choice of billing methods. Ask the following questions to help you focus, assess your practice, and determine which billing methods will allow you to reach your objectives.

OBJECTIVES AND GOALS

- Solo practitioners, firms of all sizes, and in-house counsel must set objectives and goals. Do you have firm objectives and goals?
- What are your strengths and weaknesses?
- What opportunities exist in your market that you might not have addressed?
- What services do you now provide?
- What services should you provide to address market opportunities and meet your goals and objectives?
- How do you as an owner of the firm perceive your organization in terms of its competitive advantages and disadvantages?
- Are your perceptions realistic and supported by the facts?
- How do your perceptions fit with your clients' perceptions? Prospective clients' perceptions? How will you find out?
- Who are your lawyers and staff, and what are their talents?
- What is the experience mix of your firm's lawyers, and how does it fit the needs of your clients and prospective clients?
- Who are your clients, and what are their legal needs now and in the foreseeable future?
- How do your firm's talents meet the needs of your clients?
- Do your clients believe your firm has the skills to meet their needs as they perceived them?
- Do the services you provide your clients vary in where they fit on the value curve?
- Where does your practice fit on the value curve?
- Are there services you currently provide that should be dropped due to their place on the value curve?

PRESENT AND FUTURE MARKET TRENDS

- What are the market trends?
- What is the demography of:
  - your firm?
  - your clients?
  - your legal community?
  - your community or market area?
- Who are your competitors, and where are they located?
- In what practice areas do they compete?

- What are the prevailing rates for the type of services you provide in your market, particularly price-sensitive services?
- Who are your clients?
- What are the needs of your present or potential clients?
- Are there legal needs of your current clients that are presently being handled by other firms?
- Are these areas of practice you are or should be providing?

PRESENT BILLING METHODS

- Do your present billing methods enable you to achieve a desired level of profitability?
- Do your billing methods meet client needs and preferences?
- Do they enable you to compete effectively?
- Do they enable you to further your firm's goals?
- Do they fairly measure value to the client?
- Are they consistent with trends?
- Do they promote effective marketing?
- Are they based upon written fee agreements?
- Have they been innovative? Flexible?
- Do they differ for different types of services?
- Are they competitive in your market area as to price?

WILLINGNESS TO TRY INNOVATIVE BILLING

- Have you analyzed your practice to determine those areas or types of services that might benefit from alternative or innovative billing methods?
- Are you and/or some members of your firm willing to innovate?
- Do you have clients who have requested—or might be willing to accept—alternative billing methods?
- Are you willing to take the time and make the effort to bring about a change in how you bill for legal services?
- Will your firm support the effort?

Thoughtful consideration of the preceding questions can provide insight, and completing this preliminary self-assessment is an important first step. However, a mere mental review of these questions is insufficient. As with any project, written notes add a framework and aid in retention of thoughts and observations. Providing writing materials to any lawyer analyzing these inquiries is clearly useful, if not required. The lawyer must weigh the pros and cons to determine whether the environment would allow innovative billing a chance to succeed, even if only in certain areas where it has the best chance to succeed initially. Only then is the lawyer ready for the next step: determining the cost of producing the legal services.

DETERMINING COST

Budgeting, cost tracking, and other accounting functions of law practice are often ignored by lawyers in large-firm settings, and can easily be overlooked or not addressed at all in solo or small-firm settings. The larger firms may have "back office" departments that handle all billing and accounting operations, both for money and lawyers' time, but the average lawyer in the large firm has little to do with those functions. The smaller firms may have administrators or office managers, but they usually have a variety of time-consuming duties to juggle. In all practices, monthly financial tracking and reporting are often pushed aside by the more urgent need to address client projects or prepare accurate and complete billing statements for clients. Budgets and costs are simply lost in the shuffle.

Many lawyers dislike the business aspects of law practice and are content not to deal with too many financial reports. Therefore, if the net income after paying expenses is sufficient for lawyers' needs, little attention may be paid to the specifics. The balance of this chapter covers areas that are often ignored by lawyers in their practices, but that are necessary to determine the best billing method for a particular type of work or project. Lawyers must understand and address costs before billing methods (even hourly billing) can be selected as appropriate for a task.

For the purpose of planning for alternative billing, costs of legal services can be roughly divided into two categories:

1. fixed or overhead expenses, which may be fairly constant, and
2. costs incurred in providing the actual services (the time invested) and direct costs associated with those services.

This chapter deals with both categories in analyzing a practice and determining a suitable billing method.

RETROSPECTIVE ANALYSIS OF COST AS A GUIDE

Few law offices formally base individual billing rates exclusively upon costs. Rather, the new-associate billing rate is often set by using the "rule of three" (salary times three, divided by minimum required billable hours, equals billing rate) or some modification of that rule. Other timekeeper rates are usually based upon some percentage increase over the last year, what each partner thinks about his or her own rate, some "Kentucky windage" based upon what is heard on the street or from clients, and the rates other firms charge for the same services or years of experience.

Cash collections are then estimated, based upon hours to be worked and cash collection percentages. Estimated costs are deducted. And if resulting profits are reasonably acceptable, rates are adopted.

The good news is that this approach has worked in the past. The bad news is that it does not work well today, and, for several reasons, will work even less well in the future:

- Not all costs of doing business are usually tracked. Those that are omitted may include rate adjustments to client bills, money costs, partner costs, and event costs.
- Individual client or matter profitability is not determined.
- Costs are not matched with related revenues.
- Utilization and leverage cost differences are not highlighted at the matter level.

What is needed to guide the billing process is a much broader view. That view should include all items affecting the cost of providing a service to a client, as well as the economics of supply and demand.

COST OF SERVICE VERSUS VALUE TO THE CLIENT

As discussed earlier, value is determined by the buyer of the service and may have little relation to the cost of the service. For example, at the high end of the value curve, there is essentially no relationship of value to cost. At the low end of the value curve, value and cost are almost synonymous, or the cost of the services may actually exceed the value to the client. In between these two points on the value curve, the cost/value relationship varies, depending upon where you are on the curve, as shown in Exhibit 6-1.

Note that no billing amount for a particular service has yet been set. The billing amount is (or should be) dependent upon the cost of providing a service, as well as upon the lawyer's skill in demonstrating value in the eyes of the client and his or her willingness or desire to bill that amount. This is what converts the billing process from a mechanical step to an "art." This is what is often lacking in a straight hourly billing method.

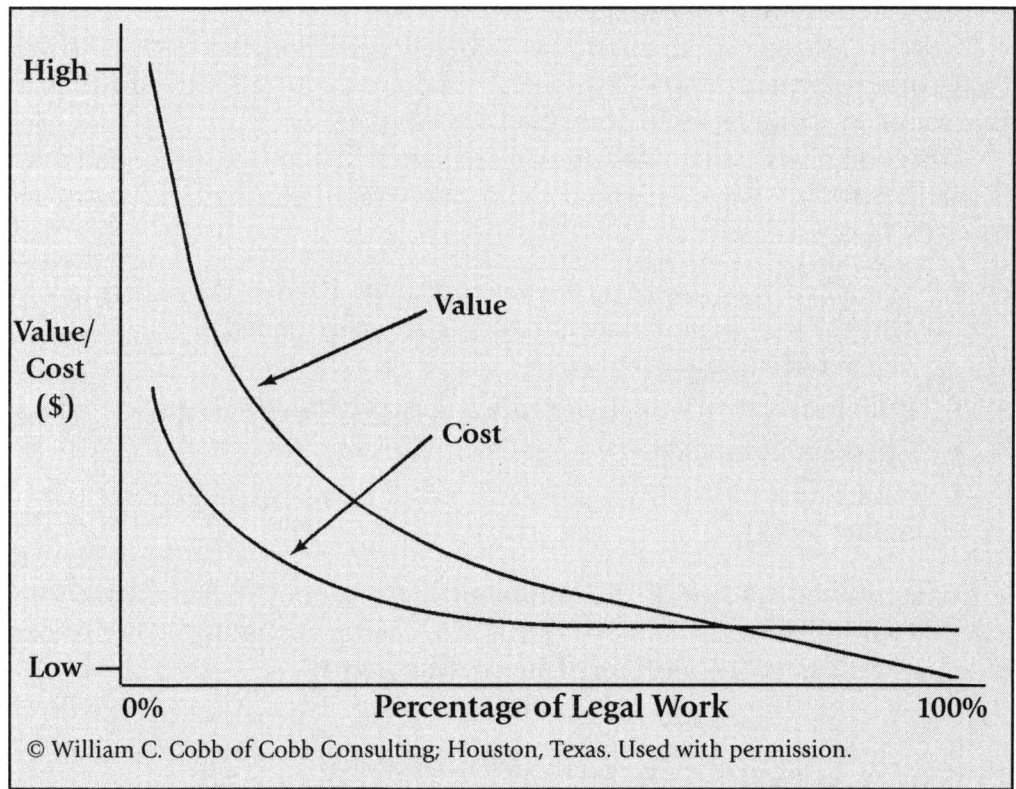

Exhibit 6-1

Value/Cost Curves in the Legal Profession

© William C. Cobb of Cobb Consulting; Houston, Texas. Used with permission.

KNOWING COSTS THROUGH DETAILED COST ACCOUNTING

Cost accounting dates back to the late 1800s and has its roots in the manufacturing industries. Only in the last few decades has this concept been applied to the service industries, and more recently to the legal profession. The reason for this delayed application is, basically, that it was not needed. As long as lawyers could increase hourly rates with little resistance from clients, the cost of delivering legal services was not very important. This has changed, and more and more law offices are finding that understanding what it costs to deliver legal services is essential in managing profitability.

The themes that emerge when lawyers start thinking about using cost accounting techniques are the KISS (Keep It Simple, Stupid) principle and fear of divisiveness. This book does not deal with the fear of divisiveness or profitability management, nor does it get into the specifics of cost accounting. However, it will be helpful to review cost accounting from the KISS viewpoint.

COSTS

Most matters involve five different types of costs. In the format of a profit-and-loss statement, they are accounted for as follows:

Revenue	$ XXX
Revenue adjustment costs	XX
Net revenue	$ XXX
Timekeeper costs	$ XX
Overhead (indirect) costs	XX
Event (support) costs	XX
Money costs	XX
Total costs	$ XX
Net profit	$ XX

At the matter or case level, each of these costs can be determined as described in the following discussion.

Revenue Adjustment Costs

For purposes of this discussion, the term "revenue adjustment costs" means those adjustments the lawyer makes to billings—either before (rate and billing adjustments or write-ups and write-downs) or after (write-offs) the bills are sent to clients. There are three types of revenue adjustment costs:

1. *Rate adjustments*: These relate to the difference between the "value" of timekeepers' time (based upon time spent and "standard" hourly rates) and the value based upon front-end agreements made with the client regarding hourly rate adjustment or other fee determination agreements. Rate adjustments can be either premiums (for additional value) or discounts (for any number of business reasons, including the desire to be in a new market or to obtain a new client).
2. *Billing adjustments*: These relate to the difference between an agreed-upon billing amount (such as an hourly rate, a premium, or a discount) and the amount billed to the client. Such adjustments may be due to inefficiencies or efficiencies that are not passed on to the client.
3. *Write-offs*: Typically these are adjustments to billed amounts for bad debts.

Timekeeper Costs

Timekeeper costs are the direct costs of individuals serving clients on a particular matter. At the level of the firm, office, and department or practice group, these costs are the actual costs incurred during the period. At the level of matter (and area of law), client (Standard Industrial Classification code, location, client type), or billing lawyer, these costs should be determined on the basis of "standard" hourly direct and indirect cost rates and would generally include an imputed cost for partners.

Overhead Costs

The firm's overhead costs are the various indirect costs associated with keeping open the doors of the law office: support staff, rent, supplies, depreciation, continuing education, and so on.

Event Costs

Event costs include the cost of nontimekeeper services provided directly to a matter. These include internal services such as document creation, copying, computerized research, and long-distance telephone charges.

Money Costs

Money costs represent the cost of borrowed funds or partner capital related to the investments made in a matter, from the time incurred until ultimately collected. Such investments may be timekeeper, overhead, and event costs plus out-of-pocket costs paid by the firm.

COST ACCOUNTING ISSUES

For some firms, all the information needed to perform this cost analysis may not be readily available. Fortunately, 100 percent accuracy is neither necessary nor desirable. Although most firms' accounting systems can be adapted to produce the information just described, many firms selectively and infrequently analyze costs outside the client accounting system, using cost accounting only for major clients and/or matters.

In carrying out this type of cost accounting, the firm must address the issue of the "cost of a partner." It is generally accepted that a partner's (or owner's) payments consist of a compensation element, a profit element (including profits from others), and, in some cases, a return-on-investment element. Firms that do not wish to delve into this level of sophistication may prefer one of these alternative approaches:

- To measure profitability by matter, client, and area of law, calculate contribution to profit (that is, excluding partner cost) per matter hour and per partner hour charged to the matter.
- To measure profitability by practice group, calculate group contribution to profit per partner, per partner point, or per partner billable hour.

These calculations will provide reasonable data for evaluating "comparative" profit performance. The data in turn can be used for resource allocation and planning.

EXERCISE IN COST ACCOUNTING

Someone already trained in elementary accounting usually spends about one college quarter learning cost accounting. The basic concepts covered in such a course must be tailored to the law office. Therefore, this section provides an overview of how each cost category is usually attributed to multiple offices, practice groups, billing lawyers, clients, and matters.

We suggest that the lawyer look at the law firm's sources of profits in layers. These layers may be depicted as a pyramid, as shown in Exhibit 6-2. (The levels of office, practice group, and billing lawyer may not exist in smaller law offices.)

Note that the working lawyer is not included here, as he or she is not considered a profit center. Rather, the working lawyer is considered a resource (cost) used to provide service to the revenue generator (that is, the matter). It should also be noted that actual costs are used mostly in the upper half of the pyramid (firm, office, practice group) and standard costs are used mostly in the lower half.

The Profitability Pyramid

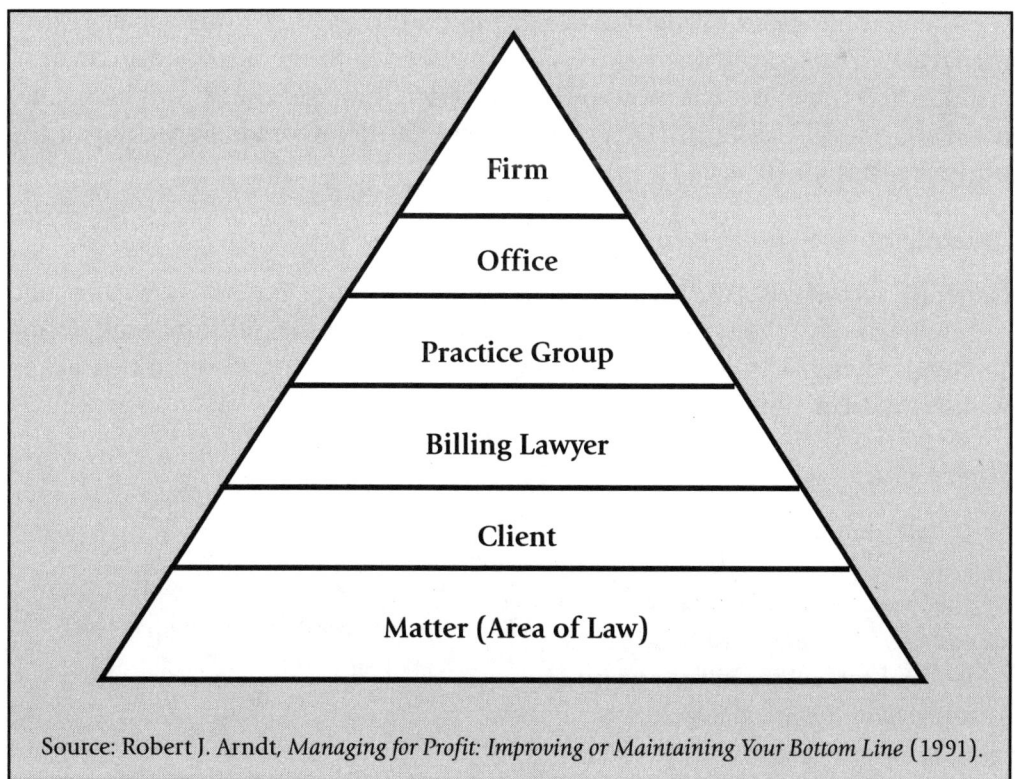

Source: Robert J. Arndt, *Managing for Profit: Improving or Maintaining Your Bottom Line* (1991).

ACCOUNTING FOR COSTS AT THE PRACTICE GROUP LEVEL

For discussion purposes, the starting point for this exercise is to determine costs at the practice group level (if the firm has multiple practice groups) or at the office level (if the firm has multiple offices). Of course, if your firm does not have multiple offices or practice groups, cost allocation is not necessary, but you still must determine revenue adjustment and money costs. So let us look at how the various costs are generally determined at the practice group level.

Revenue Adjustment Costs

The firm's client accounting system should be able to identify revenue adjustment costs by each timekeeper. If so, each practice group's revenue adjustment costs are the sum of those costs determined for each timekeeper assigned to each practice group.

Timekeeper Costs

To find timekeeper costs, add together associate and legal assistant compensation, imputed partner compensation (if used), and compensation and related fringe benefits of individuals assigned to the practice group.

Overhead Costs

The overhead costs are a portion of all other operating costs of the law office. Overhead is allocated to the practice group on the basis of timekeeper weighting factors. Thus, more overhead costs are assigned to the larger-cost consumers: partners are allocated more overhead costs than associates, and associates more than legal assistants. Determining weighting factors is particular to the practice group or firm.

Event Costs

Generally, event costs are charged to the practice groups based upon estimated or actual use of usage-type resources (word processing, long-distance telephone service, copying, and computerized legal research). These can often be tracked within the firm's billing system.

Money Costs

To calculate money costs, multiply the following factors:

The investment in unbilled work and costs plus the billed but uncollected fees and costs of the billing lawyers assigned to the practice group	x	The interest rate the firm pays on bank loans

ACCOUNTING FOR COSTS AT THE MATTER LEVEL

At the matter level, the various costs are generally determined as follows.

Revenue Adjustment Costs

Revenue adjustment costs are the revenue adjustments recognized for each matter. Some billing or client accounting systems may not track rate adjustments. If not, they can be easily calculated for each matter by tracking specific rate or billing adjustments and write-offs.

Timekeeper and Overhead Costs

To find timekeeper and overhead costs, multiply the hours charged to the matter by standard timekeeper and overhead hourly cost rates. To determine those rates, divide actual timekeeper costs and indirect costs allocated to each timekeeper (category) by the timekeeper's chargeable hours. If a timekeeper has significant amounts of nonchargeable management or firm time, add the cost of these hours to indirect costs, and use total chargeable and nonchargeable hours as the divisor in determining the timekeeper's hourly cost rate.

Event Costs

Charge event costs in the same manner as for the practice group level.

Money Costs

Determine money costs in a manner similar to that used at the practice group level. This may require modifying the firm's client accounting system.

ACCOUNTING FOR COSTS AT THE CLIENT AND BILLING LAWYER LEVELS

Costs at the client level are the sum of their matter costs. At the level of the billing lawyer, find costs by adding together the costs of clients assigned to the billing lawyer.

DETERMINING COST TO PRODUCE A PACKAGE OF SERVICES

Using the information just given, you can determine the cost of providing a service and its net profit. The following example shows how.

Revenue
- Standard value of hours (hours times hourly standard rates)

Partner A (160 × $200)	$32,000
Associate B (80 × $150)	12,000

- Revenue adjustments

Rate adjustments (160 × $20)	3,200
Billing adjustments (5%)	(2,360)
Write-offs	0
Net revenue	$44,840

Costs
- Service Provider

Direct:	Partner A (160 × $88)	$14,080
	Associate B (80 × $50)	4,000
Overhead:	Partner A (160 × $97)	15,520
	Associate B (80 × $61)	4,880

Support (events) (5 hours × $20)	100
Money (assume 6 months to pay)	2,240
Total costs	$40,820
Net profit	$ 4,020

Calculate costs per hour for the timekeepers as follows:

	Partner A	Associate B
Imputed or actual annual compensation and fringe benefits	$150,000	$ 90,000
Allocation of annual overhead	$165,000	$110,000
Budgeted hours	1,700	1,800
Costs per hour		
Compensation (direct)	$88	$50
Overhead (indirect)	$97	$61

TASK-BASED ANALYSIS

All professionals struggle with answering the client's question of how much a service will cost. The usual answer is, "I don't know because I don't know how much time it will take. I don't know how the other side will respond. I can't tell how much research is required. I can't predict how you will respond to alternatives...."

Although this answer may be correct, the client may still insist upon receiving a ballpark estimate or on knowing if the case size is of breadbox or elephant proportions. The way to solve this problem is to use solutions based upon techniques used in business and government for fifty years, called CPM (Critical Path Method) and PERT (Program Evaluation and Review Technique). These two systems use the following procedure to analyze projects:

- Segment projects into tasks and related subtasks.
- Estimate the resources required to complete each subtask.
- Estimate the time or cost of each resource.
- Identify the interdependent relationships of tasks and subtasks.
- Estimate the likely variability of each resource requirement and time estimate.

If a lawyer follows these steps, he or she will find that many, if not all, cases can easily be segmented into tasks such as these:

- Issue identification
- Discovery
- Trial preparation
- Trial
- Appeal

Further, each of these tasks can be segmented into subtasks. You should review the information in Chapter 10 on Task-Based Fees, as well as the related information in the Appendix.

When using these techniques, you will find you can estimate resource and time requirements for early tasks with more certainty (less variability) than later tasks. By way of example, it is easier to estimate resources needed for the earlier states of litigation, such as issue identification and discovery, than later stages, such as trial preparation and trial, because the requirements for each stage are often a function of what was learned in the previous stage. However, this should not prevent you from making reasonably educated estimates of *ranges* of resource and time requirements, allowing for more uncertainty (broader ranges) for each succeeding task.

This type of task plan is particularly valuable in certain discussions with clients: it helps you convey case variables and their likely effects on cost, and it also helps you communicate the value of various tasks to the overall matter.

EXAMINING CLOSED FILES TO CREATE MINISYSTEMS OR PREDICT FEES

Experience is the best tool for predicting fees. A lawyer's experience in dealing with different problems can be found in closed files and billings, which offer a treasure trove of information on how long certain procedures might take and what resources might be devoted to them. As when estimating costs, a good approach to predicting the future is to know what happened in the past. This means knowing what resources were required in similar prior cases. There are two ways to do this:

1. Examine closed files and billings.
2. Begin documenting experience on current cases by modifying current timekeeping systems so you can segment matters into tasks and subtasks.

Ideally, you should do both. Examining prior files and bills will help you identify tasks and subtasks, as well as time requirements and reasons for variability. Your closed files and old billing records can be an invaluable resource for establishing the cost of delivering legal services.

Examine closed files and bills to determine the firm's cost and the length of time required for the work involved. To get information about the average cost of production, combine files and bills that involved repetitious work. This exercise can help you predict what you should try to charge. It also may show that you have been inefficient because you did not have a case plan, a topic discussed in Chapter 9. It may point you in the direction of creating minisystems, making greater use of technology, or taking other steps to increase productivity.

In your review of closed files and bills, you may discover recurring "uncertainties" or variables that occur with certain types of services. Although the variables may differ slightly from matter to matter, if you can determine the typical range of time required to deal with the variables, you can factor that into your fees. Using the simple estate-planning example, you may find that the cost of preparing the documentation was fairly constant from matter to matter, and that the two major variables were (1) the time spent in the initial phase (conferring with clients, gathering basic facts, and helping clients decide what they want), and (2) the time spent revising documentation because the clients changed their minds about the terms of the wills you were asked to prepare. This approach is sometimes referred to as "cost pricing" (fixed cost plus variable cost plus profit). You may determine that preparation of the documents can be charged at a fixed fee, and that the conferences and analysis should be based upon an hourly rate.

Documenting current experience will help you fine-tune the knowledge gained by examining closed files and bills, and will provide a monitoring capability you can use to examine the validity of estimates made on new matters. This experience can then allow you to develop and maintain templates for different types of matters, not only to estimate matter costs (and profitability), but also to help convey value to the client.

RECURRING VARIABLES OR UNCERTAINTIES

It has been said that one cannot predict the future, but one can shape the future by planning. Variables and uncertainties are what make predictions difficult (sometimes impossible). They do so because we cannot always identify all variables and uncertainties.

However, professionals learn about common variables and uncertainties as they gain experience. Lawyers quickly learn that some of these are under their control and others are not. Though each professional should develop his or her own list, the following can be used as a starting point:

- Variables and uncertainties under the professional's control
    - effectiveness of negotiating fee and payment arrangements
    - methods used to define the "problem"
    - view regarding necessity for a "Cadillac" versus a commercially acceptable solution
    - type of resources required to develop a solution
    - resources previously developed in similar matters
    - priority placed upon matter solution
    - effectiveness of resource supervision
    - quality of resources used
    - diligence in timely billing and collection follow-up
- Variables and uncertainties not under the professional's control
    - client's view of desired solution
    - client reactions
    - actions of opposing counsel
    - court actions
    - resource availability and performance
    - new, conflicting demands affecting priorities
    - new facts and circumstances
    - acts of God

Once you develop a fairly comprehensive list of variables, you can start estimating the ranges of impact the identified variables are likely to have on the resources and time required to complete the various tasks and subtasks. Keep in mind that you need "cushions" to minimize the impact of incorrect estimates or unpredictable events.

EXAMINING PROFITABILITY AS IT RELATES TO BILLING

In all businesses, profitability depends upon relatively few key variables:

- Supply and demand
- Product or service quality
- Cost of resources
- Productivity of resources and management (effectiveness/efficiency)
- Pricing strategies and effectiveness

Assume for the moment that all the variables, except pricing strategies and effectiveness, are constant. In such case, profits depend upon the pricing strategies used. Ultimately, of course, a firm's revenues and expenses—and hence its profits, actual or desired—depend upon the risks or opportunities associated with the uncertainties of the other variables listed. Therefore, one way to look at pricing strategies (billing decisions) is in light of the various risks and opportunities involved. Here are some examples:

- There is a great deal of price elasticity (flexibility in the price range) if you are the only lawyer in town (or in the country) with a reputation for producing a certain result. Thus, you might generate a great deal of profit by billing "what the traffic will bear."
- If the external factors affecting lawyer time requirements are quite variable, this suggests billing at competitive hourly rates.
- When internal factors are substantially variable but controllable, this suggests billing at a fixed fee for the service.
- Low demand for a service may suggest a contingent-fee arrangement.
- A combination of these factors may suggest different billing arrangements for different segments of a matter, or for different matters for the same client.

Good knowledge of the resources required for—and the risks and opportunities associated with—a particular matter helps you test or model the ways different billing arrangements affect the bottom line. You can then identify an appropriate billing method and assess the economic desirability of accepting a particular representation. One example might be in the estate planning area, where an analysis of the different types of plans suggests you should charge a fixed fee for certain types of documentation, but an hourly rate for consultation and other types of work over which the lawyer has less control of the time involved. Another example might be a corporate practice, where the fees can be fixed for a simple incorporation (because of systems developed to prepare the documentation), but a different billing method—based upon the amount of negotiation required and the number of parties involved—is used for client consultations and drafting of employment and shareholder agreements.

Even if you are crossing over from a cost-based to a value-based billing philosophy, it is important to know your costs. If your cost of production exceeds the value to the client, you will be unprofitable. To offset that problem, you must make one or more of the following changes:

- Reduce the cost of production to less than the price or value of the services.
- Enhance the value of your services to meet the client's perception of value, thus raising the price above the cost of production.
- Increase productivity by using technology or systems, without increasing the cost of production.
- Failing this, eliminate a practice area, a department, an office, or a firm.

CONCLUSION

Now you are ready to try some cost accounting to determine the cost of production to be used as a guide in billing. Consider the advantage of knowing your cost of production, broken down as follows (remember that you are seeking your cost, not the fee to be charged):

- By firm
- By lawyer
- By practice area
- By department
- By office (if you have more than one)
- By staff other than paralegals (fee chargers)
- By paralegals (fee chargers)
- By the use of technology (such as word processing and computers)
- By designated matter (or package of services)

In making your analysis, be on the lookout for groups of related services that you might package and be able to define in a "scope of engagement" letter. For example, in estate planning, you might include initial conferences with the client; preparation of a will, trust agreement, durable power of attorney, and living will; and a conference for execution of the documents. This exercise will help you learn whether you made a profit on those services (which you can use the next time you enter a written fee agreement) and whether it would be possible to enter a fixed or flat fee for that package of services.

A useful technique for determining fees for services that are easily packaged and normally recurrent is to keep track of the time spent in a number of representations. At the outset, note your estimate of the minimum and maximum number of hours that will be expended to provide a defined service or package of services. Keep careful track of the actual time spent, and then compare the actual with the estimated time. See whether the actual time falls within the estimated minimum and maximum times.

After a number of such exercises, you will know whether you are a realistic estimator. Averaging the actual time spent in doing the same defined services for a number of clients, or repetitively for the same client, gives you a realistic basis for setting fees using any billing method. If you are considering billing on an hourly basis, you will have a sound basis for setting the hourly rate and giving a range of charges to your client. If you contemplate billing on a fixed-fee basis, this exercise will help you know whether the fixed fee will be satisfactory. If you work for a contingent fee, you will know whether that kind of work is profitable.

This exercise will not tell you whether your charges will be acceptable in the competitive marketplace, nor will it necessarily reflect the actual or perceived value of those services.

Although profitability is not the major focus of this chapter, the analysis that you make will enable you to determine the profitability of certain types of work. This information will be useful and may raise the following questions:

- On matters with low profit, can you increase volume, or apply technology or other forms of leverage, enough to make it desirable to continue that type of work?
- Was low profitability the result of strong competition?
- Was low profitability the result of your inefficiency, and can inefficiencies be reduced?
- Was low profitability due to inappropriate staff mix, and can that be adjusted?
- Can you justify low-profit work because it will enable you to get or keep high-profit work? (This is called a "loss leader.")
- Did you purposely set your fee low, and expect low profitability, to enter a new market? (This is called "penetration pricing" and is designed to enable you to win market share.)

CHAPTER SEVEN

Billing as Part of the Communication Process

Although there is no doubt that a primary purpose of billing is for the lawyer to be paid, one should not view it as a task done solely for the lawyer's benefit. The process of billing is a key part of communication between the lawyer and client. In fact, many times, the client focuses a great deal of attention on the billing process, perhaps at the expense of other communication and advice. Communicating the lawyer's efforts with effective and understandable billing procedures should be part of the total client relationship, commencing with the first interview. This chapter describes techniques for effective communication.

THE ROLE OF EFFECTIVE COMMUNICATION IN THE BILLING PROCESS

The price of legal services should embody the numerous values that clients receive when they buy legal services. You can select among numerous ways to set your fees. The method you select should conform to your clients' perceptions of value. If it does not, your clients will be unhappy. Unhappy clients take their business elsewhere. Thus, legal fees must not only contain your costs and profit margins, but reflect the value being delivered to the client as well.

If you choose to bill on hourly rates, learn how to wrap the rates with a bundle of values. Unfortunately, billing with time and hourly rates makes lawyers believe legal fees are the result of a mechanical process. This method lulls lawyers into believing fees exist without any concept of value. We must learn to add value to our services and accept the idea that fee setting is more an art than a mechanical process.

The quality of the attorney-client relationship rides on how effectively you communicate with your clients. Experts know that effective communication has an enormous impact on our behavior patterns. It has the same effect on clients. In *The Art of Talking So That People Will Listen* (Prentice-Hall, 1983, page 4), Dr. Paul W. Swets reminds us of the power of effective communication:

> Communication that wins a positive response from others can provide you with a new way of life. Nothing is more essential to success in any area of your life than the ability to communicate well. Nothing can compare to the joy of communicating love, of being heard and understood completely, of discovering some profound insight from another's mind, or of transmitting your own thoughts to a rapt audience. Self-concepts are enhanced, attitudes broadened, beliefs deepened, perspectives clarified, hopes restored, frustrations dissolved, hurt feelings healed.

To understand this power, we must learn more about the theoretical mechanisms that drive an effective communication process. An exhaustive study of communications theory would consume a lifetime of study, but some of the basics that apply in the attorney-client context can be briefly covered in a few pages. We do note, however, that most of us would be professionally and personally enhanced by greater insight into the communication process. If the subject matter of this chapter particularly interests you, you are encouraged to delve into other materials that cover the area in more depth.

THE LAWYER AS COMMUNICATOR

Anecdotal evidence suggests that successful lawyers are good communicators. Angry clients, broken relationships, malpractice claims, and fee disputes, on the other hand, all evolve from poor communication. Communication is more than the transmission of information; it is the sharing of meaning. We know that good listeners make powerful communicators. Many lawyers believe they understand the communication process because they spend so much time talking and writing. Unfortunately, talking may signal a failure to communicate.

It is instructive to note that a majority of the complaints filed by clients against lawyers with regulatory authorities involve communication problems between lawyer and client, usually pertaining to the failure to communicate and keep the client informed ("He won't return my telephone calls." "She doesn't respond to my letters.") or various failures within the communications process ("I was never told . . ." I didn't understand that . . ."). Though lawyers may believe they are good communicators, obviously this is not always the case.

Despite its seeming simplicity, effective communication is a complex and powerful process. Unfortunately, the dependence of the attorney-client relationship upon effective communication has not been the subject of any systematic development of theory or model that explains this process. This chapter develops a new attorney-client communication model by drawing upon research exploring how successful companies satisfy their customers' needs. The "customer satisfaction" movement offers a vocabulary for describing the attorney-client relationship and gives us tools for enhancing the process.

This new paradigm offers a promising alternative for developing better attorney-client relationships. Today, when people use the word "paradigm," they mean a model or frame of reference. Our frame of reference—in particular, the hourly rate model we use for pricing legal services—must change. We must shed this old paradigm and develop new ones for client service. Any new frame of reference should describe how clients perceive, understand, and interpret what they buy from the legal profession. It must take into account the client's idea of quality. The quality of the attorney-client relationship is an essential component of the price clients pay for legal services.

Generally speaking, communication is at the heart of the attorney-client relationship. Clients seek advice and information from the lawyer. The lawyer's training and experience are often of little value to a client if the information sought by the client is not transmitted accurately and in terms that the client can understand. Likewise, errors may occur in the representation if the lawyer does not obtain accurate information from the client. Communication occurs not only while the lawyer faces the client, but at every phase of the relationship.

Clients have certain goals in mind when they retain the services of a lawyer. Their goals must be part of the communication process. Clients, consciously or unconsciously, expect understanding, comprehension, and empathy. These features are part of the process for clients, and when they are missing, clients devalue the lawyer's services. Clients base most of their choices not upon the legal solution offered, but upon the package of values that comes with the legal solution.

ELEMENTS OF THE COMMUNICATION PROCESS

Even the simplest communication involves six basic concepts. We should quickly review these elements of the communication process: the sender, the message, the receiver, the transfer of meaning, the potential barriers to communication, and the setting/situation in which the communication occurs.

A SKILLFUL SENDER

Effective communication begins with a sender who wishes to transfer an idea, a message, an impression, or a feeling to a receiver. The mere transfer of information may not be communication. Too many times, lawyers believe they are communicating when they convey information to a client. In the classic business book *Management: Tasks, Responsibilities, Practices* (Harper & Row, 1974), Peter F. Drucker makes this point: "Communication and information are different and indeed largely opposite—yet interdependent." Communication results from a relationship between people—sender and receiver, lawyer and client.

THE MESSAGE

What is it you want to communicate? Ideally, the receiver should understand the sender's intended meaning. The principal tool we use to communicate is language, both spoken and written. Many lawyers behave as if this were the only tool. Good communicators add to this tool with gestures, tone of voice, pictures and symbols, and listening—anything that can convey their messages and intended meaning.

When you consider it, it is actually surprising that we can be as effective at communication as we are. The sender has an idea in his or her mind. In the communication process, the sender uses words as symbols to convey the idea or meaning. The goal is that the receiver ends the process with the exact same idea in his or her mind. Considering variances and nuances in the language tools used and individual differences between people (such as education, intelligence, background, ethnic heritage, and various prejudices and biases), it is a wonder that we do as well as we do.

THE RECEIVER OF THE MESSAGE

The receiver is a key component of the development of an effective communication style. Can you conceive of any need for a message unless you expect someone to receive or react to your communication? In his book, Drucker delivers a clear message when he says, "Communication is perception." He explains:

> One can communicate only in the recipient's language or in his terms. And the terms have to be experience-based. It, therefore, does very little good to try to explain terms to people. They will not be able to receive them if they are not terms of their own experience. They simply exceed their perception capacity. (Peter F. Drucker, *Management: Tasks, Responsibilities, Practices* (Harper & Row, 1974, p.484).

This principle holds enormous impact for lawyers, simply because many of us communicate with clients in the language we understand—the law. But if our purpose is to inform our clients and induce favorable responses, we must use the language of the clients.

TRANSFER OF MEANING

Drucker also says, "Communication is expectation." By this he means that we see, hear, and perceive what we want to see, hear, and perceive; therefore, before we can communicate, we must know what the recipient expects to see and hear. This is quite a challenge, because clients are unique people. Yet, in delivering legal services, lawyers often spend too little time actually listening to clients with the goal of understanding what is important to them. In fact, we are trained during law school to disregard the irrelevant and focus on only the critical. In a "no fault" divorce state, for example, a lawyer may disregard a client's tearful discussion of a cheating spouse as being irrelevant to the legal issues at hand. Although in some circumstances this fact would not affect the ultimate outcome of the case, it may nevertheless be one of the most significant facts from the client's point of view. Clients often attach a different value to a fact's importance and relevancy. A cavalier attitude toward this fact at an initial stage in the representation may color the entire relationship throughout the legal proceedings. There is little wonder that many describe lawyers as "uncaring" after experiencing or witnessing such an initial interview.

The ultimate goal of communication is the transfer of meaning—that the sender and receiver will both understand the same thing in the same way.

POTENTIAL BARRIERS TO COMMUNICATION

There are numerous potential barriers to communication, both physical and intangible.

A physical barrier to communication can be something so simple as a speaker who has a bit of lettuce on his or her teeth or who has heavily accented speech. It might be the physical pain a client is suffering from the very injury he or she is discussing with the lawyer. It may be a room that is too hot or cold, or that has unpleasant lighting. Noise can be a problem, as can a person with hearing difficulties. We have all tried to listen intently to a poor or difficult-to-understand speaker imparting information that we truly wanted to understand. We should therefore appreciate the frustrations involved when communication barriers are present.

But sometimes even more significant than the physical barriers are the intangible ones. A client may come from a totally different culture than the lawyer, with neither one fully appreciating that they have fundamentally different understandings and assumptions about the world. In much of the Western world, for example, direct eye contact is considered important and a sign of trustworthiness. That is not true in some other cultures. Although we often do not like to admit it, all of us approach life—and therefore any communication process—with our personal set of prejudices and biases. Educational backgrounds bring an important set of variables as well. Often clients see lawyers for the first time while experiencing significant emotional reactions to legal matters. These emotions can be powerful barriers to communication. They may include distress over an impending divorce or the loss of a loved one, concern about the ability to afford the legal fees, or anxiety about possible punishment in a criminal case.

As lawyers, we must cope with the special barriers to communication. We must always be aware that we use a specialized language of terms like "torts" and "presumptions." Our legal education has created for us preconceptions involving significant detail and implications associated with these terms, with which most of our clients are unfamiliar. To enhance communication with our clients, we must take care to define and explain legal terms in clear and understandable ways.

THE SETTING AND SITUATION IN WHICH COMMUNICATION OCCURS

Often the initial communication with a client occurs in the lawyer's office. The lawyer should therefore strive to have a positive setting for this important communication. Care should be taken to eliminate or minimize interruptions. Comfortable furniture is an important element. Many lawyers have two settings for office discussions, one using a coffee table or other informal setting when the goal is to have free-flowing and relaxed conversation, and the other using a massive desk and the chairs across from it when a more formal tone is required.

Lawyers are obliged to create a favorable climate that encourages respect, empathy, and understanding of each client's situation. For example, even if you do not understand or agree with a client's emotions about a particular situation, acknowledging the emotions helps minimize them as a barrier to good communication. You could say, "I understand that you are very upset about this situation, but let's spend our time looking at solutions rather than dwelling on the bad things that have happened." If you do not adequately identify and empathize with a client's situation, you run the risk that the attorney-client relationship will break down. It is this lack of understanding that causes clients to say, "You don't understand my business," or, "I can't follow that advice," or similar expressions of uncertainty. A client is someone who, driven by self-interest, has the choice of coming to you for advice or going somewhere else. Thus, there is a compelling reason for you to use the communication process to understand each client's situation fully.

We should gain a better understanding of these basic elements so we can reap the benefits of effective client communication. These benefits include:

- Greater recognition
- Satisfied clients
- Less employee turnover
- Higher productivity
- Less time and money wasted on misunderstanding and duplication
- Higher profits

KNOW WHAT YOU WANT TO COMMUNICATE

It is not enough to understand the nature of the communication process; unless you also know which needs the client wants you to satisfy, the process has no focus. Legal services must satisfy some want or need the client regards as important or desirable. Otherwise, from the client's point of view, any desirable aspects of your service are likely to prove deceptive and transitory.

Thus, the starting point for planning and delivering legal services must be to formulate a model of service that can satisfy clients. From your model should emerge a unifying theme for every phase of your service. Once the model is in place, it is up to you to use the communications process persuasively to satisfy clients and turn them into feeders for your firm.

We have enough evidence, from clients and ourselves as customers, to help us build a model of client service. We already know a lot about needs. As humans we all have needs:

- The need to feel welcome
- The need for timely service
- The need to feel comfortable
- The need for orderly service
- The need for understanding
- The need to receive help or assistance
- The need to feel important
- The need for appreciation
- The need for recognition
- The need for respect

Clients all share these needs. When they come to your office, they do not leave these personal needs at the door.

Clients have other needs. From *The Legal Needs of the Public* (William S. Hein and Company, Inc., 1977), a study by Barbara A. Curran of the American Bar Foundation, we can learn much about the unmet and unsatisfied needs of clients. Based upon the evidence she collected about the lawyer-client relationship, Curran says that one-third of the population believes lawyers do not meet the needs of clients for information about what must be done, and one-half believes that lawyers do not meet clients' needs for ongoing information about the progress of the lawyers' work. Curran also found that consumers of legal service rated lawyers lowest in these areas:

- Keeping clients informed of progress on their cases
- Interest in, and concern about, clients' problems
- Promptness

- Charging fair and reasonable fees
- Failing to report
- Slowness and failing to explain
- Working habits

These are also the primary complaints noted by dissatisfied clients when they file formal grievances. We can learn to bridge these gaps in the lawyer-client relationship with the tools of the effective communicator.

Another survey, the so-called Mobar-Pren-Hall Survey, published by Prentice-Hall and the Missouri State Bar Association, adds to the evidence of what clients want when it comes to fees. Exhibit 7-1 shows a way you can use the results from this study to improve your client fee habits.

The results of these surveys can teach us a great deal about clients' needs and wants. The clues they provide prove that clients want a large measure of satisfaction. A satisfied client is one who receives not only a solution to a legal problem, but added value from the transaction.

Exhibit 7-1

Applying the Mobar-Pren-Hall Survey Results to Your Practice

Client Fee Needs	Percentage of Time I Meet These Needs
80 percent want lawyers to discuss their fees up front.	_____ %
88 percent said not to wait until the end of the case.	_____ %
92 percent said to discuss the fee at the start of each matter.	_____ %
78 percent want to know the basis for the fee.	_____ %

Source: *Win-Win Billing Strategies: Alternatives That Satisfy Your Clients and You.* Richard C. Reed, Editor (American Bar Association Law Practice Management Section, 1992)

These studies show us how to add value and bridge the communication gap between lawyers and clients. How can we bridge this gap? One way is to satisfy these unmet needs by implementing a clear model for client services and communication.

TEN SMART WAYS TO COMMUNICATE WITH CLIENTS

The following ten ideas are practical applications of communication principles.

1. Anticipate your clients' needs for information about their legal matters and supply it periodically through update letters, detailed billing, phone calls, and other methods.
2. Encourage feedback from your clients. Your clients will tell you what they want, but you must listen.
3. You may be sure your clients want you to start the ball rolling on the subject of fees. Do not wait for them to start. Prescribing words for a fee discussion is always difficult, but here are some openings you may find helpful:
   - "Before we wind down this session, Mr. Client, I want to discuss with you our fees. I know you have an interest in what this matter will cost you. Here is how we will determine our fees for this matter."
   - "Ms. Client, I'm sure that as a businessperson you want to know what this case is going to cost you."
   - "Most people want me to explain how we set our fees, and I make it a practice to discuss fees at the beginning of every case."
4. Whatever the billing method, your billings should fairly state what you have done and, if possible, indicate how it was of value to the client. Each of the following four examples pertain to the same services and the same number of hours. Consider the effect on the client who has received each type of billing.
   - *Example 1*:
     7/13/02: Conference
   - *Example 2*:
     7/13/02: Conference with client
   - *Example 3*:
     7/13/02: Conference with Mr. Richard Roe, President of Client Corporation, to discuss proposed merger
   - *Example 4*:
     7/13/02: All-day conference with Mr. Richard Roe, President of Client Corporation, to discuss proposed merger with Greedy, Inc., involving a detailed analysis of advantages and disadvantages of proposed merger and resulting in decision to recommend to the

board of directors of Client Corporation that the merger proposal not be accepted

The fourth example describes how long the conference took, with whom, the process involved, a specific subject, and the end result that reflects value to the client in deciding a course of action. J. Harris Morgan's book, *How to Draft Bills Clients Rush to Pay* (American Bar Association, 1995), has been recognized as an excellent guide for drafting bills. He stresses that a billing description should include "action words" that convey an impression of benefit, as well as effort on the lawyer's part. The description should provide details of each activity in which the lawyer engaged on behalf of the client. Even in a fee statement without much detail, there is evidence of benefit when it looks something like this:

- FOR PROFESSIONAL SERVICES in defending against a $66,000 claim for damages arising out of the construction of the Richards Building, resulting in a settlement of $1,600 and a release freeing you from all further liability

5. Keep in touch with your clients even when no matter is pending. Build relationships.
6. Make regular visits with clients. Invite clients to visit your offices, especially to see the library and your technology resources. Visit major clients at their places of business regularly.
7. Devise effective ways of listening to your clients. Survey clients regularly. Develop effective and informal mechanisms for client feedback, and rigorously apply what you learned from the feedback. Enforce your internal policies about clients' needs; for example, return all calls from clients the same day they are received.
8. Measure client satisfaction regularly. You can do this by using surveys that generate quantitative and qualitative measures of satisfaction. Review the survey results and act. Use these measures of satisfaction to evaluate your staff and lawyers.
9. Keep *all* promises to clients, regardless of overtime costs. Set realistic dates for achieving client tasks in the first place, even if this means refusing a job. Over the long haul, what clients respect above most other lawyer traits is the ability to keep promises.
10. Develop a clear statement of philosophy about the way you perceive and treat clients. Put this statement on display, and provide a copy to all new clients.

Delivering value to clients should be a goal of all lawyer communication. You must anticipate and accommodate your clients' needs, and you must communicate effectively to demonstrate how you meet and exceed their needs. Sharing information helps keep clients informed and helps the communication process. This encourages feedback from clients. In most legal situations, the ultimate feedback you want from clients is a signal that your service satisfies their needs.

A MODEL FOR DELIVERY OF LEGAL SERVICES

Now that we understand the importance of effective communication, we must build a framework to ensure this actually takes place within the firm. Lawyers can build better lawyer-client relationships, but first they must fashion a model of service they can understand and communicate to clients. A client service model is necessary to begin a process from which the firm can verify a set of values and attitudes and, eventually, a set of methods that accurately respond to clients' needs. Without a service model, it is difficult to integrate clients' needs into the daily life of a practice. The reason is simple. Without constant, specific attention being directed to these issues, lawyers tend to revert to focusing solely upon legal services and issues.

You can forge a client service model from the evidence collected by Curran and other researchers. If you have your own evidence and beliefs about your clients' particular needs, add those needs to this model.

You build your model on the assumption that clients are a lawyer's most precious resource. Clients are the reason lawyers exist, and they make lawyers very fortunate people. You get to help others with their problems, and they pay you for it. Who could ask for anything more? Your clients deserve the best—tender loving care, your attention, your empathy, and your support. Quite simply, they deserve the best of client service.

Think of your service in terms of five central elements: timeliness, reliability, empathy, assurance, and tangibility. These elements form an acronym: TREAT. You must TREAT your clients as a precious resource—which, of course, they are! As shown in the following table, you can use the five TREAT criteria as the basis for a client service model. To do so, answer the following questions for each criterion:

- How important is this criterion in influencing your clients to retain your firm?
- How much room for improvement is there in your firm regarding this criterion?

The criteria in Exhibit 7-2 are the qualities of effective lawyers. You can use them to create a clear message of excellence for your firm. You can communicate this definition to your clients and your staff. This concept will be your service strategy—a concept that allows you to describe values you offer your

Exhibit 7-2

Criteria for Client Service

Criterion	Influence on Firm	Room for Improvement
Timeliness		
Reliability		
Empathy		
Assurance		
Tangibility		

clients. Without a service strategy, it is difficult to prove you have something different to offer.

Clients communicate with us, but often we do not seem to listen. Most lawyers have ignored the results of the Curran study, mainly because they lack a model of service that can incorporate a client's value system. We talk about value billing, but without a service strategy, it is difficult to formulate values and benefits clients receive from legal services. Listening to our clients is part of the communication process. Our clients can teach us how they want us to treat them. How we TREAT our clients refers to how we behave toward them in ways that give them special delight, pleasure, or satisfaction. People often express this kind of satisfaction with expressions such as, "They are a *treat* to do business with," or, "It was a *treat* to stay at that hotel." What do these expressions mean?

Surveys show that clients want timely service. Curran called this "promptness." A survey by *Inc.* magazine several years ago revealed that the need for timely service was high on the list of requirements that *Inc.* readers require from their lawyers. When you show you are willing and able to provide prompt service, you display that you know how to treat clients. You do this by responding to your clients' expressed timetables and by meeting all deadlines that you set or that clients impose upon you.

TIMELINESS

You must know how timely your clients expect you to be. The only way you can manage this is to analyze the time limits critical to your clients' needs (in addition to any statutory time limits). Take each area of your service and set firm standards. Then discuss these standards with your clients. If the standards do not meet the clients' needs, change the standards. Such standards should include the following:

- Do not keep a client waiting in the reception area for more than _____ minutes.
- Acknowledge agreement to accept a matter, in writing to the client, no later than _____ days after the lawyer/firm accepts the matter.
- Copies of documents should be mailed to clients within _____ days of receiving/preparing them.
- Telephone calls should be answered after no more than _____ rings.
- All telephone calls should be returned within _____ hours.
- All e-mail messages should be returned within _____ hours/days.
- Fee discussions and the agreed method of payment should be determined at first meeting with client or _____.
- A client should receive a status report every _____.
- A referral source must be thanked within _____.

RELIABILITY

Legal services must be dependable and accurate. The Model Rules of Professional Conduct demand these standards. Remember, the Curran study shows clients are interested in lawyers' working habits. Clients will make judgments about service based upon whether you perform consistently and dependably.

EMPATHY

To have empathy, you must devote individual attention to each client's situation. Attentiveness is a skill that involves understanding your clients' needs and wants. It requires you to be attuned to the human needs of your clients, not just their legal needs. You must learn to read your clients. Be sensitive to your clients' signals. What messages do they communicate to you? Empathy means you have rapport with your clients. To have rapport, you must put yourself in their shoes. You must ask, "If I were this person, what would I want?" This requires, for example, knowledge of a client's business and industry. To empathize, you must be a good listener. Here are five ways to improve your listening skills:

1. Stop talking.
2. Avoid distractions.
3. Concentrate on what the other person is saying.
4. Look for the real meaning.
5. Provide feedback to the sender.

ASSURANCE

The elements of assurance include professional credibility and competence. To convey these elements, explain the features and benefits of your services. Clients want you to keep them informed. They want to know that you have their best interests at heart. When clients say they want you to explain your fee, they are asking for the assurance of no unpleasant surprises.

TANGIBILITY

Legal services embrace not only the pure service, but also your physical support systems and other evidence of your service. Renowned Harvard marketing professor Theodore Levitt explains the importance of this evidence. In his book, *The Marketing Imagination* (Free Press, 1986, pp. 97-98), he reminds us that "[c]ommon sense tells us, and research confirms, that people use appearances to make judgments about realities." This leads to Levitt's theory that the successful marketing of a service demands that we "tangibilize" the intangible:

> When prospective customers can't taste, feel, smell, watch, or properly try the promised product in advance, the necessity of metaphorical reassurances to the marketing effort becomes amplified. Promises, being intangible, have to be tangibilized in their presentation.... Metaphors and similes become surrogates for the tangibility that cannot be provided or experienced in advance....
>
> The less tangible the generic product, the more powerfully and persistently the judgment about it is shaped by the "packaging"—how it's presented, who presents it, what's implied by the metaphor, simile, symbol, and other surrogates for reality.

Levitt uses packaging in its broadest sense. The fortune cookie is right: "You never get a second chance to make a first impression." You make first impressions every day. You succeed or fail by the impressions you create in briefings, interviews, phone calls, client conferences, conflict resolutions, and the myriad encounters of everyday practice.

With legal services, it is difficult to distinguish among what you do legally for a client, the process you use to provide the service, and the delivery system. Thus, your clients perceive quality as the interaction they have with you, your staff, and physical tools and facilities. In *Service Management* (Wiley, 1986), Richard Normann says, "The very intangibility of a service automatically forces the clientele to look for additional clues for evaluation." It is up to the lawyer to provide these clues. The fewer clues, the smaller the perceived value in the client's mind. What you need is a linkage to intangibility.

These characteristics for a service strategy come from what we already know about clients. Clients are good teachers. Try to picture your clients as your teachers. They carry around in their heads report cards on their expectations of lawyers. You can consistently score high grades on the clients' report cards if you use the evaluation factors clients apply when they think about your firm and what it offers.

You can now train your staff around a strategy. If you do a good job of communicating your service strategy to your staff and clients, you can assume you will earn high marks with clients. You become client-driven.

Our legal system is in many ways a product of the Industrial Revolution. Our corporation laws, commercial laws, and labor laws, to name a few, reflect the very nature of the Industrial Age. That age created its own demand for legal services on a scale that was, until then, unheard of. That age called for an army of legal technicians. Legal technicians dispense their advice as if the client does not exist but is merely the recipient of what the technicians have to sell. Most of us learned the law by the case method—a method that pretends fact situations are not people but cases to analyze and digest.

This is not unlike the way Henry Ford thought about his products. Ford used to say, "People can buy any color they want, as long as it's black." The economy of his day was product-driven. Consequently, Ford lacked any interest in the real needs of his customers. Many businesspeople know this era has disappeared, and they try to produce products and services in response to the wants and needs of the markets they serve. To be a market leader for any product or service today, you must be customer-driven.

SATISFACTION AND PRICE

You can become client-driven by adopting the five elements of client service. Many lawyers may yearn for simpler days, but today's market presents unlimited opportunities for lawyers willing to treat clients properly. The right client service philosophy and procedures will give you the capacity to satisfy clients' needs.

If you accept these market conditions, how do you keep—and enlarge—your client base? By realizing that clients base their choices not upon your legal skills alone, but upon the package of values that comes with the service. This package of values should come from how you treat your clients, how you satisfy their needs, and how they perceive your competency and accuracy. Obviously, the most effective and empathetic communications cannot make up for advice that proves to be wrong or predictions that fall far short of the actual outcome; but the better you treat your clients, the more highly they judge your performance, and the more satisfied they are.

The relationship between values and satisfaction is the key to pricing legal services. The more generous your package of values, the greater your clients' satisfaction. Satisfaction comes from this process. Clients compare what they expected from your service with what they perceived they got. Higher levels of satisfaction endure higher prices.

The goal must be that the customer is always satisfied—not with the outcome, for in many instances that is beyond the lawyer's control, but with all steps of the process within the lawyer's control, and with the communication about aspects of the matter outside the control of the lawyer and client.

Lawyers must understand that client satisfaction is a value-to-price relationship. If a client perceives that the value exceeds the fee, you create immediate client satisfaction. If, on the other hand, the fee exceeds the perceived value, you generate immediate dissatisfaction. Thus, satisfaction has its origin in value. If you want satisfied clients, you must know the value you intend to dispense to each client. Concepts of satisfaction should focus on one central notion: value-added services. To make this notion work, you must learn how to communicate a value-to-price relationship.

What is it you want to communicate? Clients know what they want; they want satisfaction. Think of your attempt to satisfy their needs as your "service package." A service package is the sum of what you do, what you say, how you act, and what you charge—all the services and experiences you offer to your clients. To communicate with clients, you should be able to describe, demonstrate, measure, and deliver your service package.

Picture your service package as an iceberg like the one shown in Exhibit 7-3. The client sees only the tip of the iceberg. It is your job to show each client the entire iceberg. The more of the iceberg you uncover for the client, the greater the client's satisfaction. You reduce the client's uncertainty and risk. You increase the client's perception of value, and the client will pay you for value.

The iceberg analogy may help you understand clients' perceptions of value. The intangible nature of legal services, as Levitt describes, forces clients to look for tangibility. When you purchase a car, you concentrate your evaluation process on tangibility—the car itself. You immediately see more of the iceberg. With legal services, clients rate you on other clues—equipment, premises, reputation, fees, legal skills, and the way you and other office staff treat them.

Clients will pay you well when they perceive they got more than they expected. Smart lawyers figure out what clients expect. Those who exceed their customers' expectations command higher prices for their products or services.

You must discover your clients' expectations so you can do more of what they want, which will increase their levels of satisfaction. Start with the self-assessment form in Exhibit 7-4. Place a check in the column that best describes how well your firm provides each element of client service. When you are identifying and meeting expectations, clients will recognize you as a service leader.

Exhibit 7-3

Perception of a Service Package

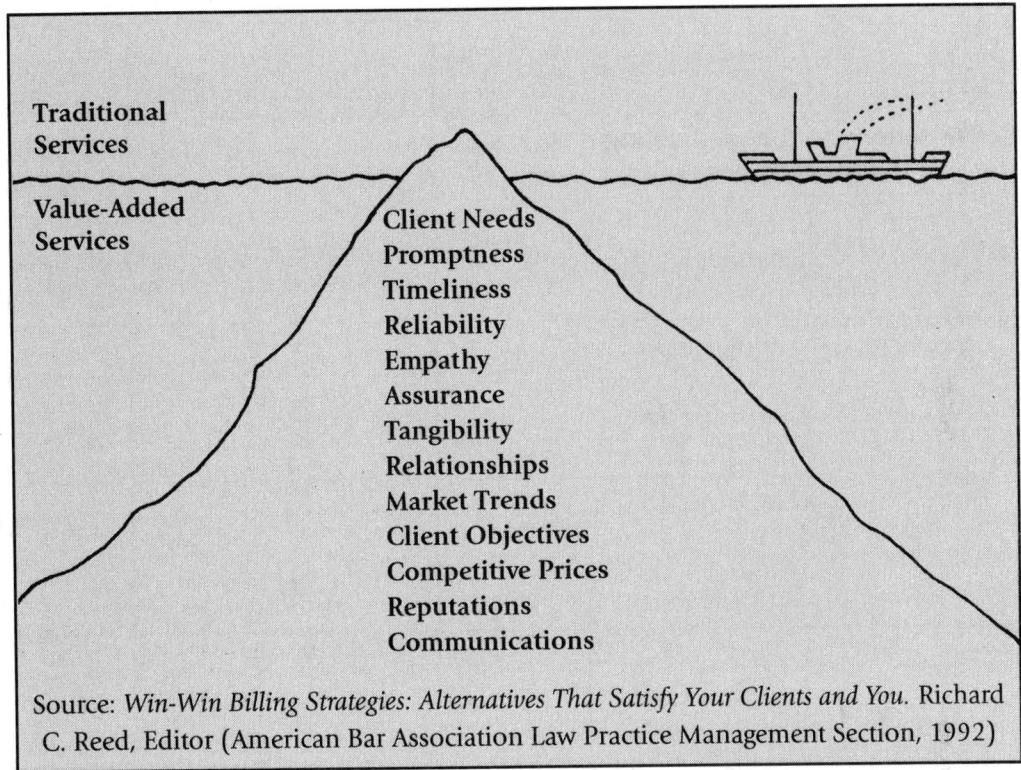

Source: *Win-Win Billing Strategies: Alternatives That Satisfy Your Clients and You.* Richard C. Reed, Editor (American Bar Association Law Practice Management Section, 1992)

HOW TO PREPARE AND PRICE YOUR SERVICE PACKAGE

A market has a sense of value that exists independently of both the costs of production and the costs of alternative solutions. We cannot recommend exact prices to charge your clients. However, if you can deliver value-added services, most clients will pay the fees that are current in your marketplace, plus a premium.

ADDING VALUE

Here are fifteen ways to increase the value of your services:

1. Exceed each client's expectations—do not merely meet them.
2. Ask questions to determine all the client's needs, not just legal needs.
3. Understand and define your client's objectives.
4. Develop a case plan or transaction plan for each client (see Chapter 9). Give the client a copy.

Exhibit 7-4

Services Satisfaction Worksheet

Dimension	Evaluation Criteria	Excellent	Adequate	Needs Improvement	Problem
Timeliness	Prompt, meeting client's deadlines				
Reliability	Consistent, dependable performance				
Empathy	Making special efforts to discover clients' special needs				
Assurance	Knowledgeable, skillful, trustworthy, and credible				
Tangibility	Attractive work product, physical facilities, and personal appearance				

Source: *Win-Win Billing Strategies: Alternatives That Satisfy Your Clients and You.* Richard C. Reed, Editor (American Bar Association Law Practice Management Section, 1992)

5. Review with the client—and make sure the client understands—the risks in any procedure or action you recommend.
6. Define the client's responsibilities.
7. Define the lawyer's responsibilities.
8. Have each client sign a representation agreement (see Chapter 12), and make sure the client understands the fee and the agreement.
9. Recommend commercially acceptable solutions.
10. Return all telephone calls promptly.
11. Shower each client with regular communications and updates.
12. Greet each client in the reception area, and make sure the client feels at home.

13. Reinforce the elements of your service strategy with an annual retreat for everyone in the firm.
14. Reward employees for being client advocates.
15. Keep all promises.

You can use your office technology to generate value-added services. For example, a lawyer can use a computer to generate a draft, or sometimes a final document, with the client present. This method fills the client's need for promptness. Lawyers can also use technology to track obligations and promises made to clients.

A FEW MORE WORDS ON COMMUNICATING VALUE

How can you communicate this process to your clients? Let them complete checklists or information sheets. In one jurisdiction, for example, a checklist for a good commercial lease covers about sixteen pages of text. If a client retains a lawyer to do a commercial lease, the lawyer can give the client a copy of the checklist and ask the client to review the checklist for items to include in the lease. This lets the client understand what must be done to draft a commercial lease. This same technique can be used in estate planning and other areas of practice. Let the client see what it takes to generate a final work product.

A list of benefits also shows you can bring value to the problem at hand. Clients do not always know the benefits you provide—you must call their attention to your good works.

What other methods can you use to make certain that a client knows about your special efforts? Draw a line down the center of a sheet of paper. In the left column, list everything "special" you did for the client on the file. In the right column, write how and when you will remind the client how good you are. Fixing a record of your efforts in the client's mind is a pathway to repeat business. Thus, the real job of the modern-day lawyer is communication with the client.

CONCLUSION

Pricing legal services must be an integrated part of a firm's overall marketing strategy. Pricing is more than an exercise in budgeting you use to set hourly rates. Fees or prices must be within ethical and professionally imposed guidelines. Yet few firms, if any, understand and use pricing as an effective lever in their competitive strategies to survive and grow.

Fees must arise from your vision of what you consider good client service. Satisfying clients means hundreds of things, such as knowledge of your area of law and a good "bedside" manner. No one model of service can ever hope to capture all the things it takes to satisfy clients. You cannot simply wish your firm into a satisfaction program; it must come from lawyers and staff who commit themselves to good client care.

You must define what you mean and how to achieve it. This requires a model and an understanding of how to communicate with clients and staff.

Client service is an acquired skill. Everyone who works in a law firm needs this skill. It cannot be the responsibility of a separate department or person. If everyone knows, understands, and receives the necessary training, a client service system can become a self-fulfilling prophecy. Like a heat-seeking missile, which constantly adjusts its flight path toward its target, each person in the firm attunes his or her actions to the firm's model of service.

Communicating well also is a critical lawyer skill. Surprisingly, many lawyers inadequately grasp the basic concepts and skills of effective communication. Many lawyers become so engrossed in what they are saying and trying to accomplish for clients that they fail to see their clients as people with ideas and feelings that need attention.

Anyone with a law degree can practice law. To succeed, you must offer more than a law degree. To add value, make the clients active participants in your service system.

You can start this process by listing all the points of contact clients have with your firm. After you figure out the contact points, go back and see how you can include the clients throughout this process.

CHAPTER EIGHT

Technology and Billing

Significant portions of this book discuss the way technology affects the manner in which lawyers produce their work and, as a result, their billing practices for producing that work. It is equally important to address how technology affects the mechanics of the billing process and how it is used to develop alternative billing strategies.

Technology can be the proverbial two-edged sword for the lawyer. Technology can relieve the lawyer from much mundane and repetitive work, shorten the time to complete tasks involving word processing, and provide nearly error-free final documents. However, because the use of technology reduces the time expended on projects, this often equates to reduced fees for lawyers who bill by the hour.

This chapter examines how technology is used in billing and collecting lawyers' bills, whether they are based upon hourly rates or alternative methods. It also explores using technology to establish fee-setting and budgets, to create systems that accommodate alternative billing strategies, and to create knowledge management tools that can lead to alternative billing strategies. The balance of the chapter addresses the use of transaction fees or expenses to share the costs and benefits of technology with clients in nonconventional fee agreements, and, finally, the use of collaborative technology in alternative fee arrangements.

TECHNOLOGY AND THE BILLING AND COLLECTION PROCESS

Effective use of technology in the actual billing process can be a true win-win situation. Because most aspects of the billing and collection process are administrative and not billable to the client or otherwise recoverable, creating efficiencies here has no negative effect on a lawyer's billings. A better billing process is a positive improvement for the lawyer, in every way.

Within a law office, billing clients typically consists of the following general processes:

- The lawyer records the time expended, the description of the work performed, and the charges, whether time-based or task-based.
- The lawyer's secretary or accounting staff then integrates the other expenses charged and payments received within the prebill or ledger of the firm's records.
- The lawyer and firm prepare a statement for the client reflecting those charges and previous payments received and retainers applied.
- The statement is then transmitted to the client in some manner.
- The lawyer receives from the client either payment or a request for clarification of the statement or additional information.
- If the statement is not paid in a timely fashion, the lawyer institutes collection efforts for the amount due.

The discipline required on the part of the lawyer for the first step—keeping concurrent and accurate time—is, of course, more of a struggle for some individuals than others. Anecdotal evidence also suggests that many law firms, particularly solo and small-firm practices, have difficulty instituting a procedure for the final step of the billing process—collection.

Let us discuss how appropriate technology can be used to facilitate or improve each of the above steps in the billing process.

RECORDING THE CHARGES, WHETHER TIME-BASED OR TASK-BASED

What recording process is used for getting the records of fee charges from the lawyer's desk to the client's hands? In the traditional paper-based system, the process goes something like this:

- The lawyer writes the time charges contemporaneously on a billing sheet or diary.
- The billing sheet or diary is later delivered to, or retrieved by, the secretary or billing department.
- The secretary or a billing clerk types the information into a computer, hopefully accurately deciphering the lawyer's handwriting.
- After all billing, payments, and other expense charges are entered, the result is printed out in lengthy drafts or prebills.

- The prebills are then sent to the lawyer for review. Hopefully, the lawyer will not delay the editing and review by being distracted by other priorities.
- Any corrections or additions are rerouted through the above steps until the bill is finalized.
- Then, after final approval, the bill is printed in final version and mailed to the client.

Contrast the above steps and potential delays with a more modern model:

- The lawyer enters time charges contemporaneously into the billing program on his or her own computer.
- The billing clerk enters payments and expenses into the billing program as they are received or incurred. The billing clerk or secretary proofs the time entries of the lawyer on a regular basis before creating a final proof.
- When it is time to finalize bills, the responsible lawyer is notified by e-mail to proof the final bill over the network. Each bill can be quickly proofed online without printing. Few changes are needed, because the lawyer made most of the entries originally, and the entries have been proofed by the lawyer's secretary or billing clerk. Note that even though electronic proofing is possible, some lawyers and some law firms prefer that the proofing be done on paper, for accountability and record-keeping purposes. Also, some people proofread much more effectively on paper than on a computer monitor.
- The bill is printed in final version and mailed to the client. (Some bills are now transmitted electronically to clients.)

Clearly, the single greatest improvement in efficiency in the billing process would occur if lawyers personally entered their time charges, whether for time or task billing, into the computer system. Many lawyers try to deny and resist this truism. Lawyers have, after all, been filling out time sheets by hand for a long time now. Some lawyers have poor keyboarding skills. But even a "two-fingered typist" can enter a brief billing notation more efficiently than several people engaging in this cycle: a lawyer handwriting information, then a third party interpreting the handwriting and entering the data, and then the lawyer or administrator proofreading the data.

There are different ways for the lawyer to enter the data. In a solo practitioner's office, the billing software may actually reside on the lawyer's computer where time is entered directly into the billing software. With several lawyers and a networked office system, the lawyers access the billing software over the network or enter the data through simple "pop-up" windows.

Another method, which is growing in popularity, is using a separate software application to record the data, which is then exported or linked to the billing software. Many lawyers and law firms use case management software to manage and track many types of information about their client files, including billing records. One advantage to using this software to enter charges is that lawyers need training in only one law office software program. Another advantage is that the lawyers have billing records within the case management system for quick referral; this can be useful at times, such as when a client asks about a particular charge for a certain task, or someone needs a refreshed memory about the date of an event when notes are unavailable. Many products are available in the case management software arena. This method of easily recording billable time or billable tasks is highly recommended, partly due to the other benefits the firm receives from using case management software.

Whether the lawyer enters data directly into the billing program or indirectly through case management software, this process clearly changes the way the lawyer interacts with the office billing system. Once the billing data becomes digital, it is more valuable. It can be used for interim reports, productivity evaluations, and many other law office internal matters far beyond billing the client. Accurate and accessible electronic billing systems allow lawyers to establish budgets and set fees for many alternative billing options. It is therefore critical that charges be entered into the system at the earliest and least error-prone stage—contemporaneously by the lawyer doing the task. Various court, business, and ethical requirements for contemporaneous maintenance of billing records have long made this abundantly clear. Because systems that avoid handwriting interpretation and proofreading help ensure the integrity of contemporaneous records, such systems will soon be universally accepted as the norm.

We could not leave a discussion of the lawyer entering billing descriptions without mentioning again the book by J. Harris Morgan, *How to Draft Bills Clients Rush to Pay* (American Bar Association, 1995). Every lawyer should be trained and regularly reminded that whenever possible, billing statements—which are often too short—should reflect the effort expended by the lawyer and the value to the client. Bills are, in fact, a critical client communication.

INTEGRATING OTHER EXPENSES AND PAYMENTS WITHIN THE STATEMENT AND FIRM'S RECORDS

When the lawyer directly enters most of the fees into a computer system, this can allow the staff more time to ensure the expenses and other accounting items are in correct form. But even here, the process can be expedited. Most firms already use some sort of accounting software package. The ultimate goal is to achieve the single entry of expense data, spread across the system as needed. Too many small law firms (and a few large ones) engage in double, triple, and even quadruple entry of the same data about an expense that should be borne by the client.

The following example of a system at its worst shows how many times data could be entered for a single check for a court filing fee: A lawyer is unsure of the exact amount of a court filing fee, and so takes a blank check along when going to the court clerk to file a document. The lawyer then handwrites the check at the court clerk's counter, hopefully receiving a receipt. Upon returning to the office, the amount of the check is entered into the checkbook register by hand. Later the checkbook entries are transferred to an accounting program. (This is already the third time someone has entered this data.) Finally, a separate data entry is made to the billing program so the expense can be charged to the client.

Whether this is a trust account or an office expense account, these steps could be consolidated into one step. If the amount of the check is known before the lawyer goes to court, the amount could be entered into the accounting software and used to print a more professional-looking check for the filing fee. The accounting program would either serve as the billing program as well, or easily share information with the billing software and any other office application that requires the information. Preparation of the check could theoretically handle all the steps listed in the preceding paragraph. Moreover, law office applications that handle all the steps seamlessly are affordable, even for solo and small-firm practices. (At press time, there were several products purporting to be law-office-specific applications that could integrate accounting and billing functions.)

PREPARING A STATEMENT FOR THE CLIENT

State-of-the-art software programs for billing allow great customization of billing statements. Law firms should take advantage of this by taking the time to design a bill format that promotes the firm's image and provides a positive brand. Though it is not always necessary to use exactly the same fonts and designs or logos that are used on the firm's stationery, it is often highly desirable. A bill statement format that complements and is compatible with the law firm's stationery, fax cover sheets, and business cards supports the law firm's efforts at branding. This tying together of a law firm's image is critically important as the legal business environment grows even more competitive.

Earlier practices of using old printers with less-than-stellar output to produce bills should be totally unacceptable to the lawyer trying to create a positive and professional image. Bills and statements are important client communications and should be treated with care. Many clients and client representatives read bills with more care and attention than copies of court pleadings and substantive documents prepared by the lawyer. There is no excuse for a bill format that looks cheap or generic, no matter what the size of the law firm.

TRANSMITTING THE STATEMENT TO THE CLIENT

This step requires little discussion, as the only real value-oriented variable here is the timeliness of the statement in relation to the end of the billing cycle, the completion of the case or project, and the client's internal needs. The lawyer should be aware of certain time frames that will encourage and expedite payment, such as consumer clients' pay periods or the times that business clients pay their monthly bills. (For example, if a business pays its monthly bills on a fixed day each month, you may want to arrange to get the bills there a week before that date to allow time for review and processing the payment.)

In the future, many more clients will request bills via e-mail. In response to such a request, the lawyer should ascertain the client's objective. Does the client want a true digital bill that can be used in-house for internal communications (for example, text that can be copied and moved into other documents or e-mails) or does the client simply want a scanned image of the bill? Is there a preferred format, like PDF? Does the client understand that careless forwarding of an "e-bill" might compromise confidentiality or reveal litigation strategy? Will the client pay electronically?

RECEIVING FROM THE CLIENT EITHER PAYMENT OR REQUESTS FOR CLARIFICATION OR INFORMATION

Improving the mechanical handling of receiving payments from clients was discussed in the section concerning the integration of expenses and payments; the goal is to minimize data entry while ensuring that proper credits are made. (This part of the process has many concerns outside the scope of this discussion, such as security against misappropriation.)

Clients who have questions or concerns about bills usually contact the lawyers in charge of their projects, typically by phone for significant complaints. In larger firms, other staff persons or departments may be designated to handle such questions or complaints. To encourage clients to contact those persons or departments, it may be wise to program a notation on the billing statements, just following the total. A sample notation might read, "If you have any questions about this bill, you may contact our billing department by phone at 123-4567."

Some may be concerned that this will encourage complaints. But many of these requests will be for information, such as whether the bill is the final bill. For disputed bills, it is still best to air disagreements and concerns as early as possible. Otherwise, the client may simply set the bill aside without paying it and another month of labor (and billing) may be done by the lawyer before a problem is recognized. As noted in Chapter 7, opportunities for clients to have feedback are critical in any service environment, but especially when alternative billing methods are being implemented.

INSTITUTING COLLECTION EFFORTS FOR BALANCES NOT TIMELY PAID

Many small law firms do not have clear collection policies, and firms of all sizes often tend to ignore their policies with special cases and other exceptions to the rules. Also, some lawyers have a tendency to identify personally with their clients and their clients' causes. It then can become difficult to assume the somewhat contradictory roles of championing the clients in court or negotiations, for example, while dunning them for payment of past-due fees.

A collection policy should be determined in advance; exceptions to the policy should be rare, with such decisions being made by committee or objective partners. Basic law office technology allows firms of all sizes to implement collection policies. Sound business judgment requires the adoption of one.

Essentially, many steps of a collection policy can be handled with a series of diaried dates and form letters. This is one situation in which using the firm's word processing system to produce a series of similar letters on specific dates becomes quite useful.

A sample policy might include the following steps (with all periods of time running from the date of initial billing):

- *20 to 25 days*: A staff person can be assigned to contact the client by telephone to make certain there are no problems with the bill and to ask when payment can be expected.
- *30 days*: When a second monthly bill is sent out with the previous balance unpaid, it is stamped "Past Due" in red ink.
- *40 days*: An internal e-mail notice is sent to the lawyer, explaining that payment has not been received. This allows the lawyer time to intervene if there has been a mistake or some alternate agreement made with the client.
- *45 days*: The first collection letter is sent to the client. This is written in the "friendly reminder" style.
- *55 days*: An internal e-mail notice is sent to the lawyer, explaining that the client is seriously delinquent and steps must soon be taken to rectify the situation. It is suggested that the lawyer telephone the client to discuss the matter.
- *60 days*: Included with this month's billing statement is a letter noting that the account is seriously past due and the firm may need to reconsider its continued representation if arrangements are not made within the next 5 days.
- *66 days*: The management committee meets with the responsible lawyer to assess any practical or ethical obstacles to withdrawing from the representation. Depending upon the situation, notices may be

sent to the client explaining that work has ceased and, in litigation matters, that a motion to withdraw has been prepared and filed.

Every lawyer and law firm must tailor the above example to serve individual needs. Some lawyers may see these dates as providing too much delay, while others may believe they are too rigid. Many will feel that a more personal one-to-one approach is appropriate.

The benefit that technology brings to this process is the rapid and inexpensive system of diarying the dates and generating the form letters. Too many times a lawyer will procrastinate in contacting a client about such an unpleasant matter, even after promising the partners that it will be done. Sending a notice to the lawyer a few days in advance of the firm's collection effort can motivate the lawyer to handle the matter personally before it reaches the next stage. A large-firm lawyer, whether partner or associate, who is concerned that too many of these delinquent client situations will reflect poorly on the lawyer in periodic evaluations may take a more proactive stance with client payment issues. The solo or small-firm lawyer who notes an inordinate amount of collection efforts by staff may determine that there is some greater problem, such as the lawyer failing to place enough emphasis on timely payment during the initial engagement process, accepting inadequate retainers, or making poor decisions during client selection.

TECHNOLOGY IN FEE-SETTING AND BUDGETS

Technology in the form of an electronically based billing system is useful not only for tracking time charges, billing, and collecting fees, but also for establishing budgets for projects similar to those already handled by the lawyer, and even for determining what can be charged in alternative billing options. In Chapter 6, where we discuss the foundations necessary to developing alternative billing methods, we outline how to go through a task-based analysis and emphasize the necessity of examining closed files (and accounting and billing records) to create minisystems and predict fees. It is through the use of technology already present within most billing systems that these processes can be implemented quickly.

Nearly all computer-based billing systems on the market today have category and coding options that allow a lawyer to track not only similar types of cases and transactions in a larger "macro" context, but also specific components or tasks within the case or project in a "micro" context. If each case or matter is coded with a category (such as Merger/Acquisition, Incorporation, or Divorce) and possibly a subcategory (Merger/Acquisition, Asset Sale; Incorporation, Oklahoma; or Divorce, Uncontested w/o Children), then it can be relatively quick and painless to sort prior activities and collections to determine the time and resources needed for the last five or ten or hundred of those projects. If the lawyer time for an Oklahoma business incorporation averaged 3.8 hours, with an average billing of $684 in fees, then perhaps establishing a fixed fee for such work at $750 might make some sense—particularly if using technology to develop an incorporation system with a document assembly program meant the lawyer could reduce his or her average time to 2.0 or even 1.5 hours!

Many billing systems allow the lawyer to separate billing slips into specific tasks, and even integrate them into task-based billing and case planning. The ability to identify the costs and time required for certain tasks that fall within a case or project enables the lawyer to develop estimates and budgets for large projects. These billing systems allow the lawyer to answer questions such as, "What did the last fifteen depositions cost in similar cases?" or, "What was the average time it took to prepare the last twenty-five revocable trusts for clients in their estate plans?" Being able to segregate information in prior matters is crucial to budgeting for future business and establishing alternative billing methods that the clients will accept.

Many large corporations and insurance companies have long championed the use of task-based billing as a means of reducing outside-counsel fees, creating efficiency in the billing process, and limiting the huge differences in fees charged by different firms for essentially identical work in contracts, claims, and litigation throughout the country. A task force of The American Corporate Counsel Association developed Uniform Task-Based Management System (UTBMS) billing codes that a number of large corporations have adopted to use with their internal legal staffs and with outside counsel. (UTBMS codes can be found in the Appendix.) When UTBMS codes are used, law firms and their clients can budget complex cases more accurately, coordinate tasks more efficiently, create acceptable and uniform bill formats, and resolve many potential billing disputes before they arise. Many large firms transmit invoices electronically, which are then integrated into the client's system to test against budgets and billing rules. The result should be an electronic payment that is quickly remitted.

SUBSTANTIVE SYSTEMS AND DOCUMENT ASSEMBLY

Perhaps the best use of technology in alternative billing is implementation of document assembly programs and systems, which generate documents in a fraction of the time it takes lawyers to produce them. By developing a substantive system and using document assembly tools—with stand-alone systems (such as HotDocs™), practice-specific programs (such as Cowles Estate Planning System™), internal systems within word processing programs (such as WordPerfect™ or Word™), or tools built into practice management systems (such as TimeMatters™, Amicus™, or ProLaw™)—a lawyer can cut the time it takes to develop initial drafts of documents and thus build a platform for charging clients for the documents provided, rather than for the time it takes to prepare them. Clients who need businesses incorporated or wills drafted likely do not care how long it takes lawyers to prepare the documents—they want to know the costs for incorporation or for estate plans. By developing a substantive system using document assembly as a tool, lawyers can provide better and faster service to clients and make more money than if they billed the work by the hour.

An organizational system applied to a substantive area of practice can be an effective tool, in addition to enhancing the delivery of high-quality legal services. A substantive legal system is a documented system for handling transactions, procedures, or work flow, which has the effect of reducing waste, optimizing productivity, and contributing to greater efficiency in the delivery of legal services. A substantive system could still be a manual forms system, but in today's world, a computerized document assembly system makes the most sense. A substantive system enables lawyers to provide top-quality legal services promptly, thoroughly, and consistently. In short, law firms that use substantive systems with document assembly can deliver high-quality legal services for fair value, while reducing the lawyer time involved in transactions and giving lawyers more time to do something else (like working, marketing, or relaxing).

Beyond their utility in freeing lawyers, substantive systems can be used in many areas of law practice to market legal services. An example is the Corporate Representation Service™, a system developed by one of the authors of this book. His firm has an extensive corporate practice that represents many small and medium-sized businesses. The firm uses a number of substantive systems to do its work, which includes business structuring, incorporation or organizational documentation, contract and employment work, mergers, acquisitions, real estate matters, dissolutions, and other general corporate work. The Corporate Representation Service prepares annual minutes, acts as a service agent, does a corporate compliance check, and prepares special meeting minutes for clients for $150 per year. (See the election form in the Appendix.) This is done with a substantive system that uses document assembly to generate the correspondence, reminders, minutes, and questionnaires; in most instances, this requires only ten to fifteen minutes of a lawyer's time per corporation per year. Some corporations may require several hours of lawyer time, but the average, spread out over several hundred corporations, still makes the work quite profitable—and yet a bargain for the clients. The firm can use this pricing strategy to attract new clients and to generate significant additional work as a result of the audit questionnaires that often uncover more legal needs of the client. By using a substantive system, the firm can better organize its corporate work while marketing additional services, and lawyers can leverage their practices.

Other substantive systems with document assembly are commercially available. The Cowles Estate Planning System is but one example of programs and complete substantive systems used throughout the country by lawyers who want to change the billing systems in their estate planning practices from hourly based fees to fixed fees. Colleen A. Cowles's book, *The Effective Estate Planning Practice: Procedures and Strategies for a Client-Focused Business* (American Bar Association, 2001), describes a substantive estate planning system in detail.

KNOWLEDGE MANAGEMENT TOOLS

If document assembly programs and systems are the current technology for alternative billing methods, then knowledge management will be the tool of the future. The most valuable asset in a law firm is its intellectual capital—not only the knowledge and wisdom of the lawyers, but the work product of those lawyers and the ability to reuse and share that work product within the firm and with clients. Knowledge management is about sharing knowledge.

Automated substantive systems are a part of knowledge management; they allow lawyers to develop and share a system with templates and forms that are used to create final documents. Practice and case management systems networked in a law office can also form a part of knowledge management. These systems can provide functions as simple as ensuring that new addresses are inputted only once and are instantly available to the entire office, and functions as complicated as placing shared transaction documents on an extranet with client access to secure electronic conference rooms. Knowledge management is about technology, but also a lot more. Knowledge management is as much about the culture of the law firm that shares knowledge as about the method and tools used to accomplish the task. For a good resource on the principles of knowledge management, see *How Organizations Manage What They Know* (Thomas H. Davenport & Laurence Prusak, Harvard Business School Press, 1998), or go online to one of the top-rated journals in the field. (See www.kmworld.com or www.brint.com for extensive resources and links.)

Law offices implemented concepts of knowledge management and reuse of prior work product long before computers existed. Paper "brief banks" and internal form books not only increased efficiency, but also helped provide a superior work product. Technological advances escalate these ideas. Thousands of briefs in research banks can be effortlessly searched using technology. Similar transactions can be replicated to start a new project for a client. Knowledge management provides the lawyer tools to look beyond the billable hour in determining a fair fee for services. If the culture of the firm is to share research, knowledge, ideas, data, and even anecdotal information, then technology can capture that knowledge and help a lawyer extract it when required for the next project, case, or client need.

Most firms are only beginning to plan for this application of technology. Many law firms now have a Director of Knowledge Management. Implementing knowledge management tools requires lawyers to invest time and change old habits. After all, the best search engines built into a document management system can retrieve documents and data only if the system is designed properly and the data are entered into the system in the first place.

TRANSACTION FEES: SHARING THE COSTS (AND BENEFITS) OF TECHNOLOGY

As the use of legal technology tools has increased, so has the lawyer's ability to share the costs of those tools with clients—particularly if the tools help reduce the fees that would otherwise be charged for the services provided. Lawyers are more frequently building the cost of specialized programs into the fees charged a client, when those programs significantly reduce the cost and time required for the client's project. Depending upon the nature of the transaction, the program costs are sometimes part of a fixed-fee arrangement, or they might be a separate charge in addition to an hourly rate or other time charge.

One common tool for which there is normally a transaction charge is one of the electronic research systems (such as Westlaw™ or LEXIS/NEXIS™). A lawyer may incur a charge for specific research or have a flat monthly cost arrangement, and then bill the charge as a flat rate or include the charge in an electronic-research hourly rate that might be different from the standard rate determined by the agreement with the client. A common tool used in securities practices is a licensed document assembly system that generates blue sky forms and certain Securities and Exchange Commission filings, for which the law firm might charge a fixed fee per filing, to cover both the technology license and the paralegal/lawyer time expended in completing the documents.

Some lawyers may be concerned that exposing too much law office technology to clients could affect clients' perceptions of their lawyers' value. However, modern-day clients expect their lawyers to incorporate technological tools in their practices, in the same way that many of these clients have been forced to rethink their business processes in light of new technological capabilities.

COLLABORATIVE TECHNOLOGIES

Lawyers sharing information with one another and with clients can be critical for moving beyond hourly billing as the only measure of value provided by lawyers to their clients. Technology can be used to share information over the Internet through extranets accessible to clients, lawyers, and other members of projects or case teams. Extranets can provide cost-effective and secure Internet-based storage centers, which allow documents, e-mail, discussion group threads, and other information to be stored in secure areas that can be accessed by those needing to participate. Different areas of an extranet can have different levels of security and access. Law firms are already building extranets for their clients as part of the normal delivery of legal services. These firms are not only generating revenues from the use of such technology collaborations, but also cementing relationships with clients. The immediate access to all relevant information that these clients enjoy makes other law firms without such tools less attractive.

Law firms and individual practitioners also use the Internet and document assembly technology combined with expert systems to work with clients in developing standard documents for routine transactions, for which fixed fees—rather than hourly billings—are frequently the norm. An Iowa firm has a Web site where individuals can enter information online for their own simple wills. Another firm has established a loan document system, where the lender and borrower provide the information electronically and the documents are generated, reviewed, finalized, and e-mailed for closing without a paper draft copy being printed—all for a fixed fee. An international financial printer has developed secure Web sites to which multiple law firms, issuers, and underwriters have access, and where they can create, post, and edit documents for the workgroup to use before electronically filing them with the Securities and Exchange Commission.

CONCLUSION

This chapter provides some examples and ideas demonstrating how lawyers can use technology to increase efficiency in their billing processes and to think beyond the billable hour. Many applications of technology are discussed elsewhere in the book, and some that we touched upon only lightly (or even ignored) are used regularly by practitioners. Technology can be the great equalizer between large firms and solo/small firms—not only by enhancing the practice environment but also by fostering creative ways to provide value to clients and bill appropriately for that value.

CHAPTER NINE

Developing the Case Plan or Transaction Plan

The "case plan" or "transaction plan" is a systematic, written outline of what must be done to accomplish the client's objectives in a particular case or transaction. The detail and complexity may vary, depending upon the assignment. In some circumstances you will be able to foresee the scope of services and what is required, while more complex matters may involve unknowns that will require you to revise your plan periodically. Use of an alternative billing scenario increases the need for such an outline in advance, so that both client and lawyer can have a mutual road map as the matter proceeds.

The principle that underlies the case plan or transaction plan is that at the outset of any representation, you should map out or plan what must be done to reach the client's objectives. "Case plan" suggests litigation, and "transaction plan" suggests something other than litigation, but that is the only distinction between these labels.

WHY SHOULD I BOTHER WITH A PLAN?

Whether you are a solo practitioner or practice in a firm, it is important that you communicate with your client about some fundamental items: What have you been hired to do for the client? How much will it cost? When will it be completed? Although business clients in complex transactions may insist upon written plans, solo practitioners' consumer clients often need them more, because they are usually inexperienced and unfamiliar with the legal process, have little or no basis upon which to evaluate the technical or procedural nuances of the legal problem, and generally are nervous when dealing with lawyers. Whether in the fee agreement, a checklist, or a written plan, you must define the client's problems and needs, communicate your competence in addressing those problems and needs, and agree upon a fee arrangement.

Developing a plan is an early stage of communication between you and your client. It is a game plan that forces both you and your client to develop and agree upon what is to be achieved. It requires a commitment of resources and can suggest the appropriate billing method. Ultimately, it can be the standard for measuring the value received. The goal is to give the client some certainty about the cost (or at least the process), which allows the client to make an assessment of value.

The steps that occur in organized practice management should start before you agree to accept the representation. These preliminary steps include (1) analyzing your prospective client, the objectives sought, and the type of issue presented; (2) making a preliminary examination of the facts; and (3) verifying the legal principles and the availability of enough expertise and staffing to undertake the representation. Developing a case/transaction plan is a logical way to carry out these steps.

The plan you develop is much like a game plan developed by a coach in an athletic event or a battle plan developed by a military commander. The common thread is to devise an approach that defines the problem to be solved and the resources that will be available, recognizing that there may be many variables or unknowns that will require adjustment as the matter proceeds.

For some legal matters that are reasonably routine, the plan can become part of the office practice manual or minisystem, prepared in advance and communicated to the client through the legal representation agreement, standardized checklists, and correspondence. For example, for a nonjudicial deed-of-trust foreclosure, each step can be systematized. The client's objective is to complete the foreclosure, to postpone the foreclosure, to reinstate the obligation, or to cancel the proceedings. Once started, the process can proceed until one of those conclusions occurs. If the deed-of-trust foreclosure is contested, the steps to be taken differ from the nonjudicial process, but the course is determined. All this can be clearly outlined to the client in the legal representation agreement, a standardized checklist, or correspondence that is prepared and already in a system. Many would not consider this simple illustration to be a "plan," but it is.

Both computer-based and manual systems (such as incorporation systems for business lawyers or estate planning systems for lawyers working in estates and probate) can be developed internally or purchased from vendors who have developed proprietary systems to handle those types of transactions. Such systems lend themselves readily to establishing fixed fees, which provide value to the client and higher realization rates to the lawyer.

However, many representations are not so simple. Because the steps to be taken vary by practice setting, area of practice, type of matter, and client objectives, you should work with the client to develop a plan specific to the representation. (Refer to Chapter 7 for the importance of good lawyer-client communications.)

ELEMENTS OF THE CASE/TRANSACTION PLAN

A typical plan, whether for litigation or transactional representations, should be in writing and should be the common product of lawyer and client. The fact that it should be a common product does not negate the lawyer's obligation to have forms and other document assembly tools in place to make drafting a plan operate very quickly. After all, the goal is for the client to have the plan in hand at the earliest possible stage. For smaller and routine matters, this means that the client should be given the case plan at the same meeting where the lawyer is retained. All plans should include the following elements, although in simple or routine matters, these may be combined with other elements and/or may not require detailed analysis:

1. Definition of the client's problems (both legal and nonlegal)
2. Gathering of the facts
3. Initial legal analysis
4. Statement of client goals and expectations
5. Prescription of steps necessary to succeed
6. Anticipation of uncertainties, unknowns, and possible alternatives
7. Definition of the scope of the work
8. Determination of the resources required
9. Forecast of schedules for each part of the process
10. Definition of the client's duties
11. Definition of the lawyer's duties
12. Determination of the range of dollar values or the importance of what is at stake for the case/transaction, and for the legal expense
13. Evaluation of the risks to the client and to the lawyer
14. Agreement regarding how the risks will be shared
15. Determination of the billing method to be used
16. Procedure for modifying the plan, which must provide for contingencies, unknowns, factors beyond control, changed conditions, and the need for possible revision in the case/transaction planning to meet changing conditions

Some of the issues to be resolved in the development of the case/transaction plan should be included in the legal representation agreement. In simple or routine consumer matters, perhaps all the elements could be in the fee agreement. However, the case/transaction plan as a planning method can be more specific and detailed, particularly in more complex matters. It may involve checklists so that as steps are completed, you can have a written record of where you are and what needs to be done.

For example, in a complex case, a detailed plan might include names and addresses of known possible witnesses—favorable and adverse—with a schedule for interviews and possible depositions. All discovery would be included, again with a method for summarizing the filing of the testimony when discovery is completed for each witness. Key documents would be cataloged and indexed with an appropriate filing system for required retrieval. As the case evolved, all this information would be gathered in preparation for the ultimate trial.

If you were asked to do estate planning, the transaction plan would involve the necessary asset information, the names of the legatees or beneficiaries, and the client's objectives in connection with providing for family needs or minimizing specific taxes.

Once you grasp the concept and recognize the value of the type of analysis required to develop a specific case/transaction plan, you can adapt the general principles and features for your use on any matter—simple or complex.

PREPARING IN ADVANCE

Establishing a case/transaction plan actually begins when you finish the last similar case or transaction. How many of us do a thorough review and analysis of a case or transaction at its conclusion? Determine what we did right or did wrong? Choose what we can extract from the case for future use—briefs, forms, research, ideas? How can technology assist us in providing this same service and value at a lower cost? Nearly every other profession goes through this or a similar process at the conclusion of an engagement. A "post mortem" meeting or project review after each engagement provides information that is invaluable in making the next similar engagement better and more profitable.

One of a lawyer's greatest assets is his or her old files, which can—and should—be prospected and mined for information and ideas to aid in the next engagement. Billing records hold critical information on the time and cost required to provide services of a similar or identical nature, which helps in establishing fixed fees or estimating fees in a case/transaction plan.

SETTING CLIENT GOALS AND EXPECTATIONS

Early in the process of developing the case/transaction plan, you should elicit from the client his or her goals and expectations in the matter. This may not be easy, as the client often has not formulated a goal or may have an objective that is not disclosed specifically to the lawyer. Defining objectives may be an ongoing process.

It also is critical to determine, as early as possible, and based upon the then-known facts, whether the client's goals and expectations are reasonable and attainable. For example, a personal injury claimant may have in mind a recovery of $5 million in a case that appears at the outset to have a settlement value of $10,000. No matter how good a job you do, the client will be dissatisfied if your appraisal turns out to be the final result. The stronger your agreement with the client that his or her objectives are reasonable, the better your relationship will be.

It is difficult to measure the "value" you will provide to the client until you know the client's objectives. Take as an example four variations in a simple marriage dissolution representation:

1. The client wants an amicable dissolution that is fair to both spouses, done quietly, without antagonism, and with adequate provision for family support. *The objective is fairness.*
2. The client indicates that although the dissolution of the marriage is inevitable, the entry of any decree should be delayed as much as possible, at least until after a major business transaction has been closed. *The objective is delay.*
3. The client indicates an intent to remarry at the earliest possible date and states that no matter what the cost in terms of property settlement, you should get the marriage dissolved as soon as possible. *The objective is speed.*
4. The client is angry and vindictive, wanting to strike back against the other spouse in any way possible to repay the wounding the client has suffered. *The objective is revenge.*

If the lawyer does not understand the client's motives and objectives, there may be a mismatch. If the lawyer's approach in handling the dissolution is counter to the client's objectives, the client will be dissatisfied with the value received no matter how technically good the representation might have been. There may also be combinations of these objectives in varying degrees of intensity. Often, helping a client clarify the most important objective is an important part of the representation process.

If you think in terms of a real estate acquisition rather than litigation, you can develop the same type of scenarios to reflect different client objectives. To illustrate, the client may wish to negotiate for a parcel of land (1) to buy at any price because the parcel is indispensable for a planned development, (2) to buy for investment if the parcel can be acquired at a reasonably fair market value, or (3) to buy for speculation only if the parcel can be acquired at a bargain price. Negotiating techniques might vary depending upon the client's true wishes.

Setting realistic client expectations about time frames is important as well. In marital dissolution, a series of events usually follow in regular order. These may include filing and service of the initial pleadings, a response by the defendant, a temporary order hearing, various discovery procedures, a pretrial conference, court-ordered mediation or settlement attempts, and, finally, the hearing on the merits. Because most domestic clients are negotiating unfamiliar waters, time lines are a useful part of case plans. Although lawyers always orally explain these time frames to their clients, providing them with written documents that they can take home and periodically review gives clients greater value.

DETERMINING BILLING METHODS

Satisfaction of client objectives is tied to the choice of billing methods; the ultimate fee to be charged must relate to both the client's perception of value and the cost of providing the services to the client. You will learn more about the matter as you and your client develop the plan, and, as you do so, you can determine an appropriate billing method that is fair to both you and the client. As with any other undertaking, the more times you develop a plan, the more skilled and effective you become.

CHAPTER TEN

Alternative Methods of Billing

This chapter defines fifteen different approaches to billing and summarizes their advantages, disadvantages, and characteristics. If used correctly, these descriptions can be springboards to innovative billing.

Alternative methods of billing as they now exist fall into several general types. The key to selecting a billing method is to pair the client's needs and expectations with the method that most equitably measures the value of the lawyer's services. For all but the most routine matters, this involves drafting a case or transaction plan as discussed in Chapter 9.

FIXED OR FLAT FEE

A fixed or flat fee is the price that will be charged for defined services. It may be the entire fee for the engagement or may apply to segments of the total services. It may stand alone or be combined with either an hourly fee or a contingent fee. An example might be a fixed fee for incorporating a business or preparing a will or a trust agreement.

ADVANTAGES

- Forces agreement between the lawyer and client regarding which services will be required and furnished
- Requires the lawyer to know the cost of providing the defined services
- Allows the client to know what the fee will be
- Can be competitive with the market

- Can be useful in marketing services
- Not dependent upon the time spent
- Can be keyed to the value of the benefits to client

DISADVANTAGES

- Unprofitable if the cost of providing the services exceeds the fee
- Unprofitable if the services are not performed efficiently
- Unprofitable if included services are not specifically defined and the fee arrangement does not account for unforeseen problems that might arise and require extra work (unless that is clearly covered by the representation agreement)
- Should not be used when there are foreseeable uncertainties

WHEN TO USE

- For routine services where experience shows what is normally required, so the lawyer can foresee and define the included services and limit the excluded services
- When the lawyer can estimate both the time required and the mix of standard billing rates or costs
- For commodity services in a highly competitive market
- For repetitive, high-volume work
- When the lawyer is comfortable accepting the risk of unprofitability if the cost of production exceeds the fixed fee

PREDICTABILITY OF TOTAL FEE

- Excellent ability to let clients know what the fee will be

INCENTIVE FOR EFFICIENCY

- Encourages the development and use of systems, appropriate delegation of work, and technology

RECOGNITION OF VALUE TO CLIENT

- Can be priced to reflect the value to the client
- Allows the value to the client, rather than the time expended, to be the standard in setting the fee (subject to competitive market conditions)

CONTINGENT FEE

The contingent fee is a charge that depends upon the results achieved. It requires clear agreement regarding the desired results, as well as the items the fee does not cover. Those results may be positive (direct), in the sense of achieving a desired objective, or negative (reverse), in the sense of avoiding exposure to liability. A contingent fee may be combined with a fixed or flat fee, or with hourly billing. A common example is a personal injury case in which the fee is based upon the recovery. An example of mixing a contingent fee with a fixed fee might be a fixed fee for preparing a securities offering and a contingent or "success" fee if the offering closes and is funded.

ADVANTAGES

- No payment of the fee by the client unless a favorable result is achieved
- Provides legal representation for clients who might otherwise be unable to pay (The lawyer assumes the risk of providing services without assurance of payment.)
- Possibly lucrative, if the lawyer is careful in accepting the representation and properly screens cases before agreeing to the representation
- Requires payment to depend upon the results, not the time expended in obtaining results
- Clearly defined terms of representation in the fee agreement

DISADVANTAGES

- Assumption of risk by the lawyer, without assurance of being paid for services
- Carrying costs (The expense of litigation is advanced or carried by the lawyer if the client is unable to pay.)
- Limited contingency percentages in some jurisdictions in prescribed cases
- Uneven cash flow for the lawyer
- Possibility of time and effort exceeding estimates
- Conflicts with ethical rules in certain types of situations (for example, criminal defense or marital dissolutions)

WHEN TO USE

- When it is desirable to represent individuals who are otherwise unable to pay

- When your expertise and reputation attract good cases
- When you can skillfully screen the desirability of a representation, so you accept only cases with a likelihood of success

PREDICTABILITY OF TOTAL FEE

- Clear formula for measuring results that determine the amount of the fee, even though the exact fee is not known at the outset

INCENTIVE FOR EFFICIENCY

- Excellent—motivates the lawyer to maximize results with the least expenditure of time and effort (However, complications can arise if the lawyer and client disagree about whether to settle or try a matter.)
- Separates payment from time spent

RECOGNITION OF VALUE TO CLIENT

- Tied directly to the results achieved, so presumably reflects value to the client (If the matter is mishandled and good results are not obtained, the client will not receive value, even though no fee, or a low fee, is paid.)

HOURLY RATE

Since the late 1960s, hourly billing (sometimes referred to as time-rate billing) has predominated. It is predicated on the keeping of accurate, contemporaneous records of time expended by lawyers, legal assistants, and other staff members. The hourly rate for each fee charger is intended to represent the cost of production plus a profit factor. Therefore, knowing the cost of production is important (although many lawyers do not have reliable cost data to determine their costs in delivering legal services). To some extent, hourly rates are market-driven, particularly at the commodity level, and can reflect lawyer expertise and anticipated value at the high end of the value curve. (See Chapter 4 for a discussion of the value curve.)

Hourly billing has developed some components unrelated to the time actually spent on a matter, such as a minimum time charged for a particular service (for example, minimum time entries of one-quarter hour, or minimum entries for each letter or phone call). These should be—but often are not—clearly explained to clients in fee agreements.

Many firms have different rates for different fee chargers, and different rates for a specific lawyer, depending upon the type of service, the client, the subject matter, or other variables. These variations recognize that value to the client differs and that time spent does not necessarily measure the fee accurately.

This method can be combined with contingent fees or fixed/flat fees.

ADVANTAGES

- Comfort of lawyers and clients with this method, due to its longtime use
- The ability of lawyers to set, quote, and use rate schedules, along with the ability of clients to check, monitor, and compare those rates
- Nearly automatic billing process, particularly with computerized billing systems that can multiply the time recorded by preestablished rates per hour to produce statements
- Eliminates subjective judgments in billing
- Requires a chronology of the work done and a means of communication with the client, due to detailed itemized statements based upon contemporaneous time entries
- Due to the detailed itemized statements, creates the appearance of objectivity and evidence of the services provided, to justify the charge being made
- Allows all risks (except the risk of nonpayment of the fee) to be placed upon the client

DISADVANTAGES

- Inability of the client to know what the total charges will be
- Possible lack of relationship between the fee charged and the value of benefits received by the client
- Reduced incentive to reach an early conclusion and provide efficient, cost-effective services
- Resistance of clients to the high cost of legal services they perceive to result from hourly billing
- Assumption of all risks by the client, including lawyer inefficiency
- Lack of method's ability to recognize the benefits of using systems and technology, or to compensate adequately for the cost of developing such systems and technology
- Inadequate compensation for lawyers in high-value and high-responsibility matters
- Lack of recognition of extraordinary, priority, and emergency services
- Caps on gross income, due to finite limits for annual billable hours and for hourly billing rates

- Reduced incentive to find better ways to provide legal services at a reasonable cost to the client

WHEN TO USE

- When the client demands hourly billing and will not consider alternative methods
- When there are variables that cannot be foreseen with reasonable accuracy
- When no reasonably fair alternative method can be used
- When the lawyer is willing to accept the representation but not willing to accept any risk
- When the lawyer needs court approval of fees, and the only method the court recognizes is hourly billing

PREDICTABILITY OF TOTAL FEE

- Difficult, unless there is a guaranteed maximum
- Possible that sophisticated clients who have experience with similar matters and/or the same lawyer can anticipate the range of the fee
- Limited, even with case control by the client
- Depends upon the lawyer's willingness to write down a fee for the client based upon retrospective review

INCENTIVE FOR EFFICIENCY

- Not inherent, except generally to please the client and preserve the lawyer-client relationship
- Generally perceived to promote inefficiency, and to disregard relationship between fees for services and value to the client

RECOGNITION OF VALUE TO CLIENT

- Generally unrelated to value to the client, which may penalize either the lawyer or the client

BLENDED HOURLY RATE

The blended hourly rate is a hybrid of the hourly rate. Instead of specific hourly rates for individual fee chargers, one rate applies to all hours billed on a matter.

This fee arrangement is found more often in larger law firms, in large cases or in transactions where the client has negotiated the fee.

ADVANTAGES

- Generally the same advantages as for the hourly method
- Thought to be simpler to negotiate and administer than using specific rates for each fee charger
- Can be advantageous to the lawyer if work can be performed by individuals with lower normal hourly billing rates (This depends upon the capabilities of those individuals and the retained right of the lawyer, not the client, to direct who will do the work.)
- May encourage delegation of work

DISADVANTAGES

- Generally the same disadvantages as for the hourly method
- Appears simple, but still depends upon knowing the cost of production
- May endanger the quality of the work product through improper delegation, unless quality controls are in place
- Will be unprofitable if the blend in practice is at the high end of the hourly rate structure

WHEN TO USE

- When the type of work involves a typical pattern, and the fee-charger "mix" needed to do the work is reasonably foreseeable
- Should not be used uniformly if the matters subject to the agreement vary in the required level of expertise and specialization or in the responsibility assumed by the lawyer or firm

PREDICTABILITY OF TOTAL FEE

- Same as for hourly billing

INCENTIVE FOR EFFICIENCY

- Encourages more efficient use of individual skills, due to incentive to delegate (Care must be taken to ensure high-quality products, and to avoid increased costs to clients, if low-end personnel are markedly less efficient than high-end individuals.)

RECOGNITION OF VALUE TO CLIENT

- Generally unrelated to value to the client, which may penalize either the lawyer or the client

FIXED OR FLAT FEE PLUS HOURLY RATE

In this hybrid method, the portions of the services that have a definable scope are charged on a fixed-fee or flat-fee basis, and the portions of the services that are not capable of being defined because of variables or uncertainties are charged on an hourly or a time-rate basis. This method can be used in both litigation and transactional matters. Numerous variations can occur, and the sequence of the method of charging may vary.

To illustrate the method in a transactional matter: In an estate planning assignment, the charges can be billed on an hourly basis during the initial phase, when the client's objectives are being determined, asset information is being gathered, and tax ramifications are being assessed. When the plan has been determined and the requirements defined, the preparation of documents and services necessary to complete the assignment can be charged on a fixed-fee or flat-fee basis.

To illustrate the method in litigation: A flat fee can be charged for handling what appears to be routine litigation, with some agreement regarding which services are included in that fee. If it is necessary to do extra work, there can be an hourly charge for services beyond the original defined scope.

ADVANTAGES

- Compromise or balancing in the risk sharing and predictability of the fee
- Combines and modifies advantages of the hourly and fixed/flat fee methods
- Provides the client with an economic basis upon which to decide to proceed, once the lawyer quotes a fixed/flat fee after some variables or unknowns are removed

DISADVANTAGES

- Compromise or balancing in risk sharing and predictability of the fee
- Combines and modifies disadvantages of the hourly and fixed/flat fee methods

WHEN TO USE

- When some, but not all, of the contemplated services can be defined, so that a fixed or flat fee can be quoted (At the outset, the general approach to charging can be specified, even though the precise fixed or flat fee cannot be specified until some of the variables or unknowns have been removed.)

PREDICTABILITY OF TOTAL FEE

- Allows predictability for the fixed/flat-fee portion of the total fee, not for the hourly portion

INCENTIVE FOR EFFICIENCY

- Combines the incentives described for the fixed/flat fee and hourly fee methods

RECOGNITION OF VALUE TO CLIENT

- Creates a compromise between the two methods

HOURLY RATE PLUS A CONTINGENCY

By combining hourly billing and a contingency factor, the client and lawyer share risks within the limitations of the representation agreement. Because a portion of the fee is based upon hourly billing, the lawyer is guaranteed a minimum amount. This is true whether the hourly fee is based upon regular hourly rates or agreed-upon hourly rates that are lower than the regular rates. That guarantees the lawyer some payment, but also leaves the client with some risk. As with straight contingency agreements, the client and lawyer are both motivated to obtain the maximum results, because both will benefit.

The method for measuring the contingent fee must be clearly defined. If the achieved result justifying the contingent fee is not directly expressed in dollars, the agreement must explain the amount of the contingent fee and how it will be measured. For example, the basis for the contingent fee might be obtaining a rezoning, acquiring a business, or obtaining a restraining order, any of which would need to be assigned a value or tied to the fee amount that will be paid.

ADVANTAGES

- Sharing of risks and benefits between the lawyer and client
- Allows the hourly portion of the fee to offset the lawyer's cost of carrying the matter
- Creates a situation where the client does not pay the full hourly rate if the objective is not achieved, and shares only proportionately if there are benefits
- Provides a client who is otherwise unable to pay for services the opportunity to achieve a result for which he or she can pay

DISADVANTAGES

- As with any contingency-fee agreement, requires the lawyer to define the chances of success and to exercise care in accepting the representation
- Creates potential for disagreement if the fee agreement does not clearly define how the contingency fee will be computed
- Except to the extent of the compromise, has the same disadvantages as both the hourly and contingent-fee methods

WHEN TO USE

- With carefully selected clients
- After careful appraisal of the chances of success
- When the potential dollar value is significant (The potential contingent fee must more than offset the reduced hourly fee.)

PREDICTABILITY OF TOTAL FEE

- Raises the minimum total fee and generally lowers the maximum potential fee, as compared with the straight contingency fee

INCENTIVE FOR EFFICIENCY

- Generally the same as with any contingent-fee representation

RECOGNITION OF VALUE TO CLIENT

- Close relationship to value because of contingency factor and the way success will be measured

PERCENTAGE FEE

Typically, a percentage fee is based upon a schedule of fees related to the amount involved in the matter being handled. The amount may be predetermined or may, in some instances, be related to the amount ultimately determined. Examples include fees representing a percentage of the value of a probated estate, the amount of a real estate transaction, or the amount of a bond issue. The percentage rate may be constant or graduated.

ADVANTAGES

- Relatively easy to state the terms in the representation agreement
- Reflects the amount involved and the lawyer's exposure to liability
- Does not depend upon the time spent
- Has the same advantages as a fixed/flat fee, if the percentage and the amount of the transaction are predetermined
- Has the same advantages as a contingent fee, if the percentage is known but the amount of the transaction is not known

DISADVANTAGES

- If set too high, may not be competitive
- If set too low, may be unprofitable
- Forces the lawyer to bear the risk if complications arise and extra services are required, unless the representation agreement closely defines which services are and are not included
- Has the same disadvantages as a fixed/flat fee, if the percentage and the amount of the transaction are predetermined
- Has the same disadvantages as a contingent fee, if the percentage is known but the amount of the transaction is not known

WHEN TO USE

- In situations shown in the above examples
- Possibly in awarding fees in common-fund fee approvals, in lieu of the lodestar or hourly methods

PREDICTABILITY OF TOTAL FEE

- Allows for the method to be known, even if the amount of the fee cannot be calculated until the amount of the transaction is determined

INCENTIVE FOR EFFICIENCY

- Fosters efficiency, because the fee is not tied to the hours spent or the duration of the transaction
- Provides an incentive to use the most effective and most economical personnel to complete the assignment and to maximize the results

RECOGNITION OF VALUE TO CLIENT

- Presumably reflects value to the client in some cases (such as agent for a professional athlete) where the fee is tied directly to the results achieved, but in other situations, reflects the responsibility and potential liability associated with the project

TASK-BASED FEE

The task-based fee method is a hybrid of a fixed-fee arrangement, in which the fee is based upon identified tasks or components of the transaction, such as the total square feet being developed, the loan amount, or the tasks or phases of a litigation matter. The measuring method is usually predetermined based upon the task, the anticipated development, or the transaction, but may in some instances be adjusted due to changes encountered during the representation. The task-based method can also be used in budgeting complex matters, even when the billing method is completely or partly based upon hourly rates and time spent on particular tasks. Many larger businesses require task-based budgeting in litigation matters, with approval required before billings can exceed the budget for the defined task.

ADVANTAGES

- Relatively easy to state the terms in the representation agreement
- Allows sharing of risks and benefits between the lawyer and client
- Does not depend upon the time spent
- Same advantages as for a fixed or flat fee

DISADVANTAGES

- If set too high, may not be competitive
- If set too low, may be unprofitable
- Requires the lawyer to have a good understanding of the amount of work needed and the costs associated with the work

- Forces the lawyer to bear the risk if complications arise and extra services are required, unless the representation agreement clearly defines which services are and are not included
- Has same disadvantages as fixed/flat fees, if the tasks in the transaction or case are predetermined

WHEN TO USE

- In situations shown in the above examples

PREDICTABILITY OF TOTAL FEE

- Allows for the method to be known, even if the amount of the fee cannot be calculated until the size or amount of the transaction is determined

INCENTIVE FOR EFFICIENCY

- Fosters efficiency, because the fee is not tied to the hours spent or the duration of the transaction
- Provides an incentive to use the most effective and most economical personnel to complete the assignment and to maximize the results

RECOGNITION OF VALUE TO CLIENT

- Provides the client a clear understanding of the service received in return for the fee

RETROSPECTIVE FEE BASED UPON VALUE

The retrospective fee based upon value differs in approach from most of the alternative billing methods, in that the exact amount of the fee is not known to either the lawyer or client until the matter is concluded. However, the representation agreement can set forth the factors to be considered in setting the final fee. Often these are the factors set forth in the Model Rules of Professional Conduct. It is possible to provide either a maximum or minimum fee that will be charged. The amount may be combined with an hourly fee in setting a minimum. The amount of the fee should be determined by the lawyer, not the client.

ADVANTAGES

- Allows a retrospective determination of the fee when there are no longer uncertainties and unknowns
- Attempts to equate the amount of the fee with the value to the client of the services performed
- Depends upon the benefits conferred, rather than solely upon the time spent
- Can be more equitable than some mechanical systems, because the judgment regarding the fee amount is subjective

DISADVANTAGES

- Prevents the client and lawyer from knowing the fee amount in advance
- Depends upon a close and trusting lawyer-client relationship
- Contributes to wariness—in sophisticated purchasers of legal services—of potential abuses and inability to budget or monitor legal expenses
- Should cut two ways, with reduction of the fee below normal hourly rates, when value is not achieved despite efforts to do so
- Creates the potential for disagreement, because the lawyer's determination of value may differ from the client's perception of value received
- If no payment is made until conclusion of the matter, requires the lawyer to bear the cost of carrying the matter with limited cash flow, unless the client has agreed to make partial payments of fees as the matter progresses, subject to final adjustment

WHEN TO USE

- Selectively, depending upon the client and the nature of the matter being handled
- When the lawyer and client have a trusting relationship characterized by good communication, and the client is aware of the work that was done and the true value of the results
- When the lawyer and client each have confidence that the other will act fairly

PREDICTABILITY OF TOTAL FEE

- Difficult, unless a maximum or minimum range is established, with clearly defined criteria for setting the fee

INCENTIVE FOR EFFICIENCY

- Generally fosters efficiency, because the time spent is not necessarily a major criterion

RECOGNITION OF VALUE TO CLIENT

- By definition, if applied fairly and equitably, offers the best way to relate the fee charged to value to the client

UNIT FEE

The unit fee is a subspecies of the fixed or flat fee, in that the lawyer charges a fixed amount for a specific service, regardless of the actual time spent in providing that service. For example, a lawyer could have fixed charges for each letter, phone call, and deposition. This approach normally is combined with hourly billing for services not included in the unit billing. Some representation agreements provide that for a specified service, the lawyer will charge either the unit fee or the hourly rate fee, whichever is greater.

ADVANTAGES

- Simplifies time recording somewhat
- Reduces the time lost from inadequate record keeping
- Allows for the addition of a premium over straight hourly billing

DISADVANTAGES

- Distorts time records if records are used for purposes other than billing
- May be deceptive if the client believes the lawyer will charge a fee on an hourly basis
- Requires that the representation agreement clearly explain what the unit charges will be

WHEN TO USE

- When the lawyer has accurate knowledge of the typical time required to provide a specific service
- When the client will agree to this method

PREDICTABILITY OF TOTAL FEE

- Same as for hourly billing

INCENTIVE FOR EFFICIENCY

- Encourages efficiency in connection with the services covered by the unit fee portion of the representation agreement
- Encourages minimum time expenditure for a specific service

RECOGNITION OF VALUE TO CLIENT

- Not keyed to value unless unit price is below hourly rate

RELATIVE-VALUE METHOD

The relative-value method of billing involves creating schedules that separate the lawyer's services by subject matter and by task, and assigning a "relative value" or multiplier to each. Each fee charger can be assigned a different basic rate or charge, which is then factored into the equation. Individual practitioners who have developed their own schedules create variations in this method. Proprietary systems also exist.

Inherent in this approach is a determination or judgment of the value of each component service or task. This assumes that tasks performed by a lawyer differ in value, whereas straight hourly billing assumes that all time spent in performing various tasks has equal value. Once the relative-value schedules have been established, the base rate factor can be changed, thereby changing the fee.

The relative-value method combines elements of hourly, value, and fixed/flat-fee billing.

ADVANTAGES

- If uniformly used within a law firm, tends to provide more uniform or consistent statements
- Addresses value in the development of the schedules
- Permits fine-tuning in fee determination

DISADVANTAGES

- Time-consuming to prepare and maintain schedules of relative value
- Thought to be cumbersome to use

- May disregard whether the client's perception of "value" coincides with values assigned in the schedules
- Unless final charges are reviewed, may ignore factors such as results achieved or responsibility assumed

WHEN TO USE

- When the tasks to be performed can be classified and are reasonably predictable

PREDICTABILITY OF TOTAL FEE

- Limited, except in routine matters that fall into a billing pattern

INCENTIVE FOR EFFICIENCY

- Depends upon whether the system is task-oriented rather than time-oriented

RECOGNITION OF VALUE TO CLIENT

- Requires a determination of value in the production of legal services (This may or may not coincide with the client's perception of value.)

LODESTAR METHOD

The lodestar method of setting fees had its origin in the federal court system in *Lindy Brothers Builders, Inc. v. American Radiator & Standard Sanitary Corp.*, 487 F.2d 161 (3d Cir. 1973), and has been adopted in some states. The method was initiated as an attempt to create an objective system that could be applied by the courts with some consistency. It involves multiplying the hours spent by a reasonable billing rate per hour to determine the "lodestar," and then multiplying the lodestar by a factor—such as 1.4, 1.7, 3.0, or 0.8—to recognize factors other than time spent.

Courts have restricted the factors that may be considered multipliers, contending that those factors are "subsumed" in the hourly billing rate. For example, "expertise" originally was a factor in determining the amount of the multiplier but now is generally considered to be reflected by the hourly billing rate. Uncertainty of payment remains a factor for the multiplier.

Courts often set billing rates that are below the market, and sometimes will disallow portions of the hours expended if they deem the hours unnecessarily spent. One objection to the lodestar method is that using it to approve fees takes too much court time.

ADVANTAGES

- In theory, permits the hourly rate to be modified upward or downward based upon criteria other than the time spent

DISADVANTAGES

- Same as for hourly billing method
- Tendency of courts to disallow portions of the hours expended
- Encourages inefficiency, discourages early settlement, and is too complicated, according to many
- As in any court approval process, permits second-guessing of what was required
- Allows situations where awards may not reflect the market value of the services

WHEN TO USE

- When required by the court

PREDICTABILITY OF TOTAL FEE

- Little predictability

INCENTIVE FOR EFFICIENCY

- Very limited; encourages padding if the lawyer believes the court may not allow all hours recorded

RECOGNITION OF VALUE TO CLIENT

- None

STATUTORY OR OTHER SCHEDULED FEE SYSTEM

Sometimes, the amounts to be paid for legal services are prescribed in statutory enactments, in schedules for prepaid legal service plans, or by purchasers of legal services on a volume basis. Some fees are imposed; some are negotiated. Some fees are fixed or flat; some systems prescribe methodology. Some schedules are in fee-shifting situations; some reflect government-imposed social policies.

ADVANTAGES

- Allows the lawyer to know in advance what the fee will be or how it will be computed
- Allows the client or the plan to negotiate the fee amount
- Aids in cost containment, from the client's point of view

DISADVANTAGES

- Often rigid and/or arbitrary
- May not recognize the cost of production
- May be out-of-date if not revised frequently

WHEN TO USE

- When compelled to do so
- When the fee will fairly pay for the services provided

PREDICTABILITY OF TOTAL FEE

- Reasonably predictable

INCENTIVE FOR EFFICIENCY

- Creates an incentive for efficiency if the fee is fixed and does not depend upon time spent

RECOGNITION OF VALUE TO CLIENT

- Typically not much correlation

AVAILABILITY-ONLY RETAINER

The availability-only retainer, sometimes referred to as a "pure retainer" or "right-to-call retainer," is characterized by payment to the lawyer of a fee for which no direct services (or limited services as specified) will be performed. In exchange for that fee, the lawyer makes a commitment to be available when requested and, for a specified time period, to refrain from representing parties adverse to the client or competitors of the client. This method is not widely used, and normally involves a lawyer who has high-level expertise or prestige.

The funds, when received, belong to the lawyer and should not be deposited into the client's trust account. The majority rule in jurisdictions that have considered the issue recognizes the distinction between "advance fee deposits," which are client funds and must be put into trust accounts, and "retainers," which are funds paid by clients to secure lawyer availability over a given period of time. The retainer funds are considered earned at the time of payment, and need *not* be put into client trust accounts.

ADVANTAGES

- Creates no expectation that the lawyer will do any work for the fee
- Ensures representation by the lawyer of the client's choice
- Assures the client that the lawyer will not represent any party adverse to the client or any competitor of the client
- Creates belief by some clients that the lawyer's prestige will add to their prestige

DISADVANTAGES

- May prevent the lawyer from accepting desirable work from other clients
- May lead the client to decide that the amount paid does not bring expected benefits
- May create a situation where the lawyer's loss of business opportunities exceeds the amount of the retainer

WHEN TO USE

- When the monetary amount is significant enough to justify the disqualification from taking work from other clients

PREDICTABILITY OF TOTAL FEE

- Entirely predictable

INCENTIVE FOR EFFICIENCY

- Not relevant, because no services are provided

RECOGNITION OF VALUE TO CLIENT

- Should be reflected in the negotiated amount of the availability-only retainer

RETAINER AS A DEPOSIT AGAINST FUTURE SERVICES

The retainer as a deposit against future services, which differs from an "availability-only retainer," is not a billing method per se, but a credit technique that ensures the client will pay for services to be rendered or disbursements to be made on the client's behalf. Upon receiving these funds, the lawyer must deposit them into a client trust account, and may withdraw them only after performing services or making disbursements on behalf of the client. At the conclusion of the representation, the lawyer must return any balance to the client.

Some agreements require the client to keep the funds on deposit at a certain level and replenish them when they drop below that level. This is done to maintain an even cash flow for the lawyer and to ensure that funds will be available to pay the final bill. This arrangement can be used with a variety of billing methods, as it is a deposit against future charges, however computed.

ADVANTAGES

- Requires the client to make a financial commitment at the start of the representation
- Minimizes fee collection problems if the retainer balance is kept at an agreed-upon level throughout the representation
- Enables the lawyer to know throughout the representation that he or she will be paid

DISADVANTAGES

- Requires the client to have up-front funds
- May create collection problems for the lawyer if the balance at the end of the representation is insufficient to cover the final charges
- May present a timing problem for the client regarding when the client can take a tax deduction for legal expenses

WHEN TO USE

- From the standpoint of the lawyer, whenever possible for cash-flow purposes
- When the lawyer wants protection against certain malpractice claims (If there is doubt concerning when the lawyer was hired and obligated to the representation, an agreement that specifies the representation will start only when funds have been deposited helps protect the lawyer against certain malpractice claims.)

PREDICTABILITY OF TOTAL FEE

- Not relevant

INCENTIVE FOR EFFICIENCY

- Not relevant

RECOGNITION OF VALUE TO CLIENT

- Depends upon the billing method chosen

CHAPTER ELEVEN

Implementing Value-Based Billing

Using value-based billing requires you to rethink the billing process. You must manage your entire practice to ensure that clients are receiving value for their money. Thus, the ideas in this chapter are intended to stimulate thinking on innovative approaches not only to billing, but also to the conduct of the practice of law.

In changing from one billing method to another, you must consider what the change is, the effects of the change, the reasons why the change will be resisted, and how to find ways to overcome that resistance.

The old way of thinking associated with the cost-plus billing method was that hours equal value, and leverage equals profit. As costs go up, rates rise as a multiple of costs. A whole generation of lawyers and clients grew up with—and became accustomed to—hourly or cost-based billing as the predominant method. There is comfort in doing what is familiar. Whenever change is contemplated, it is necessary to analyze whether current conditions are the same as the conditions that existed earlier. If problems are different, the solutions should be different.

The cost-plus method essentially favored lawyers, without regard to the benefit or value produced for their clients. This led to dissatisfaction on the part of many clients. As described earlier, when the market for legal services was expanding, the hourly billing method was seldom challenged and even came to be accepted almost as the standard approach.

In contrast, value billing is an attempt to equate the amount of the charge to the client's perception of value, or to tailor the billing method to meet the client's preferences. Implementing this method is more than just *billing for value;* it is *managing for value.* Managing for value means doing only those things that will produce a benefit. It means that lawyers exist to serve clients, not clients for the benefit of lawyers.

Implementing a change to a core office function, particularly one involving money, will no doubt stimulate a response and discussion among lawyers and clients alike. This chapter discusses the actual implementation of the new system.

VALUE BILLING AND PROFITABILITY

No matter what billing method you use, your legitimate interest is to be compensated adequately. The premise of value billing is that clients who receive value are satisfied clients, and satisfied clients make for a profitable and successful law practice. Moving away from cost-plus billing does not mean lower profitability; in fact, if value is produced, there will be mutual benefit.

The "realization rate," when traditionally and more narrowly defined, means the extent to which collections of fees equal fee billings. In the broader context, "realization" can be defined as the extent to which you are fully paid for all services performed. This implies that you are doing the right things and that what you do provides a benefit to the client. Thus, profits are linked to planning, wise choices of steps taken, expertise, and managing for value to the client.

The rate of realization then depends upon both external and internal factors. External factors include client satisfaction (the perceived quality of the work product, the perceived efficiency in the generation of the product), market characteristics, client characteristics, and the rates as compared with competitors' rates for similarly valued legal services. Internal factors include efficiency in generating the product, the mix of the persons doing the work (delegation, paralegals), the effective use of systems and technology, timely billing and collection, legal and industry specialties, management attention to quality and value, and provision of assured quality to the clients.

The objective of value billing is to optimize realization by matching the fee to the value of the services and to deliver services profitably, given the client's perception of value. Value billing therefore forces you to understand the economics of your practice and focus on ways you can maximize the net income per partner. Here are at least five ways:

1. Increase chargeable hours per charging person (utilization). That is, people can work harder, longer, and more productively.
2. Increase overall fee realization. Do this by eliminating unnecessary work that provides no benefit to clients.
3. Increase the book of business per lawyer. The "book of business" means the amount of desirable and profitable legal work per lawyer that results from doing good work, having satisfied clients, effectively

marketing services, and otherwise adding to the volume of the type of work that produces value.
4. Reduce costs.
5. Increase operating leverage by adding associates and paralegals and reducing the number of partners.

These techniques apply regardless of the billing method used.

STRATEGIES FOR PROFITABLE VALUE BILLING

How can value billing make your practice more profitable? This approach to managing your practice suggests several possible strategies.

SEEK A HIGHER DOLLAR REALIZATION

First, you can move in the direction of work with a higher dollar realization. Two ways of doing this are to prune the client base and prune the lawyer base. You can also use marketing techniques designed to attract the kind of work you seek. For example, the marketing effort might have these objectives:

- Promoting the firm's reputation
- Promoting clients' loyalty to the firm
- Establishing new loyalties and expanding upon the existing base

Finally, you can seek work with a higher dollar realization through the selective hiring of lateral partners whose expertise or reputations will attract higher-quality work.

RAISE THE VALUE OF YOUR SERVICE

You can also enhance profitability by increasing the actual or perceived value of your services. To increase the actual value of services, you might use these approaches:

- Through research and development, stay ahead of the pack.
- Do more for the client; redesign your product to be more effective.
- Use innovative approaches to dispute resolution.
- Focus on industry niches.
- Increase the quality of your services.

Here are some ways to increase the perceived value of your services:

- Improve communications.

- Improve speed and responsiveness.
- Improve availability.
- Increase senior counsel involvement and visibility.

IMPROVE QUALITY

Improve quality as a means of increasing "value." For example, as computers have evolved from mainframes to personal computers, the price of computing has come down despite an increase in the capabilities and performance of smaller, less costly personal computers. Similarly, when handheld, battery-operated calculators first came on the market, they had limited capabilities and were relatively high in price. The manufacturers of personal computers and handheld calculators enhanced the quality and capabilities of their products and provided better value in relation to cost, which resulted in widespread use of the products.

REDUCE THE COST PER UNIT OF SERVICE

By cutting the firm's cost of providing a unit of service, you can boost the amount of revenue going to the bottom line if you do not change the fees received for the units of service. The most obvious way to do this is to optimize productivity (output of legal product per lawyer per time period). There are numerous sources of enhanced productivity:

- Better-trained lawyers and staff
- Paralegals
- Forms and systems
- Automated research tools
- Expert systems (computer applications designed to assist in decision making)
- Practice management and quality controls
- Controlled mix of lawyer experience

Also, consider implementing a two-tier practice structure to recognize that in most law practices, some legal business is routine (the "commodity work" described in Chapter 4) and other practice areas are "unique." Most law firms tend to treat all matters as having the same value from the viewpoints of both lawyers and clients. Physical surroundings, skill of personnel, and even office locations can be restructured to reflect the difference in expertise required for different types of work. Once these distinctions have been made, the firm can selectively recruit personnel based upon demands of either "volume" business or "custom" business.

USE TECHNOLOGY

You can create value by using technology to automate and improve services. Your office can use substantive law expert systems, document assembly, case management, and budgeting software. Using technology to create value normally involves the following steps:

1. Decide what you want to accomplish.
2. Consider the impact of technology on existing methods.
3. Determine the cost-effectiveness of the technology.
4. Select what to automate.
5. Select and develop specific systems.
6. Determine pricing for services.
7. Explain the new techniques to clients.

Being at the forefront in the evolving use of technology gives pioneering firms competitive advantages. The promise of technology for the legal profession is that it will give law firms the flexibility to pursue alternative billing methods by lowering the costs of producing legal documents and services. See Chapter 8 for a more comprehensive discussion of technology.

The payoff for the effective use of technology is rapid and flexible adjustment of pricing policy to market conditions. Not insignificantly, with efficient use of technology, pricing no longer needs to be determined solely by the amount of billable time required to produce the service.

POSITION ON THE VALUE CURVE

The principle of the value curve, introduced in Chapter 4, suggests that the curve itself probably will not change a great deal. Changes likely would be at either the high end or low end, depending upon whether the proportion of unique services increases as the law evolves or whether more and more services are produced routinely.

To the extent there is change, it would be primarily on an industrywide basis and influenced by outside forces. However, the dollar value at any point on the curve might change, depending upon the number of lawyers competing or the amount of services performed by nonlawyers.

Although the value curve itself remains quite constant, a lawyer or law firm may be able to move up on the curve in total practice, or by practice area, by fitting into both the external and internal factors. This is called "positioning," which involves fitting into a slot on the curve by taking a selective approach to law practice. For example, if you do commodity work, you can reduce that type of work and develop expertise in work that is at the high end of the curve. The curve does not change, but your position on the curve will have changed:

- If you increase the "actual value" by turning out a better product, you will move up the curve.
- If your clients have an increased perception and appreciation of value—the ultimate test—the effect will be to move you up the curve.

CLIENTS' PERCEPTION OF VALUE

There are ways to increase clients' perception of value. Perceptions can change if you concentrate on, and improve, some or all of the following factors:

- Image
- Lawyer-client communication
- Timeliness of services
- Availability
- Dependability
- Response time
- Convenience to the client
- Efficiency
- Effectiveness
- Stability
- Accountability
- Fairness
- Education of clients so they understand the value of the services
- Education of clients so they better understand the responsibility assumed by the lawyer
- Conveyance of a caring attitude
- Doing the right thing

These factors permit differentiation, which involves distinguishing the services that you can perform from those performed by other lawyers. The differences may be actual or perceived, but either type of difference is reflected as value in the marketplace.

GUARANTEES

Another way to build client loyalty is to guarantee performance, a concept that is not prevalent in the service industries. In contrast, guarantees of manufactured products are common. Some are restricted in scope while others guarantee total satisfaction. For example, the manufacturers of Zippo™ lighters guarantee they will repair or replace any Zippo lighter without charge. The customer merely sends the lighter to the company, and back comes a lighter in good working order. No questions are asked! In maintaining a high level of service, Nordstrom™ stores accept the return of merchandise for credit or refund, again with no questions asked. What kind of guarantee could a law firm give that would be meaningful and would develop client loyalty and be of value? Here are some realistic possibilities:

- *Any phone call received from a client before 3:00 P.M. will be returned the same day.* If the lawyer is unable to do so, someone else will return the call to explain why the lawyer cannot return the call, set a time when the call will be returned, and ascertain the problem or the message or provide the necessary information.
- *Agreed-upon deadlines will be met.* If the deadline for performance cannot be met because of uncontrollable factors, the client will be advised to that effect before the original deadline.
- *Written work products will be free of typographical and spelling errors.*
- *A written status report will be supplied at specific intervals.*
- *All appointments will be kept promptly.* No clients will be kept waiting more than ten minutes beyond the scheduled appointment time.
- *There will be no charge for the initial conference with each new client.*
- *Copies of all documents and correspondence will be sent to the client.*
- *There will be no charge for phone calls to or from clients of less than ten minutes' duration per day.*
- *At the end of each matter, a client satisfaction survey will be sent to the client.*
- *For each client, there will be a backup person who is knowledgeable of the status of the matters being handled for that client.*

Many of these suggested guarantees would cure some common client complaints. Perhaps more important, a commitment to these guaranteed performance standards would set the internal law firm requirements for client service. As part of the program for guaranteed performance, the firm should specify some adequate monetary benefit to the client in case the guaranteed commitments are not met.

CHANGE: HOW TO BRING IT ABOUT

As with any change, sometimes it is easier to start on a small scale (for example, with one or two partners in a small firm, in only one practice area, or in one department of a large firm). That way, not everyone need be involved, as some will resist change or be slow to change. Remember, the lawyer or firm must first be convinced that there are reasons to change the methods of billing.

Before you approach the client, you must undertake some internal analysis. Review a few closed files to note the fees charged, the number of hours characteristically spent by everyone who worked on those files, and the procedures followed. (See Chapter 6 for a more thorough discussion of reviewing closed files and bills.) Think about how those closed files could have been handled more efficiently. Then ask some "what if" questions about those same closed files. Assume you were considering a change from hourly billing to a fixed fee per case. Compute what the results would have been with the closed files if you had handled those matters for a fixed fee. How would that billing method have affected you? How would it have affected the client? What volume of work would you have needed to reach profitability on an average case?

If after completing your analysis you conclude that a fixed fee could be charged on particular types of cases, think about which clients send you that type of work. Which clients are most likely to be willing to innovate, to try something different? Pick the client that appears to be the best candidate. You need not, and perhaps should not, adopt the change across the board. Have a test run under the best circumstances.

Once that decision has been made, you must educate the client about the proposed change and convince the client to try it. An example of a successful approach occurred when a banking client and outside law firm agreed to test the alternative method. A number of cases were assigned for handling, with half on a contractual-fee basis and the other half on an hourly billing basis. After the cases were concluded, the outside firm and corporate counsel analyzed the results and negotiated a mutually acceptable ongoing representation agreement.

It is not always the law firm that wants to alter the billing method. Sometimes a client wants to change how the lawyer bills for services. For example, in-house counsel may be dissatisfied with hourly billing and want to innovate. Corporate counsel who have arranged alternative billing methods tend to use the procedure just described. It starts with reviewing how cases have been handled and charged by outside counsel. When corporate counsel can view volumes of cases that have been handled by more than one outside firm, they can establish patterns. Whether the impetus for change comes from the lawyer or the client, both parties must practice good communication and be willing to try something different.

Often the push toward innovation comes from below. Assistant in-house counsel may need to convince the general counsel to change, just as a lawyer may need to convince partners, departmental chairs, the managing partner, and the executive committee of the benefits of innovation.

CASE STUDY: COULD THIS HAPPEN IN YOUR OFFICE?

The associate in a law firm, John Young, enters the office of the department chair, Sara Head.

"Hi, Sara. Do you have time now to discuss an idea that I've been developing for some time?"

"Sure, John, tell me what's on your mind."

"You know that we've been handling a lot of nonjudicial deed-of-trust foreclosures for three or four banking clients. Most of them have been assigned to me, and my legal assistant, Jackie, has worked closely with me. In fact, with the systems we've developed, it seems we can do most of the cases on a routine basis."

"Yes, John, I'm aware of what you've been doing in handling those foreclosures."

"Jackie and I have gone back and reviewed all the foreclosures that we had in the past year or so. We know how much time was spent on each and by whom. We know the billing rates and the total fees that were charged. We averaged the time spent and the fee charged on a per case basis. I can give you a summary of what we found."

"That's interesting, John, and I'd like to look it over more closely. What do you propose?"

"Well, I think we could handle cases of the type included in our study for a fixed fee per case. Here on this schedule is what I think we could include by way of services and what we could charge per case. If the foreclosure became contested or if a stay order was entered by some bankruptcy court, we could cover that in the fee agreement. I know we might earn less on a few cases, but if we had enough volume, that should average out, particularly if one or more of our banking clients would give us all their work instead of splitting it as they now do. At the fee I suggested, we would have a profit, especially if we can improve our methods for processing the work to eliminate any unnecessary steps. The clients would be paying us less per case than the average fee paid during the past year, so they should be happy."

"This sounds interesting. Assuming we go ahead, where would you start?"

"Sara, I get along well with Sam Workout at First Savings. I think it would be best if we approached him with this idea to get his reaction. Then we could try the new method for a batch of cases. If it works for First Savings, we could then go to Second Savings and make the same proposition. I think the fixed fee would be attractive to them, because they always seem to worry about the total fee when we bill on an hourly basis."

"I'll study your figures, John. Let's meet tomorrow morning at ten o'clock to discuss this further. At the moment, it seems like a great idea. See you in the morning."

This scenario could lead to a fixed-fee billing method, but, with variations, one of the other methods of billing could be proposed. Similarly, the cast of a junior lawyer proposing innovation to the chair of a department could be changed to a partner convincing another partner, a law firm convincing the chief operating officer of a corporate client, a law firm convincing in-house counsel, an assistant in-house counsel convincing the general counsel, or in-house counsel convincing outside counsel.

The process starts with a willingness to innovate, an analysis of existing practices, a thoughtful review of the method of delivering services, a systematized method of producing legal services, a review of closed files to ask "what if" questions, a client relationship that is characterized by good communication, and a willingness on the part of the lawyer and the client to try something different.

ARGUMENTS IN FAVOR OF CHANGING BILLING METHODS

GENERAL ARGUMENTS

Following are some general arguments supporting a change from hourly billing to another method.

Match of Billing Methods to Client Needs

Aside from total costs, clients are concerned about the predictability of legal costs and risk sharing. Chapter 10 describes the characteristics of a number of billing methods. Anticipate what each client desires and try to match that need.

Increased Client Satisfaction

Clients expect to pay for legal services, but if they are dissatisfied with the billing methods, they may sooner or later be dissatisfied with the services provided. Displaying a willingness to change can itself result in more satisfied clients.

Increased Incentive for Efficiency and Effectiveness

The analysis process should heighten the firm's ability to work efficiently and effectively; that is, to do things right and to do the right things. This is because analysis forces a review of what and how things are done. Once the firm abandons billing on the time-rate method, it will have less of a tendency to do unnecessary things or to procrastinate.

Fairness

The injection of the concept of value, together with the recognition of the importance of the client's perception of value, direct attention to finding and using a method that most fairly measures the value of the services provided.

Recognition of Economic Realities

With increased competition and the fungibility of many types of legal services, services that are in the commodity end of the value curve are price-sensitive. This creates an imperative for efficiency, value, and appropriate pricing.

Reduction of Pressure for Expansion

Pyramidal organizational structures and reliance on leveraging through numbers have forced law firms to expand. As general economic conditions become less favorable, the way law practice is conducted becomes more important. If firms can increase profits through improved use of technology and more efficient production, they will be under less pressure to grow constantly.

Leverage for Profit, Not for Numbers

With increased efficiency promoted by the use of methods other than cost-based billing, plus hoped-for increased client satisfaction, law firms can concentrate on the "mean-and-lean" approach to profitability. Unbridled growth may be a thing of the past.

Increased Predictability of Legal Expense

When the time spent is the only basis for charging fees, a client cannot know in advance the total expense that will be incurred. Many of the billing methods described in Chapter 10 provide for predictable fees, thus satisfying a basic client demand.

Opportunity for Risk Sharing

Several of the billing methods described in Chapter 10 involve some sharing of risks between lawyers and clients. Risk sharing can promote efficiency, motivate lawyers and staff to produce better results, and demonstrate confidence in clients' causes. Thus, sharing risks can be mutually beneficial.

SPECIFIC ARGUMENTS

Following are some illustrations of changing how lawyers bill, techniques for convincing others to change, and reasons that can be advanced—in sum, a series of scenarios that you might use.

Associate Convincing Partner

I can use my time more efficiently, so there will be higher utilization to increase billable hours. You will not have to write off as many hours if:

1. we use project management so assigned lawyers will know what products are needed when and what the budgets are,
2. there are fewer wild-goose chases and not as many surprises when the billing memorandum arrives on your desk, and
3. we focus on internal budgets combined with alternative billing to increase my attention to budgets, and to improve my—and the team's—realization on your projects.

I can apply my ability to use computers and conduct computerized research. My training in use of the computer, combined with alternative billing, will allow me to get a higher return on my time, allow me to be more efficient without loss of fee revenue, and allow the client to get what he or she wants quickly and at a reasonable and fair cost. Also, my understanding of the computer and the discipline imposed by alternative billing will motivate me to create substantive systems with accumulated knowledge of the firm, because with fixed fees we will realize a higher return on my hours.

Partner Convincing Partner

We can achieve higher realization on your time and the time of those you leverage in client matters. Your time is too valuable to spend on legal tasks that others with lower billing rates can perform. By using alternative billing, you will be motivated to delegate more effectively. The time of those you leverage will be billed at higher rates, with fewer write-downs of time. When effective billing rates increase, there will be less pressure to keep all your associates and paralegals generating very high (but low-realization) hours. You can spend more time training them in the things that will make real profit for the firm.

There will be higher net income per partner, due to improved realization on your clients and matters. Your contribution will be greater than for partners who rely only upon billable hours to generate fees. There are several reasons for this:

- Your effective collection rate, and therefore your realization, will go up, making a more significant contribution to the net of the firm.
- Your time will be better spent on high-value work.
- Your increase in realization on your time will allow you to work fewer hours or do more work in the same amount of time.

Partner(s) Convincing Department Chair or Management Committee

We can make better use of our accumulated knowledge in the department (or firm). There will be a higher return on the hourly rates when fixed fees are billed for tasks or legal products produced by substantive systems. Also, partners in your department will spend less time on associate work and therefore allow a higher return on their own billing rates (higher realization).

We can also make better use of our systems and technology. Alternative billing will enable your professionals and administrative staff to see a return and a reward for better use of systems and technology, so they will be motivated to use them. More timely service will give you a competitive edge with clients and with other partners in the firm.

You can increase the realization of your department in the long term. The revenue generation per partner in your department will improve as the revenue per lawyer increases through alternative billing and higher realization. Therefore, overhead will decrease as a percentage of revenue dollars. Your department will become one of the high-profit departments that this firm is willing to develop by investing more resources. Also, your partners will excel in relation to partners of other departments (who perform work at hourly rates), giving them more income per partner. Furthermore, your associates will have a better chance at partnership because they earn a favorable revenue per lawyer and because they will acquire the skills required by the firm.

Demands on your time for assimilating a large number of new associates will decrease. You will not need as many professionals to get the work done; they will be more efficient.

Finally, quality control will increase as the department moves to alternative billing and quality assurance techniques come into play. This is a result of increased return from the use of alternative billing techniques that motivate effectiveness and efficiency.

Law Firm Convincing the Client CEO (or CFO)

This is how we will increase the quality in your work and improve timeliness, while reducing the cost of your legal services.

Alternative billing will make our firm and your personnel focus more effectively on what must be done and when. We will work more closely with your people in laying out the scope of the project to meet your performance, cost, and schedule requirements, because we will be motivated to lower your cost and increase our profits. Also, there will be far more coordination and status reporting to ensure we are on track in managing the matter to stay within budget.

Your legal fees will be more consistent. The items listed under fixed-fee arrangements will always cost the same, so you will know the fee before selecting a course of action. The items listed under the blended rate will give you a consistent fee per hour that will not creep up due to the involvement of too many high-billing-rate lawyers. Furthermore, you will be able to accrue legal fees more accurately over the year, instead of getting hit in one quarter with a surprising and large amount.

You will be better able to budget the legal fees for the firm. To implement these alternative billing techniques, we must be more disciplined in budgeting phases of work ahead of time. This will give you warning regarding quarterly and annual legal budgets.

You will have more information for the board and the CFO. To establish a proper scope for the work, we will have to become much more involved in understanding the factors that affect the profitability of your business. Also, because of the project management techniques we must use to implement alternative billing techniques, your officers and board will have better information to understand risk versus cost.

Law Firm Convincing In-House Counsel

Most of the arguments used with the CEO (or CFO) also apply here, and there are some additional approaches you can take.

Alternative billing methods lead to better quarterly budgeting of legal fees. To draft engagement letters for all the work and for specific projects, your people and our people will need to lay out the scope of work more accurately, thus allowing better projection of legal fees.

We will also provide better project management (planning, organization, staffing, direction, and control of matters) for the client. A higher level of coordination in project management will protect you against surprises on legal bills. We will be more responsive to your needs and schedules. You will have better information for staffing projects in-house, because everyone will better understand the scope of work, course of action, required tasks, and legal products.

You will be more protected from surprise actions by the other side. The project planning required for alternative billing will make us dissect previous work to see how the other side has come at us. Debriefing of major projects will become part of the bundle of services offered to you in our efforts to create efficiencies and plan subsequent projects more effectively.

You will be able to make better scope estimates for in-house counsel staffing. Continued use of alternative billing, and the management that must support it in the firm and in-house, will give your personnel more information for projecting future in-house staffing needs.

Assistant In-House Counsel Convincing General Counsel

Many of the arguments in the preceding illustration should be used here. In addition, there are other benefits to assert:

- Better quarterly budgets and estimates are possible.
- Staffing needs of in-house counsel are more easily defined.

- Lower legal fees
- Better information for in-house reports to management

In-House Counsel Convincing Outside Counsel

You will have better profits per hour, because you will receive fair fees for fixed-fee items, blended-rate work, and hourly fee work if you make the proper adjustments in your structure for delivering legal services.

You will not need to grow as quickly and invest all that money in new staffing.

We can make some of the required investments in project management systems, to release your capital for other purposes.

You will have the continued loyalty of our lawyers, who will learn how to manage cases from your top people.

I want my bills reduced, and this is the only way I will accept your relationship with our company. I think that if we work together on this, you will make a reasonable profit while I lower my legal costs. If you are not willing to invest the time and effort, I am sure that some law firm out there is willing to work with us.

IMPEDIMENTS TO CHANGE

Despite the benefits, there are some understandable impediments to changing billing methods. Following are the ones most frequently enunciated:

- *Inertia*: "We have been doing all right. Why change?"
- *Lack of understanding of the concepts*: "This value billing seems like a lot of theory. It may work for others, but I don't see how it will work for us because we have a different kind of law practice."
- *Fear of change*: "I know how things work with hourly billing, but I don't know what would happen if we changed." (It is better to dislike the known than to fear the unknown.)
- *Compensation systems based upon billable hours*: "If we did away with billing on an hourly basis, how would we know how to compensate our lawyers? We have always relied heavily upon billable hours recorded." (The answer is to forget about billable hours as the major criterion for compensation and talk about total fees produced and received. Count dollars in the bank account, not hours logged.)
- *Fear that if systems and technology are major methods of producing services, and project management becomes a major role of lawyers, this would not be "practicing law"*: "I didn't go to law school to be just a mechanic."

- *Generational difference*: "For the past forty years, we have been doing hourly billing. Now you new guys want to change what has worked in the past."
- *Threat to the personal security of individuals whose role would be changed*: "For years I have logged more billable hours than anyone else in the firm, and now you guys want to change the rules."
- *Threat to the relative political power of the partner who generates a lot of hours, or to those associates who work for that partner but achieve relatively low realization rates on billings*: "I've got a good thing going, so why change it?"
- *Courts' reliance upon time records in awarding fees*: "The courts may not recognize other billing methods, at least not for many years." (This is a valid objection, in light of the typical time lag between new methods of law practice and courts' adjustment to those methods. After minimum-fee schedules were abolished, it took the courts a long time to adjust to hourly billing and time records. Nevertheless, only a small percentage of fees are set by the courts.)
- *Concern that under the Model Rules of Professional Conduct, a legal fee must be "reasonable"*: "Under some of the methods of billing, would this be a problem?"
- *Uncertainty about the time needed to handle a case*: "What if this is a worst-case scenario? I can't estimate the whole project. There is no way a lawyer can anticipate all that might occur."

Overcoming these (and other) impediments to changing billing methods is what this book is all about. Identify the roadblocks in your firm and use the information in this book to change your firm and your practice for the better.

CONCERNS OF CORPORATE COUNSEL

Since the first book in this series, *Beyond the Billable Hour*, was published, quite a few corporate counsel—as major and sophisticated purchasers of legal services—have expressed doubts about changing from hourly billing. One doubt is about "value billing." Some equate value billing with "premium billing" and object to the notion of being charged at a higher level. Others interpret "value billing" as a judgment about value made by the lawyer after the matter is concluded. The objection on this basis is that clients do not want to be at the mercy of the lawyer in setting the amount of the fee when there are no preagreed standards for making a fee decision.

Corporate counsel have diverse views about the billing methods of outside counsel, but at the same time, they express some common notions. In their role as clients engaging outside counsel, corporate counsel have these major objectives: cost containment (in terms of total dollars), predictability of charges (allowing budgeting and analyzing of the risks and benefits of a given course of action), cost efficiency (knowing that only what is required is being done and that it is being done effectively and efficiently), and risk sharing.

Legal services are generally recognized as covering a wide range of matters, from the repetitive and routine on the one hand to the risky and complex and infinitely complicated on the other. In between are nonroutine litigation and complex transactional matters, where the variables and uncertainties are difficult to foresee because of factors that are not controllable at the outset. Once these distinctions are recognized, it is possible to fashion appropriate billing methods.

Sophisticated clients who support hourly billing appear to do so only partly because of inertia. Generally, proponents of hourly billing believe they understand how the method works, what the costs of producing legal services are or should be, and that they as clients can control the outside costs by requiring budgeting and discount rates based upon volume, restricting what is done, prescribing who will do the work, and, ultimately, having the leverage to force work to be done on their terms because the outside firms wish to receive further work assignments. In the past decade, the increased role of inside counsel in managing outside legal work, or retaining specific legal work for processing by inside counsel, has made monitoring and controlling outside legal costs more effective.

In litigation matters where there are unknowns, a common technique is to use task-based billing to compartmentalize or segment the handling of the matter and to require a fixed fee or cap for a specific phase of the litigation, such as pretrial discovery. Periodic reviews are made at progressive stages, with the law firm and the client agreeing upon a course of action and a fee arrangement appropriate for the next phase.

Some clients agree to pay a bonus for certain results, along with using the basic hourly billing method. This arrangement is designed to provide an incentive for effort, results, or speedy resolution of the matter being handled.

Increasingly, in-house counsel give legal work to lawyers or firms with specialized expertise in the subject matter being assigned. There appears to be less of a tendency to give all outside legal work to a single firm.

In 1990, corporate counsel were asked to name the factors that would cause them to stop using an outside firm. Interestingly, the highest response was poor-quality work. The second-highest response was total legal cost, and the third, the method of billing. Generally, corporate counsel who were reluctant to change from the hourly billing method decried the perceived abuses of that method, but believed they had developed ways to control those abuses, at least enough to limit their enthusiasm about alternative methods.

CONCLUSION

The multiple-value curve described in Chapter 6 suggests that the services performed by a given lawyer or law firm may fit at different points on the curve. You may attempt to move up the curve by the means suggested in this chapter, or abandon certain low-value practice areas.

When changing from a cost-based billing approach to a value-based system, you must adjust the price of certain services. Some clients may perceive that some fees based upon cost are overpriced. On the other hand, some fees based upon cost may be underpriced, in that they provide value, in the perception of the clients, that is greater than now charged. Value billing is not "premium billing" as some contend, but an attempt to equate the price to perceived value.

Implementation of these concepts into office policies and new models of client service is not easy. Many lawyers have expressed belief in these concepts, but have failed to achieve significant acceptance and create real change. Hopefully this chapter has provided you with the tools to create real change.

CHAPTER TWELVE

Legal Representation Agreements

Besides setting forth general provisions for legal representation agreements, this chapter and the Appendix at the end of this book provide illustrations of how firms are adapting innovative billing approaches in various substantive practice areas. As the examples show, many practicing lawyers are using innovative approaches to billing. Thus, we are talking about real-life situations, not just theory.

MATTERS TO ADDRESS IN ALL LEGAL REPRESENTATION AGREEMENTS

Some types of representation mandate written fee agreements. Similarly, some jurisdictions specify which fee agreements must be in writing (contingency-fee agreements, for example) and the parameters for such agreements. Rule 1.5 of the Model Rules of Professional Conduct provides that a lawyer who has not regularly represented a client must communicate to the client the basis or rate of the fee, preferably in writing, before or within a reasonable time after commencing the representation.

Prudence and good business practice suggest that the services to be provided, as well as the basis for the fee to be charged, should always be put in writing. A legal representation agreement defines the scope of the engagement, the duties and rights of the lawyer and the client, and the way the fee will be determined. Thus, it is broader and more comprehensive than a "fee contract."

Negotiating a representation agreement minimizes the possibility of misunderstanding. Perhaps even more important, it forces the parties to analyze what needs to be done, who will do it, and how the fee will be computed.

Whatever the billing method, all legal representation agreements should address certain matters. James W. McRae identifies those matters in *Legal Fees and Representation Agreements* 42–44 (American Bar Association, 1983):

1. Scope of the engagement:

    - Specify exactly whom you represent. (This sounds simple, but it can be tricky when multiple interests are involved.)
    - Describe the specific functions you expect to perform and the results you hope to achieve.
    - Identify the personnel from your firm who are likely to play roles in the representation.
    - Identify the functions that will be performed by the client and by other persons not associated with your firm.
    - Include a general timetable of activities (hedged to give you the flexibility you need to deal with unanticipated developments).
    - Include express authorization from the client for you to act on his or her behalf, to the extent of the specific functions you have been retained to perform.
    - Provide for control points, or specific decisions that must be made by the client before you are authorized to proceed further.

2. Legal fees and expenses:

    - Describe the method to be used in determining the proper amount of the legal fee.
    - Specify whether the lawyer or the client is responsible for significant payments for expenses (for items such as court reporters, court costs, investigators, title examiners, airline tickets, or associated counsel).
    - Specify whether the lawyer or the client is responsible for nominal out-of-pocket disbursements (for items such as photocopies, messenger services, telephone charges, postage, travel expenses, or secretarial overtime).
    - Include a clear statement of your understanding regarding the timing of payments for both fees and expenses, including any retainer or fee to be paid in advance and the manner in which it will be applied or refunded.
    - Specify the extent of detailed data to be included in statements.

3. General matters:

    - Provide that the work product produced in the course of the representation should remain as your property, although the client should be given reasonable access to it.
    - Reserve the right to withdraw from the representation, and to be paid on some basis for all services rendered before the date of such withdrawal, if the client fails to honor the agreement.
    - Provide that the client has the right to terminate the representation if you fail to honor the agreement, and that in such event, you

waive any further rights to compensation related to the representation.
- Consider whether any disputes regarding fees or failures to honor the agreement should be submitted to arbitration for prompt resolution. (Ethics rules in some jurisdictions may limit your ability to do this, and care should be taken to inform the client that agreeing to arbitration means both parties waive the right to sue. Independent legal counsel for the client about this provision may be required under certain circumstances. See Rule 1.8(h) of the Model Rules of Professional Conduct, which provides that a lawyer shall not make an agreement prospectively limiting the lawyer's liability to a client for the lawyer's personal malpractice, or settle a claim for such liability with an unrepresented client or former client, without first advising that person in writing that independent representation is appropriate.)
- Provide that upon any termination of the representation, you will cooperate with any successor counsel to accommodate a smooth transition of the representation.
- Provide that the client has the right to direct that the representation be transferred, without penalty to the client, in the event the lawyer who is principally handing the matter, or who is the principal contact, dies, becomes disabled, or is temporarily or permanently disassociated from the firm.
- Explain that the representation will not commence until you receive a copy of the legal representation agreement signed by the client (together with any advance fee that may then be due) on or before a specified date.

When you contemplate making some adjustment for factors other than time, consider the following optional provision, also suggested by James W. McRae in *Legal Fees and Representation Agreements* 88 (American Bar Association, 1983):

Client acknowledges that, although time expended is the major fee-determining criterion, ultimately the total and final fees will be based on a more comprehensive measure of the reasonable value of the Counsel's services. Factors other than the amount of time required, such as the novelty and complexity of the questions involved, the skill required to provide proper legal representation, familiarity with the specific area of law involved, the preclusion of other engagements caused by the acceptance of this engagement, the magnitude of the Matter, the results achieved, customary fees for similar legal services, the nature and length of the Counsel's relationship with the Client, the time limitations imposed by the Client or by circumstances will all have a significant bearing on the reasonable value of the services performed. Therefore, it is agreed that the final fees to be charged by the Counsel may be revised upward or downward from the total fee amount as calculated above, at the discretion of the Counsel, to properly reflect such factors as those listed above, as well as other considerations which may arise during the course of the representation.

CAVEAT

In connection with all representation agreements, be careful to comply with all state and federal laws and regulations. Because those provisions vary from state to state and are subject to periodic changes, no specific statutes or regulations are cited here.

Pay special attention to requirements for the extension of credit, disclosure, maximum charges, contracts written in a language other than English, and other provisions designed to protect the consumer. Traditional approaches used by lawyers may directly—or by extension or interpretation—be deemed subject to such requirements. Legal representation agreements that permit the extension of credit or include interest or finance charges for consumers are subject to particular scrutiny. Violators of fair credit laws are subject to civil and criminal penalties.

CHAPTER THIRTEEN

Evaluating Results of the Use of Alternative Billing Methods

Evaluating the results of your billing process is an ongoing task. Conducting this evaluation will tell you whether you are making progress in becoming a win-win lawyer or law firm.

Remember that before you adopt any alternative billing method, you should determine your cost of doing business, set a desired profit margin, and attempt to predict the consequences—monetary and otherwise—of a change in billing methods. For example, Chapter 11 described how counsel for a bank and its outside counsel ran a test before entering a final agreement. That test involved handling a number of cases, comparing hourly billing with billing on a fixed-fee basis. Then, by mutual agreement, corporate counsel and outside counsel fashioned a more permanent representation agreement (reprinted in the Appendix).

REVIEW OF CLOSED FILES

As part of the effective management of your practice, you should institute a process for continuing review of your billing methods. Closed files can provide a wealth of information if you make the effort to review them. For example, you can compare cases that were handled under a new billing method with similar cases that were handled with the previous billing method.

Move in the direction of analyzing each file or transaction when you either close the file or complete the transaction. Use the results of this case-by-case analysis to fine-tune your billing methods.

When you open a new file for a new client (or begin a new matter for an existing client), you probably use a routine form and follow a standard procedure. It is equally important to have a regular routine for closing a file, which allows you to evaluate results and review how you handled the representation. A form for file closing and evaluation appears as Exhibit 13-1.

If you have the case plan or transaction plan that set forth the objectives you and your client agreed would be sought, compare them with the actual results and determine the extent to which those objectives were reached. That will tell you two things: the extent to which the client received benefits from your services, and your skill level in projecting reasonably attainable objectives.

As part of this end-of-matter review, ask yourself these questions:

- What value did my efforts bring to the client?
- Were the results reasonably close to our projections?
- How could I have done a better job?
- How could I have been more efficient?
- If I had it to do again, how would I have done things differently?

From a review of similar cases, you may discern common features and procedures that can be converted to minisystems or complete systems. Frequently, once a lawyer or firm performs a service, clients make more requests for the same service. What may have started as a one-of-a-kind matter develops into repetitive work that can be systematized.

A retrospective review should lead to improved efficiency. For example, as individuals within the firm become familiar with processing a given kind of work, you can delegate increasing amounts of the work to the least expensive unit of labor competent to perform that service. A review of closed files can also disclose forms and agreements that you can convert from customized agreements to generic forms or agreements. Failing that, the review will at least lead to the preservation and indexing of prior work products for future use.

Analyzing profitability is part of the review process, so some sort of cost accounting will be advantageous. Once you regularly assess the profitability of a specific type of work, you can move toward eliminating the unprofitable work and increasing the type of representation that will place you higher on the value curve.

CLIENT AUDITS

An important aspect of evaluating results of the use of alternative billing methods lies in determining the extent of client satisfaction with that prior work. How do you do that? As noted in earlier chapters, communication between the lawyer and the client is critical. Lawyer-client communication includes learning the client's degree of satisfaction and perception of value.

Exhibit 13-1

Checklist for Closing a File

File name and number	
Responsible lawyer	
General description of the matter (include code)	
Was there a written representation agreement?	Yes No
Billing method used	
Did actual time/cost exceed the opening estimate?	Yes No
Was there a case/transaction plan?	Yes No
To what extent did the actual results reach the initial stated objectives?	
What value did you bring to your client?	
How could you have done a better job for your client?	
What would you have done differently?	
Can any systems or minisystems be developed from this file?	Yes No
Identify any forms, pleadings, or memos for the forms file	
Are there forms that can be made into generic forms for the form file?	Yes No
Do you anticipate work of a similar nature in the future?	Yes No
Was this matter profitable to the firm?	Yes No
Have you discussed with the client whether the client was satisfied with the handling of this matter?	Yes No
Summarize the client interview	
Did you do any cross-selling with the client?	Yes No
If you had it to do over, would you use the same billing method?	Yes No
If no, what method would you use?	
What technology was used on this matter?	
Could this matter have been handled more profitably by some other individual or method?	Yes No
Additional comments:	

I certify that I personally completed this form on this _____ day

of_____, 20 ____.

_____
Responsible lawyer

As part of the procedure for closing files, firms often use client audits, surveys, or questionnaires. These ask a client his or her feelings about the handling of the matter just completed. If there is a problem that needs correction, the audit may point the lawyer in the direction of rectifying the shortfall. A form questionnaire appears as Exhibit 13-2.

If the client expresses satisfaction, the door is open for cross-selling additional legal services, which is yet another important reason for conducting a review process. There should be a systematic procedure for following up on any cross-selling opportunities that are identified.

PERFORMANCE EVALUATION

Another benefit of the review process is the opportunity to evaluate the level of competence of the person or persons who performed the services. Performance evaluations can be tied to compensation decisions, and can provide the basis for expanded responsibilities in making future work assignments.

PROFITABILITY ANALYSIS

Billing methods will vary from firm to firm, from department to department, and from individual lawyer to individual lawyer. The type of work may dictate a certain billing method. Some lawyers will be more innovative than others. Individual lawyers may experiment with alternative billing methods on one or two matters or cases before adopting them for all matters of the same type. A practice group may decide to experiment with some alternative billing method, even though the firm as a whole has not recognized the advantages of innovating.

Consequently, it may prove interesting to make some in-house comparisons of profitability based upon these differences. If two lawyers within a firm do the same type of legal work but use different billing methods (such as time/rate by one and fixed fee by the other), you could compare their profitability. Determine whether the difference in profitability is due to different billing techniques.

QUALITY OF LIFE AND QUALITY OF WORK PRODUCT

Another component of the review process, although it may be difficult to quantify, is determining whether there is any apparent difference in the lawyers' quality of life resulting from the use of a specific billing method. Criticism has been leveled at the hourly rate billing method because it places such high em-

Exhibit 13-2

Confidential Questionnaire

	Y	N	Comments
1. Are you treated by the attorneys and staff in a courteous and professional manner? If not, please elaborate.			
2. When the firm handled a legal matter for you, were you kept fully informed of all pertinent matters relating to that matter?			
3. Have the legal fees and other charges been clearly and adequately explained to you? If not, how can we better explain them?			
4. Are our fees reasonable in light of the nature of the services we have provided you?			
5. During the last 2 years, have you used other lawyers to represent you? In what areas? Have you been satified with their services? With their fees? If not, why?			
6. Have you referred others to our firm? Would you refer others to our firm? If not, why?			

7. Please make any comments you feel would assist us in better serving you in your legal needs:

_____
_____
_____
_____
_____
_____

8. Optional:

Name:_____

Address:_____

Telephone #:_____ Fax #:_____

CLIENT QUESTIONNAIRE B

phasis on recorded billable hours. Stress, pressures, and the resultant lack of job satisfaction are sometimes attributed to some firms' requirements for billable hours.

The review process can help lawyers evaluate work product quality. Lawyers and firms can look for differences in the levels of client satisfaction and work product quality that can be attributed to the billing method chosen, and can use what they learn to help correct poor-quality work. The review process can also target for reward those individuals whose work is consistently good.

We should all attend well to our personal lives outside of the office. It is easy to take stress home from the office. It is also problematic that lawyers who strive for personal and financial success often find that "billing more hours" is the path to that success. There is nothing wrong with hard work. But there is everything wrong with a system that provides the only paths to success at the expense of personal, civic, and family time.

A review of the lawyer's quality of life issues may be somewhat subjective, but a marked change in pressure and stress might be the most important and far-reaching result of the implementation of these ideas.

CONCLUSION

Systematically evaluating results requires discipline, as does consistently using written representation agreements and developing case or transaction plans. However, the discipline required to institute these methods results in a win-win law practice.

Appendix

Fee Letters, Agreements, and Other Resources

To illustrate the practical application of some of the concepts discussed in this book, this Appendix reproduces some actual fee and representation agreements from firms of all sizes around the country. In some instances, at the request of either the lawyers or the clients involved in those agreements, we have deleted the names of the parties or other identifying information, as well as dollar amounts. This is to protect the rights of privacy, confidentiality, or in some instances perceived competitive position. All illustrations are real-life approaches to the problem of billing fairly.

Exhibit 1: Standard Fee Letter
Exhibit 2: Letter Giving Alternative Fee Options to Client
Exhibit 3: Formal Fee Agreement (Hourly or Contingent)
Exhibit 4: Increased Hourly Rate for Negotiations; Contingent Fee if Litigation Is Required
Exhibit 5: Alternative Billing Proposal for Either Hourly Rates or Reduced Hourly Rates with a Contingency Fee if the Business Is Acquired
Exhibit 6: Guidelines for Use of Outside Counsel; Not Dependent on Any Specific Type of Billing Method
Exhibit 7: Agreement for Fixed-Fee Representation of a Bank for Major Collection Litigation with Bonus Clause

Exhibit 8: Fixed Fee Corporation Representation Service Election Form
Exhibit 9: Fixed Fee for First-Year Services to Emerging Business
Exhibit 10: Fixed-Fee Retainer Agreement for Handling Insurance Defense Cases Based on a Prescribed Volume of Cases
Exhibit 11: Fixed Fee with an Hourly Rate if the Time Exceeds an Agreed Number of Hours
Exhibit 12: Fee Agreement Incorporating Hourly, Fixed, and Unit Fees for a Real Estate Development Project
Exhibit 13: Uniformed Task-Based Management System
Exhibit 14: Probate Case Plan

Standard Fee Letter

The fee letter in Exhibit 1 is a model letter that can be used by a law firm to fit a variety of fee arrangements. The letter as presented covers fees billed using a standard hourly rate and based upon the time it takes to handle the particular matter. It provides for an adjustment in the hourly rates upon prior notification and has a provision that can be included to estimate the range of the fee. The retainer provisions call for the funds to be placed in the law firm's trust account and remain there until the end of the engagement with the proviso that if a monthly bill goes unpaid, the retainer may be applied to the unpaid bill and the engagement terminated.

ROBERTSON & WILLIAMS
Attorneys and Counselors At Law

3033 N.W. 63rd Street, Suite 200
Oklahoma City, Oklahoma 73116-3607
(405) 848-1944 · Fax (405) 843-6707

Mark A. Robertson
E-mail: marobert@robertsonwilliams.com

[Date]

[Name Prefix] [First Name] [Last Name] [Name Suffix] [Title]
[Organization]
[Address 1]
[Address 2]
[City], [State/Province] [Postal Code]

Re: <u>Legal Representation and Fee Agreement</u>

Dear [Salutation]:

It is a pleasure having the opportunity to be considered for representing you as counsel in [_____]. We are pleased to undertake this representation. I think that it is both appropriate and helpful to a client for me to outline in writing the scope of the engagement and this firm's fee policy. I believe it to be good business practice to discuss the subject of fees with a client at the beginning of our representation and outline how the fees will be computed and how we expect payment. I prefer to use a fee letter that both the client and the law firm agree to.

Scope of Representation. As I understand the scope of our employment, we will be [_____].

Communications and Responsible Attorney. In an attorney-client relationship, it is important to communicate to us all the important information concerning the engagement and to call whenever you have questions or wish to discuss your matter. We will endeavor to keep you informed as well. I will be responsible on a day-to-day basis for the supervision of the representation in this matter. Other attorneys and members of our professional staff who will assist me are [_____].

Fees. We take into account many factors in billing for legal services, and I will review all statements before they are issued to ensure that the amount charged is appropriate. The firm's fees for this type of work are significantly influenced by, but not entirely based upon, the hourly rates assigned to attorneys or assistants in performing the legal services. Due consideration is also given to other factors, which the American Bar Association Code of Professional Responsibility states must be taken into account, including the complexity, difficulty, and novelty of the issues involved; the degree of expertise required to handle the project; the time constraints imposed upon the firm; and results obtained on the client's behalf. The nature of the project will often determine how the fees are charged.

For the type of work outlined above, our fees will be based upon the time it takes to handle the matter.

Our schedule of hourly rates for attorneys and other members of our professional staff are based on years of experience, specialization in training and practice, and the level of professional attainment. Periodically, we review the hourly rates in the firm and make adjustments based on those factors. Our present rates for matters of this nature are $225 per hour for attorneys and $60 per hour for legal interns and clerks. We will notify you in advance of any rate changes. [Since the nature of what will be required is not defined, it is impossible to estimate what the fees will be in this matter.][We estimate the fees will run approximately $_____ based upon _____.]

Billing Procedures. We keep detailed records of the time we spend on a project and bill the work monthly to keep the client informed of our activities. Each statement is carefully reviewed to determine whether a charge is justified before it is sent. Unless otherwise requested, the monthly statements will contain a brief summary of the nature of the work and the costs advanced. In addition to the fees, you will be billed monthly for all costs and expenses advanced on your behalf, including filing fees, court costs, photocopies, facsimile charges, long distance, travel, and other out-of-pocket expenses. A schedule of our current charges is available on request. Any large or extraordinary expenses will be billed to you directly by the provider and are due on receipt. Our policy of billing monthly provides the client with a current summary of what was done on a particular matter. We encourage clients to ask questions and discuss our services and fees when the statement is received.

Terms of Payment. Payment of the monthly statement is due upon receipt. If a statement is not paid by the first day of the following month, we reserve the right to charge interest on all overdue amounts at one and one-half percent (1-1/2%) per month on the past due balances. We have the right to terminate our representation if payments are not made promptly.

Retainer. It is our firm's policy to require a retainer from all clients until a satisfactory payment history is established. The amount of the retainer is based upon the nature of the representation. We are requesting from you a retainer of $[_____]. The retainer will be put in the firm's client trust account and will be applied to the bill at the end of our representation in this matter. If a monthly statement remains unpaid at the end of the month it is rendered, the retainer will be applied against that statement and our representation will be terminated. Any funds remaining from the retainer after all fees and expenses have been paid will be returned to you.

Our firm would like to serve as your legal counsel. With this position comes the responsibility to advise and counsel you on matters we are competent to handle and, if requested, to assist you in obtaining suitable representation from outside lawyers in areas we cannot handle for you. We view ourselves as an asset to our clients by providing timely, accurate legal services that are affordable to both the client and the firm. We are pleased that you have selected our firm to represent you. We look forward to serving you and will use our best efforts on your behalf.

If this proposal is acceptable to you, please sign the enclosed copy of this letter and return it to me together with a check for the $[_____] retainer at your earliest convenience. Upon receipt of a signed copy and the retainer, we will proceed promptly to undertake the matter outlined above. If you wish to discuss the proposal or have any questions, please do not hesitate to call.

Very truly yours,

Mark A. Robertson
For the Firm

Agreed to and accepted personally and on behalf of [Organization] this ____ day of _____, 200__.

[First Name] [Last Name]
MAR:djt

Exhibit 2

Letter Giving Alternative Fee Options to Client

The fee letter in Exhibit 2 uses model letter found in Exhibit 1 and provides the client with three fee options. The letter covers a proposed engagement to assist in preparing a private placement memorandum for the client to sell interests in a limited liability company. After an analysis of similar work, the law firm was able to present clients with different alternatives on how they wanted the fees to be charged—a fixed fee with a contingent success payment, a reduced hourly rate with a premium payment at closing, and a regular hourly rate arrangement based upon the time it takes to handle the matter. It has been the author's experience that in most instances, clients prefer a fixed fee that can be budgeted—even in matters as complex as securities offerings. Over the last 10 years, more than 90 percent of our private placement fees have been on a fixed fee with contingent payment, with an average realization rate of nearly 150 percent of our standard hourly rate.

ROBERTSON & WILLIAMS
Attorneys and Counselors At Law

3033 N.W. 63rd Street, Suite 200
Oklahoma City, Oklahoma 73116-3607
(405) 848-1944 · Fax (405) 843-6707

Mark A. Robertson
E-mail: marobert@robertsonwilliams.com

[Date]

[Name Prefix] [First Name] [Last Name] [Name Suffix] [Title]
[Organization]
[Address 1]
[Address 2]
[City], [State/Province] [Postal Code]

Re: Legal Representation and Fee Agreement

Dear [Salutation]:

It is a pleasure having the opportunity to represent [organization] as corporate/securities counsel for the proposed private placement for the _____ project. We are pleased to undertake this representation. The remainder of this letter will outline the scope of the current private placement project and representation and the legal fee proposal for your consideration.

Scope of Representation.

The scope of the work required for a private placement by your Company (using a Regulation D offering) is to prepare the Private Placement Memorandum (together with the exhibits) for use in selling the member interests in the limited liability company. We will also need to file exemption notices or requests with appropriate state regulatory authorities.

In addition to the foregoing, Robertson & Williams will assist in preparing any state and federal reports, forms and other filings for selling. We will also assist in preparing the appropriate escrow agreement and other documentation for use in the offering at whatever bank in [_____] you select to act as escrow agent.

Fee Proposal

I think that it is both appropriate and helpful to a client for me to outline in writing this firm's legal fee structure and, when possible, estimate the legal fees or give a fixed quote for the required representation. I believe it to be good business practice to discuss the subject of fees with a client at the beginning of our representation.

The fees charged for legal services traditionally are based upon a combination of the following factors: (a) the complexity of the matter and the degree of expertise required to handle the project; (b) the amount of time involved; and (c) sometimes the results obtained on the client's behalf. The nature of the project will often determine how the fees are charged. The fee arrangement should be established at the beginning of the representation and should be clearly outlined in writing or thoroughly discussed with the client so there are no misunderstandings. I prefer to use a fee letter that both the client and the law firm agree to.

The present scope of the legal work required is outlined under <u>Scope of Representation</u> above. I am confident that Robertson & Williams can handle the work required in a timely manner and for a fee that is fair to the Company. The fees for securities work done by most qualified law firms are charged at a premium over standard rates due to the specialized skills and high risks involved. I have found most clients in today's economy have requested a fixed fee quote for securities work as an alternative to an hourly rate, since it is easier to budget. I would like to suggest the following **alternative** fee arrangements, which incorporate these requests and have worked for several clients in the last few years:

☐ **Fixed Fee with Contingent Payment**

  * Payment of a fixed non-refundable fee of $9,000 payable as follows: $4,500 upon the acceptance of this fee arrangement and $4,500 upon the Private Placement Memorandum being completed and delivered to you. This would

be for the securities, tax, blue sky in [_____] and [_____], and the other work outlined above for the offering under <u>Scope of Representation</u>.

* If the offering is successful and sufficient subscriptions are received to do an initial closing, an additional fee of $9,000 would be due at that closing.

* Any additional state filing work (outside of [_____] and [_____]) would be on an hourly rate basis at a reduced rate of $180 per hour (regular rate is $225 per hour) plus any filing fees, costs, etc. We will need to identify those states you wish to sell in before we can estimate the fees and expenses.

☐ **Reduced Hourly Rate with Premium Payment on Closing**

* We would do the securities, tax, blue sky, and other work outlined above for the offering under <u>Scope of Representation</u> at a reduced hourly rate of $180 per hour (our regular rate is $225 per hour). Instead of requiring a retainer, billing will be done every other Friday, delivered electronically, and paid by the following Tuesday.

* If the offering is successful and sufficient subscriptions are received to do an initial closing, we would charge **an additional** $90 per hour for the work already performed. All work following the closing would be charged at regular hourly rates at the time (currently $225 per hour).

☐ **Regular Hourly Rate**

* We would do the securities, tax, blue sky, and other work outlined above for the offering under <u>Scope of Representation</u> at our regular hourly rate of $225 per hour. Instead of requiring a retainer, billing will be done every other Friday, delivered electronically, and paid by the following Tuesday.

Other Required Payments and Fees

* All major expense items such as filing and registration fees, travel, and printing expenses will be paid directly by the Company. Expenses advanced by the firm such as long distance, copies, fax, etc., using our published rates will be billed monthly and are due on receipt.

I believe the fee quote is quite reasonable for a private placement; our normal hourly estimate for a private placement of a partnership or limited liability offering runs $15,000 to $22,000 (due to the tax issues that need to be addressed) and can run over $24,000 if problems arise or there are a large number of states in which the offering is being sold.

Billing Procedures. We keep detailed records of the expenses we incur and, where appropriate, the time we spend on a project, and bill the work regularly to keep the client informed of our activities on his behalf. Each statement is carefully reviewed to determine whether a charge is justified before it is sent. Unless otherwise requested, the statements will contain a brief summary of the nature of the work and the costs advanced. In addition to the fees, you will be billed for all costs and expenses advanced on your behalf including filing fees, court costs, photocopies, facsimile charges, long distance, travel, and other out-of-pocket expenses. A schedule of our current charges is available on request. Any large or extraordinary expenses will be billed to you directly by the provider and are due on receipt. Our policy of provides the client with a current summary of what was done on a particular matter. We encourage clients to ask questions and discuss our services and fees when the statement is received.

<u>Summary</u>

After you have had an opportunity to review this, please give me a call and we can discuss which option you prefer.

                                          Very truly yours,

                                          Mark A. Robertson
                                          For the Firm

MAR:djl

Exhibit 3

Formal Fee Agreement
(Hourly or Contingent)

The following Exhibit 3 is a formal fee agreement that has optional provisions that can be used to cover both an hourly billing arrangement and a contingency fee arrangement. The form also includes a guaranty of payment.

LEGAL REPRESENTATION AGREEMENT

Effective Date: , 20   [City], [State]

This Agreement is made between [Name of Client(s)] ["Client(s)"], [Address of Client(s)]; and [Law Firm], [Address], [City], [State] 73116 ["the Law Firm"].

STATEMENT AND SUBJECT OF EMPLOYMENT

Client(s) retain(s) the Law Firm to represent Client(s) as counsel for Client(s) in a matter involving [name(s) of defendant(s)] and potentially other parties, based upon investigation, regarding [describe general nature of case] ("the Matter"). ("The Responsible Attorney") will be the attorney in the Law Firm who will have primary responsibility for handling the Matter, although other attorneys in the Law Firm may participate in the Matter. The Matter may actually compose more than one file [e.g., if separate claims are made on behalf of Client(s) against Defendant or other persons or entities whether or not the other persons or entities are parties to this case; or if separate claims are made by Plaintiff against Client(s)]. Regardless of the number of files the Law Firm opens for the Matter, all files related to the same subject matter are considered one transaction and constitute one Matter.

Client(s) authorize(s) the Law Firm to investigate the facts and research the law pertaining to the Matter, including potential claims and/or defenses, to determine the factual, legal, and economic viability of the Matter. Client(s) further authorize(s) the Law Firm to effect a resolution of the Matter and to settle or institute such legal action, including preparing documents, filing a claim against Plaintiff or another person or entity not a party to the suit, answering the petition or counterclaim, conducting discovery, and presenting the Matter for trial, as may be advisable in the Responsible Attorney's judgment.

Client(s) authorize(s) Law Firm to employ personnel inside and outside the Law Firm to perform necessary services to facilitate Client('s s') Matter. Representation of Client(s) by the Law Firm in the Matter will not commence until Client(s) and the Responsible Attorney have signed this agreement and any retainer payable at the outset of this representation is in fact paid by Client(s).

Representation of Client(s) by the Law Firm in an appeal related to the Matter is not included in this agreement. The Law Firm's representation of Client(s) in any appeal related to the Matter, if agreed upon between the Law Firm and Client(s), must be included by a written addendum or in a separate written fee agreement signed by Client(s) and the Responsible Attorney. Although the Law Firm may agree to represent Client(s) in an appeal related to the Matter, the Law Firm is not obligated to represent Client(s) in any appeal related to the Matter, and representation on appeal will not commence until Client(s) and the Responsible Attorney have signed a written addendum to this agreement or a separate written agreement dealing with representation on appeal, and any retainer, if applicable to representation on appeal, is in fact paid by Client(s).

ATTORNEY FEES

[CONTINGENCY FEE]

Client(s) agree(s) to pay the Law Firm a fee contingent upon the outcome and based upon the recovery received from any party in any file obtained in the Matter. When the term "recovery" is used in this agreement, the term includes any recovery from one or more parties. Thus, if the Matter involves multiple parties and a separate recovery is obtained from more than one party, recovery includes each separate recovery. The recovery is deemed to include all cash, property (tangible and intangible), and any and all other items of value of every type and description which Client(s) receive(s) in this Matter, including but not limited to executory rights. The present value of all items, other than cash, which are included in the recovery, or any partial recovery from any party paying any claim related to the Matter, will be determined for the purpose of calculating the total recovery for use in determining the amount on which the Law Firm's fee is calculated. Unless Client(s) and the Law Firm agree on the amount of all items included in the recovery, other than cash, Client(s) and the Law Firm will share equally in the expense of retaining a duly qualified certified public accountant or other appropriate expert(s) to determine the present value of the items, other than cash, which are included in the recovery. Client(s) shall pay the Law Firm as attorney fees for representation in the Matter according to the following schedule:

1. $33\frac{1}{3}\%$ of the value of all items included in the recovery if the Matter is resolved and settled prior to the beginning of the pretrial conference.

2. 40% of the value of all items included in the recovery if the Matter is resolved and settled after the beginning of the pretrial conference, but before any notice of appeal is filed.

3. 50% of the value of all items included in the recovery if the Matter is resolved after either party files a notice of appeal, petition in error, or other instrument that initiates an appeal, whether the case is presented in a jury or bench trial.

Client(s) authorize(s) the Law Firm to advance the costs and expenses of the Matter, including the costs and expenses of litigation, if applicable, which Client(s) agree(s) to reimburse. All expenses advanced by the Law Firm that have not been previously paid by the Client(s) will be subtracted from Client('s s') portion of any recovery after the Law Firm's fee portion of the recovery is deducted from the amount recovered. If the fees due the Law Firm equal 50% of the recovery, then the costs and expenses will be paid from the Law Firm's portion of the recovery.

In the event of a structured settlement resulting in periodic future payments, all costs and expenses advanced by the Law Firm shall be paid in full before any recovery is paid to Client(s) [or any beneficiary of the Estate] or attorney fees are paid to the Law Firm. After all costs and expenses of the Matter advanced by the Law Firm are paid, each payment on the structured settlement will be divided pro rata between Client(s) and the Law Firm according to the appropriate percentage set out above. In the event no recovery is made, Client(s) will owe no attorney fees. However, Client(s) will be responsible for all costs and expenses incurred in the Matter, regardless of the outcome, even if there is no recovery.

[HOURLY FEE]
Client(s) shall pay the Law Firm as attorney fees for representation in the Matter according to the following schedule:

Billing Rates

Billing rates for the Matter are as follows:

- Responsible Attorney $ 000.00 per hour.

- [Senior / Associate] Attorney $ 000.00 per hour.

- [Senior / Associate] Attorney $ 000.00 per hour.

- [Senior / Associate] Attorney $ 000.00 per hour.

- Law Clerk / Legal Assistant $ 000.00 per hour.

A minimum of 0.20 hour will be charged for activities performed by the Law Firm and other office personnel assisting with the case, including telephone calls. Client(s) authorize(s) the Law Firm to advance the costs and expenses of the Matter, including the costs and expenses of litigation, if applicable, which Client(s) agree(s) to reimburse.

["RETAINER": OPTIONAL FOR CONTINGENCY OR HOURLY MATTERS]

Retainer

CHOOSE AN OPTION:

1. Client(s) will pay a retainer of $, which will be deposited in the Law Firm's trust account to be billed against at the hourly rates provided in this agreement. The retainer is payable upon Client('s s') acceptance and return of this agreement to the Law Firm. The Law Firm will bill Client(s) monthly for time, costs, and expenses charged to the Matter. Client(s) shall replenish the retainer each month so that the amount of the original retainer is constantly maintained in the trust account, until the Matter is concluded or until this agreement is terminated. Failure of Client(s) to pay any retainer or replenish any retainer when due will justify the Law Firm's withdrawal from representing Client(s) in the Matter.

2. Client(s) will pay a retainer of $, which will be deposited in the Law Firm's trust account to be billed against at the hourly rates provided in this agreement. The retainer is payable upon Client('s s') acceptance and return of this agreement to the Law Firm. The Law Firm will bill Client(s) monthly for time, costs, and expenses charged to the Matter. If the retainer is fully expended, the Matter is not concluded, and this agreement is not terminated, Client(s) shall replenish the retainer in the amount of the original retainer, and the Law Firm will bill against the replenished retainer as with the original retainer. Failure of Client(s) to pay any retainer or replenish any retainer when due will justify the Law Firm's withdrawal from representing Client(s) in the Matter.

3. In the event Client('s s') account becomes past due more than thirty (30) days (i.e., any statement is not paid within thirty (30) days of the statement date), Client(s) will pay a retainer of $, which will be deposited in the Law Firm's trust account to be billed against at the hourly rates provided in this agreement. The Law Firm will bill Client(s) monthly for time, costs, and expenses charged to the Matter. Client(s) shall replenish the retainer each month so that the amount of the original retainer is constantly maintained in the trust account, until the Matter is concluded or until this agreement is terminated. Client(s) shall continue replenishing the retainer as provided until the Matter is concluded or until this agreement is terminated. Failure of Client(s) to pay any retainer or replenish any retainer when due will justify the Law Firm's withdrawal from representing Client(s) in the Matter.

Billing Statements
[CHOOSE AN OPTION: [1.] FOR CONTINGENCY CASES; [2.] FOR HOURLY FEE CASES.]

[1.] The Law Firm will provide Client(s) a detailed monthly statement for costs and expenses incurred during the month. Each statement will contain an accounting of the charges made to Client('s s') account. All billing statements are due in full upon receipt by Client(s). Client(s) agree(s) to pay, or authorize(s) the Law Firm to pay from the retainer (if applicable), each statement in full upon receipt. Failure to pay any balance when due will justify the Law Firm's withdrawal from representing Client(s) in the Matter.

Each monthly billing cycle begins on the first business day of the month. Any statement not paid in full by the beginning of the next billing cycle is considered past due. For example, a billing statement sent in January for the charges related to the previous December is due upon receipt in January. The January statement would be past due on the first business day in February, which is when the next billing cycle begins.

[2.] The Law Firm will provide Client(s) a detailed monthly statement for attorney fees, costs, and expenses incurred during the month. Each statement will contain an accounting of the charges made to Client('s s') account. All billing statements are due in full upon receipt by Client(s). Client(s) agree(s) to pay, or authorize(s) the Law Firm to pay from the retainer (if applicable), each statement in full upon receipt. Failure to pay any balance when due will justify the Law Firm's withdrawal from representing Client(s) in the Matter.

Each monthly billing cycle begins on the first business day of the month. Any statement not paid in full by the beginning of the next billing cycle is considered past due. For example, a billing statement sent in January for the charges related to the previous December is due upon receipt in January. The January statement would be past due on the first business day in February, which is when the next billing cycle begins.

Interest Charges to Aged Accounts
Any outstanding balances not paid when due as provided in this agreement will accrue an interest charge of eighteen percent [18.0 %] per annum (i.e., one and one-half percent [1.5%] per month) from the due date until paid. Interest charges will apply to the full unpaid balance as shown on the billing statement. Interest charges will continue to accrue until the full balance, including interest, is paid in full. In the event an account becomes past due, payments on the account will be credited first to accrued interest, then to past due balances, then to the current balance due.

ATTORNEY FEE AND COST CASES

Client('s s') Matter may involve a case in which the Court may make an award of attorney fees and/or court costs, if allowed by law. Client(s) agree(s) and acknowledge(s) that Client(s) is/are solely responsible for payment of the Law Firm's, costs, and expenses, even if the Matter is one in which attorney fees and court costs are allowed under law, and even if the Court in fact makes an award to Client(s) for attorney fees and court costs against any opposing party. Client(s) agree(s) and acknowledge(s) that the Matter in which the Law Firm is representing Client(s) does not include or involve any action to collect or recover from any opposing party any award for attorney fees and/or costs if allowed by the Court. OPTION IN CONTINGENCY CASES: [In the event the law allows recovery of attorney fees for the Matter, the attorney fees collected by the Law Firm shall be considered additional attorney fees and will be included in the total amount recovered as part of fees due the Law Firm described above.]

LEGAL RISKS

Client(s) further acknowledge(s) that the Matter is the type of case which may provide for the recovery of attorney fees and/or costs by the prevailing party. Client(s) acknowledge(s) that the Responsible Attorney has fully informed Client(s) of the legal risk(s) associated with pursuing this matter in connection with the possible award of attorney fees and/or costs to the opposing party in the Matter in the event the opposing party should prevail. Client(s) also acknowledge(s) that the Responsible Attorney has advised Client(s) of all potential risks related to the Matter. Client(s) acknowledge(s) to the Law Firm that Client(s) is/are fully informed and is/are willing to accept the legal risks related to the Matter.

COSTS AND EXPENSES

Although the Law Firm may advance costs and expenses of the Matter, Client(s) is/are responsible for all costs and expenses arising out of the investigation, preparation, discovery, and litigation of the Matter, as applicable. The costs of the Matter include, but are not limited to: filing fees, costs of service of process, witness fees (including experts), and deposition costs. The expenses of the Matter include, but are not limited to: postage, photocopy expense, travel, facsimile charges, computer assisted legal research, and long distance telephone calls. Photocopies will be charged at $0.25 per page, and telecopier transmissions/receptions will be charged at $0.25 per page. Fees generated by outside parties will be billed to Client(s) at the same cost the Law Firm is billed.

LEGAL INSURANCE

In the event Client(s) has/have any insurance policy that may cover attorney fees, costs, or expenses incurred by Client(s) related to the Matter, this paragraph applies. Payment on Client(s) account is to be made in full by Client(s) on receipt of the statement for the current month. It is Client('s s') responsibility to obtain reimbursement by an insurance company, if applicable. The Law Firm will provide any information, subject to reasonable charges for photocopies, etc., needed to assist Client(s) in filing any claim with an insurance company to recover fees, costs and/or expenses related to the Matter. Client(s) agree(s) to pay all fees, costs, and expenses which are not covered by the Client's insurance policy. Client(s) agree(s) that the Law Firm has not verified that the services provided in this agreement are covered by Client('s s') insurance policy. Further, Client(s) agree(s) that the Law Firm is not responsible for ensuring that the services rendered under this agreement are covered by Client('s s') insurance policy. It shall be Client('s s') sole responsibility to ensure compliance with all terms and conditions of Client('s s') insurance policy.

ATTORNEY'S LIEN

To the extent allowed and permissible by law and as applicable to this particular Matter, Client(s) agree(s) that the Law Firm has a lien on the claim or cause of action related to the Matter in which Client has an interest, on any sum recovered through settlement or through judgment related to the Matter. The lien is in the amount of the sum and share described in this agreement as attorney fees and shall total the full amount due the Law Firm under this agreement, including the costs and expenses of litigation advanced by the Law Firm. The Law Firm shall have general, possessory, or retaining liens, and all special or charging liens known to common law.

TERMINATION OF AGREEMENT

This agreement will terminate upon completion of the Matter described in this agreement. This agreement will also terminate upon withdrawal of the Law Firm, with or without cause, as counsel to Client(s) in this Matter, on reasonable notice to Client(s). In the event of withdrawal, the Law Firm shall retain an attorney's lien for the fee due the Law Firm based upon [**CHOOSE 1. OR 2.: 1. CONTINGENCY CASES:** the quantum merit value of services rendered by the Law Firm in the Matter, in connection with the contingency fee schedule stated above, **2. HOURLY CASES:** the number of hours worked by all attorneys in the Law Firm], and for all costs and expenses the Law Firm has advanced on the Matter. Any balance remaining in the Law Firm's trust account in connection with the Matter will be refunded to Client(s) after an audit of Client('s s') account and payment of any outstanding balance due on the account.

CONFLICT OF INTEREST

After considering the Responsible Attorney's consultation, Client(s) has/have concluded that no conflict of interest exists or appears imminent which would materially prejudice Client(s) in this Matter, and Client(s) consent(s) to the Law Firm's representation in the Matter. In the event a conflict of interest arises during the course of this representation which cannot be resolved, the Law Firm will withdraw from representation of Client(s) [and/or the Estate] and Client(s) [on behalf of the Estate] shall be liable for all attorney fees, costs, and expenses due in this Matter.

SETTLEMENT OF CASE

Client(s) will not make any settlement agreement in this case without the Responsible Attorney's knowledge and consent.

FAVORABLE OUTCOME NOT WARRANTED

The Law Firm makes no warranties to Client(s) concerning the possible successful outcome of the Matter.

This agreement is signed and effective on the date first written above and at the address for the Law Firm stated above. Client(s) acknowledge(s) receipt of a signed copy of this agreement.

"CLIENT"   [NAME OF CLIENT, IF A COMPANY]

By: [Name of officer or responsible person], [Title]

"LAW FIRM"   [Law Firm]

By:
                    [Lawyer]

GUARANTY OF PAYMENT OF ATTORNEY FEES, COSTS, AND EXPENSES

[name of guarantor(s)], [address of guarantor(s)] ("Guarantor(s)"), as the [relationship of guarantor to Client, e.g., parent(s)], of Client(s), agree(s) to pay all attorney fees, costs, and expenses on behalf of Client(s) under this agreement. Guarantor(s) agree(s) to be bound by all of the terms of this agreement in connection with payment of all attorney fees, costs, and expenses incurred in the Matter for which Client(s) is/are responsible.

Guarantor(s) specifically acknowledge(s) and agree(s) that the duty of the Law Firm and Responsible Attorney is solely to Client(s) and not to Guarantor(s), and that the attorney-client relationship is solely between the Law Firm/Responsible Attorney and Client(s), and that no attorney-client relationship exists between the Law Firm/Responsible Attorney and Guarantor(s). Guarantor(s) acknowledge(s) and agree(s) that all decisions made by the Law Firm/Responsible Attorney in connection with the Matter are to be made in connection with Client(s) consent and best interests, without any consideration to Guarantor('s s') preferences.

Guarantor(s) further specifically acknowledge(s) and agree(s) that all client confidences are to be maintained between the Law Firm/Responsible Attorney and will not be disclosed to Guarantor(s) without specific consent of Client(s). Guarantor(s) will not inquire into Client('s s') Matter without specific consent of the Client(s), and Guarantor(s) will not attempt to influence the Law Firm's/Responsible Attorney's decisions concerning representation of Client(s), but that

Client(s) shall make all decisions related to the Law Firm's/Responsible Attorney's representation of Client(s) in the Matter.

"GUARANTOR(S)"

[Name of Guarantor]   [Name of Guarantor]

I/We have read this section entitled "Guaranty of Payment of Attorney Fees, Costs, and Expenses", and I/we consent to the agreement of Guarantor(s) to pay on my/our behalf the attorney fees, costs, and expenses incurred in the Matter for which I/we am/are responsible.

"CLIENT"

[Name of Client]

"LAW FIRM"   [Law Firm]

By:
                              [Lawyer]

Exhibit 4

Increased Hourly Rate for Negotiations; Contingent Fee if Litigation Is Required

The Holland & Hart fee agreement in Exhibit 4 reflects innovative - win-win billing practices. The client, a half owner of a small corporation, had been locked out for years by the other half owner, who controlled the board of directors. When the client came to Holland & Hart, he was cash poor and had been for several years. The corporation had not declared any dividends, and he was not being paid as an employee of the company. Needless to say, the other half owner was living rather well.

The other owner had tried to buy out the client, offering $800,000 to be paid over a long period of time. On the surface, it appeared as if the client's share of the company was worth more than that. The client had tried to get a number of lawyers to represent him on some sort of contingent fee basis. All of them wanted the standard one-third to one-half of any recovery, whether by settlement or litigation. The client felt that he might as well take the $800,000 offered to him, because he would lose so much on attorneys' fees.

Holland & Hart, taking a different approach, offered to charge two and one-half times its regular hourly rates for negotiation services and, if a suitable negotiated settlement could not be achieved, to proceed to litigation when so directed by the client on a standard one-third contingency.

The firm was paid $55,000, two and one-half times its normal hourly rates. The firm was happy; the client was happy to have avoided paying more than $500,000 in attorneys' fees and was overjoyed to receive $1,545,000—almost twice the amount originally offered.

Factors influencing the use of this approach include prior successful litigation by this firm against the other half-owner of the corporation, a preliminary evaluation that the value of the stock was greater than the initial amount offered for the stock, and the reputation of the firm for being vigorous litigators.

CONTRACT OF EMPLOYMENT
(Modified Contingency Fee Agreement)

This Contract of Employment is made on December _____, 2002, between Holland & Hart, attorneys at law, whose address is Post Office Box 8749, Denver, Colorado 80201 ("counsel") and_____, whose address is _____ ("client").

RECITALS

A. Client has requested counsel to provide legal services with respect to _____.

B. To avoid any misunderstanding, client and counsel wish to formalize their agreement regarding employment by this written contract.

C. _____ of Holland & Hart informed _____ of the hourly rates charged by attorneys at Holland & Hart and its policy for charging fees based upon time and other considerations. Instead of that regular fee arrangement, client has requested counsel to provide representation based upon a modified contingency fee arrangement, as further set forth in this agreement.

THEREFORE, client and counsel agree as follows:

1. **Attorneys Fees:** Client agrees to pay counsel a fee contingent upon the outcome of the matter in accordance with the following:

    a. Prior to the filing of litigation, client agrees to pay counsel a fee equal to two and one-half times the regular hourly rate charged by counsel for work done on behalf of its clients. Client has been advised that the regular hourly rates charged by Holland & Hart vary depending upon the level of seniority of the attorneys involved and other factors including the complexity of the work and extraordinary time demands. The regular hourly rate for _____ is presently $_____. Rates for attorneys with a lower level of seniority are typically lower than this amount and rates for attorneys with higher seniority are typically higher. Regular hourly rates are subject to change from time-to-time in accordance with firm practice.

    b. If counsel is directed to bring suit, client agrees to pay counsel a fee equal to $33^{1}/_{3}\%$ of all sums recovered by the client as a result of that litigation.

    c. Counsel agrees to provide client with regular fee statements and to notify client each time fees reach increments of $5,000, i.e., $5,000, $10,000, etc.

2. **Expenses:** Client acknowledges counsel will incur various expenses in providing services to client. It is understood that client will be responsible for all expenses incurred in this matter regardless of any recovery and will remit those expenses promptly to counsel upon receipt of an invoice. Some examples of these expenses are charges for court filings, depositions, expert witness fees, investigation costs, reports, photocopying, telephone charges, and the costs of hiring accountants to review books and records of _____. If expenses are not remitted promptly upon request, client agrees to pay interest at the annual rate of 18% on all amounts owing more than 30 days.

    Counsel estimates that the expenses involved in this matter may range from approximately $_____ to $_____ but notes that it is unable to make such a prediction with any accuracy because the amount of expenses incurred will necessarily depend upon factors beyond counsel's control, including decisions made by the client, and the efforts of opposing counsel. Client's express approval will be secured for any single expense in excess of $1,000. Furthermore, client's written approval will be secured if and when the expenses exceed $5,000.

3. **Termination of Contract:** Client may terminate this contract by notifying counsel in writing. If permission for withdrawal from employment is required by the rules of any court, counsel shall withdraw upon permission of the court. Counsel may withdraw as counsel for client and terminate this contract for any just reason by notifying client in writing. Some examples of reasons for termination include, but are not limited to, client's failure to cooperate with counsel or any request by client which would require counsel to violate the Code of Professional Responsibility approved by the Supreme Court of Colorado.

If counsel withdraws as client's counsel and terminates this contract, it will take reasonable precautions to avoid any prejudice to the rights of client by allowing a reasonable time for employment of other counsel, delivering to client all papers and property to which client is entitled, and complying with all applicable laws and rules.

If representation is terminated by client or by counsel for any reason, counsel shall be entitled to be compensated at its usual rates in effect as of the date this agreement is signed, but only in the event the client is ultimately successful on the claim or in client's negotiations and receives any amounts from _____ or any other defendant.

4. **Miscellaneous:**

This contract contains the entire agreement of client and counsel regarding counsel's employment. This contract shall not be modified or revoked except by written agreement between client and counsel.

This contract shall be binding upon the client and counsel and their heirs, executors, legal representatives, successors and assigns.

This contract shall be construed and governed by the laws of the State of Colorado.

In the event of litigation or arbitration concerning this contract, reasonable fees and costs shall be awarded to the prevailing party.

Client acknowledges having read this contract in its entirety and declares it to be fair and reasonable.

CLIENT   COUNSEL
                                                HOLLAND & HART
                                                Post Office Box 8749
                                                Denver, CO 80201
                                                303-295-8000

_____   By: _____

Date: _____   Date: _____

Exhibit 5

Alternative Billing Proposal for Either Hourly Rates or Reduced Hourly Rates with a Contingency Fee if the Business Is Acquired

The following form has been used by a Houston law firm when clients desired to acquire a business. The law firm agreed to work on either a normal hourly basis or, if the acquisition is abandoned or not consummated before a prescribed date, accept a defined percent of the normal fees. If the percent fee is paid promptly, the balance of accrued time is forgiven.

If the acquisition is consummated, a fee at the normal hourly rate will be paid, with all or a portion of the fee evidenced by an interest-bearing note in quarterly installments. As an inducement to use the firm's services after closing, the firm will forgive up to one-half of the principal amount of the note in an amount equal to 50 percent of the fees collected from legal services rendered by the firm to the acquiring corporation within one year after the time of the closing.

For example, assume the principal amount of the note is $100,000, and within one year after the closing, the acquiring corporation pays the firm $50,000 in legal fees before making any principal payments. In that case, the principal amount of the note will be reduced to $75,000 ($50,000 X 50% with a cap of 50 percent of the then unpaid principal amount of the note = $25,000).

This arrangement has worked well where prospective entrepreneurs are attempting an acquisition that seems sound, the lawyers are willing to share risks and are willing to make concessions initially with the hope that the acquisition will be consummated, and the acquiring corporation will continue to use the legal services of the firm after closing.

It demonstrates that the choice of a billing method, some risk sharing, and some recognition of the economic needs of the clients can be tools for developing new clients—the gamble being that the acquisition will be consummated, that the business acquired will be successful, and that the company will continue to use the services of the firm.

FEE AGREEMENT

Personal & Confidential

ABC Client
Success Tower
Houston, Texas
Gentlemen:

The purpose of this letter is to summarize our understanding with respect to the engagement of [_____] (the "Firm") in connection with the acquisition (the "Acquisition") by you and the individuals who have executed the last page of this agreement (collectively, the "Acquirers") of Target Corporation (the "Company"). The engagement will involve (i) conferences with, among others, the Acquirers, the Company's officers, directors, investment bankers and independent certified accountants; (ii) the review and/or preparation of documents to evidence the Acquisition of the Company; and (iii) such other services that are necessary.

Our agreement with respect to the engagement is as follows:

(a) The hourly rates we charge for legal services range from $200 to $300 per hour for all time expended by principals of the Firm, $90 to $175 per hour for associates and $50 to $70 per hour for legal assistants. I will be responsible on a day-to-day basis for the supervision of the representation in connection with matters such as the Acquisition. Other attorneys who probably will render legal services in connection with this matter are [_____] and [_____], whose hourly billing rates are $225 and $175, respectively. The determination of whether a principal, an associate or a legal assistant renders services to you depends upon the nature of the work and the qualifications of the person needed to perform that particular aspect of the engagement. Attached hereto as Exhibit "A" is a list of the hourly billing rates you will be charged for the Firm's attorneys and legal assistants.

(b) We estimate that legal fees in connection with this representation will range from approximately $100,000 to $125,000. While we will endeavor to keep the fees to a minimum, please recognize that this estimate is merely a rough approximation based upon our prior experience, and the ultimate fees may vary depending upon the actual facts and the services rendered in connection with the engagement. Should it appear that the legal fees will be in excess of the estimate, you will be notified as soon as practicable.

(c) Prior to calling on the Firm to render services, you and the Acquirers will unanimously agree as to the manner by which we will be paid for such services. The two alternatives we are willing to accept are described in Exhibit "B." On the last page of this agreement, either Alternative A or Alternative B has been marked by you and the Acquirers, and the parties agree to be jointly and severally bound by the terms of this agreement and that Alternative.

On a monthly basis, the Firm will furnish you and the Acquirers detailed invoices of the services rendered and the amount of fees and reimbursable disbursements (including, but not limited to, filing fees, parking fees, overtime charges for secretarial services, copying costs, and long-distance telephone charges) incurred on your behalf. Overtime charges for secretarial services will only be charged if the hiring of one or more secretaries is necessary in order to meet deadlines. The invoices will explain in detail the nature and date of the services rendered and reimbursable expenses. If you or any of the Acquirers do not agree with the charges set forth on the invoices, I will be notified within two weeks of receipt of the invoices. If I am not notified that there is a question or that someone disagrees with the charges, it will be irrebuttably presumed that the charges are fair and reasonable.

(d) If the Firm's invoices are not paid when due, you and the Acquirers will also be billed the standard hourly rates for all time expended by the Firm's attorneys in the Firm's collection efforts and $25 per hour for all administrative time expended in collection efforts. Furthermore, you and the Acquirers will also be responsible for all expenses incurred in connection with the collection of amounts due to the Firm, including fees of attorneys who are not employees of the Firm, should such collection efforts become necessary.

(e) This agreement shall be construed in accordance with the laws of the State of Texas and all obligations of the parties are performable in Harris County, Texas. This agreement shall be binding upon and inure to the benefit of the parties and their respective heirs, executors, administrators, legal representatives, successors and assigns.

(f) In case any one or more of the provisions contained shall be held to be invalid, illegal or unenforceable in any respect, such invalidity, illegality or unenforceability shall not affect any other provision, and this agreement shall be construed as if such invalid, illegal or unenforceable provision did not exist.

(g) Once executed, this agreement constitutes the only agreement of the parties with respect to matters involving the engagement of the Firm, the payment of fees in connection therewith, and supersedes any prior understandings or written or oral agreements between the parties respecting such subject matter.

(h) This agreement may be executed in multiple counterparts, each of which shall be deemed an original, but all of which shall constitute one and the same instrument.

Gentlemen, I apologize for the formal tone of this agreement, but it is important that we fully understand what is expected of one another. Therefore, if this letter accurately sets forth the agreement as to the basis upon which the Firm has been engaged, please have this agreement signed and return the signed copy to me. The second copy is for your records.

We are looking forward to working with you on this matter and anticipate a long and mutually beneficial relationship.

Very truly yours,

[_____]

[_____]

AGREED AND ACCEPTED this day of _____, 200__.
ABC Client
   By:
      (Name Printed)   (Title)

Also, the undersigned jointly and severally agree to (i) be bound by the terms of this agreement; (ii) the Alternative marked below; and (iii) pay any amounts due to the Firm hereunder pursuant to the terms of this agreement.
[ ] Alternative A
[ ] Alternative B
(Name Printed)   (Name Printed)

EXHIBIT "A"

Hourly Billing Rates from October 1, 2001, through September 30, 2002

Hourly
<u>Billing Rate</u>

Principals
Associates
Legal Assistants

EXHIBIT "B"

Alternative A

The Firm's invoices are due upon presentment. The invoice for services in a particular month is usually mailed between the 10th and 15th day of the following month (the "Month of Receipt"). Any invoice that is not paid by the first day of the month following the Month of Receipt will bear interest at the rate of eighteen percent (18%) per annum commencing on the first day of the month following the Month of Receipt. For example, an invoice for fees and out-of-pocket expenditures for March 2002 will be mailed between April 10 and April 15. If such invoice is not paid in full by May 1, 2002, interest will accrue on the unpaid amount commencing May ___, 200__.

Alternative B

In the event the Acquisition is abandoned or not consummated on or before August 31, 2002 (the earlier to occur of either abandonment or August 31, 2002 being the "Termination Date"), the Acquirers will pay the Firm within 14 days of the Termination Date (the "Payment Date") an amount equal to the aggregate of the out-of-pocket disbursements incurred by the Firm through the Termination Date. In addition to the foregoing, on the Payment Date you and the Acquirers will pay the Firm an amount equal to ___% of the legal fees incurred in connection with the Acquisition. If the firm receives on or before the Payment Date the amount you and the Acquirers owe the Firm, the remaining ___% of the fees incurred will be forgiven and you the Acquirers will have no liability therefor. However, if such payment is not received on or before the Payment Date, you and the Acquirers will remain responsible for all legal fees rendered in addition to any charges arising pursuant to paragraph (d) of the agreement to which this Exhibit "B" is attached.

In the event the Acquisition is consummated (the "Closing"), the aggregate amount (legal fees and out-of-pocket disbursements) set forth on the Firm's invoices to you the Acquirers will be paid at the time of the Closing plus any fees not covered by the following described Note. In addition to paying the Firm the amounts set forth on the Firm's invoices at the time of the Closing, at that time you and the Acquirers will execute and deliver to the Firm a promissory note (the "Note") in an amount equal to ___% of the amount of legal fees incurred through the day of Closing. The Note will (i) provide for the payment of interest at 10% per annum; and (ii) be payable monthly with four equal quarterly payments of principal, each in an amount equal to 25% of the original principal amount of the Note. In addition, you and the Acquirers and any corporation(s) and/or partnership(s) that are organized for the Acquisition or acquired in connection therewith (collectively, the "Acq. Corp.") shall be a maker of such Note. The Note shall be substantially in the form attached hereto as Exhibit "__."

As an inducement for you and the Acquirers to utilize the Firm's services after the time of the Closing, the Firm will forgive up to one-half of the principal amount of the Note in an amount equal to 50% of the fees collected from legal services rendered by the Firm to the Acq. Corp. within one year subsequent to the time of the Closing. It is acknowledged that such credit will be based upon collections, not billings, received by the Firm within one year from the time of the Closing.

For example, if the principal amount of the Note is $100,000 and, within one year subsequent to the Closing, the Acq. Corp. pays the Firm $50,000 in legal fees before any principal payments are made, the principal amount of the Note will be reduced to $75,000 ($50,000 X 50% with a cap of 50% of the then unpaid principal amount of the Note = $25,000).

Any amount that is not paid when due under this Alternative B, either at the time of the Closing or the Termination Date, will bear interest at the rate of eighteen percent (18%) per annum commencing on the first day of the month following the due date. In addition, you and the Acquirers will be responsible for the charges arising pursuing to paragraph (d) of the agreement to which this Exhibit "__" is attached.

Exhibit 6

Guidelines for Use of Outside Counsel

Numerous corporations have taken a systematic approach to the retention of outside legal counsel. Many strictly use an hourly billing basis. Typically, the corporations impose various controls in an attempt to contain costs and to permit in-house budgeting. Many controls involve evaluating the performance of outside counsel.

The guidelines reprinted in Exhibit 6 were chosen for two major reasons. First, they illustrate the procedures and requirements typically followed in retaining outside counsel. Second, unlike many approaches, they recognize that alternative fee arrangements can be advantageous. Each appendix to the guidelines is typical of approaches taken by various corporations as major purchasers of outside legal services.

I. **Selection and Retention of Outside Counsel**
   A. **General**
   In order to better manage the legal affairs of the Corporation, it is the policy of the Law Department to perform as much legal work in-house as is practicable. It is understood, however, that sound management will require the use of outside counsel. In allocating work to either in-house or outside counsel, the following criteria should be considered:
   1. degree of subject matter—expertise of in-house staff;
   2. existing workloads and availability;
   3. need for an "independent" legal opinion;
   4. need for special qualifications such as language skills, access to or familiarity with local governmental bodies or customs and laws or membership in local bar;
   5. proximity to the problem; and
   6. client acceptability or expectation resulting from established track record for particular problems.

   B. **Authority to Employ Outside Counsel**
   When possible, selected counsel should be chosen from the list of "approved counsel" and should be cleared with the appropriate level of supervision (e.g., an Assistant General Counsel or the General Counsel where the legal fees are anticipated to exceed $_____ in the aggregate or if the importance of the matter otherwise dictates General Counsel approval).

C. **Initial Contact**
  1. The initial contact with the outside counsel should be made either by the in-house counsel in charge of managing the referred matter ("managing attorney") or, where appropriate, the General Counsel. During the initial conversation with the outside counsel, the managing attorney must be prepared to discuss the facts and legal issues connected with the case and the general expectations of the outside counsel. As a minimum, the following points should be discussed during the first contact:
     a. identify the corporation and its subsidiaries and the opponent to avoid possible conflicts of interest;
     b. summarize the facts and legal questions;
     c. discuss the areas of expertise of the outside counsel and the support staff available;
     d. confirm which attorney will be lead counsel;
     e. discuss the hourly rate and billing practices; and
     f. confirm the communication channel between the firm and the Law Department.
  2. After the outside counsel has been selected, the managing attorney should send a retention letter (Appendix I) and a copy of the Corporation's General Procedures for Outside Counsel (Appendix II).

     Once the referral is made, the managing attorney should complete the Case Digest (Appendix III) for litigation matters or the Project Digest (Appendix IV) for other matters.

II. **Working Relationship with Outside Counsel**
  A. **General**
    1. The managing attorney should work closely with outside counsel on any significant matter to make certain that:
       a. the quality of the work is high;
       b. the fees charged are appropriate;
       c. all actions on behalf of the Corporation are consistent with the Corporation's policies and general interest;
       d. deadlines are met;
       e. facts are properly developed; and
       f. as much of the work as practicable is performed by in-house counsel.
    2. In carrying out these guidelines, the managing attorney should remain sensitive to the professional status of outside counsel and should use care to foster a relationship based on mutual trust and respect.

  B. **Who Does the Work**
    1. In any significant matter in which outside counsel is retained, the minimum participation of the managing attorney should be a general review of the work performed by the outside counsel.

2. It should be made clear that the Corporation has retained the outside firm because specific attorneys in the firm have the skills needed to accomplish a particular task. For this reason it is expected that the designated attorney will continue to be responsible for the matter through its completion and that such responsibility will not be delegated without the Corporation's consent.
3. Should delegation of the work be required to accomplish greater efficiency, the following factors should be considered:
   a. Other members of the firm may be assigned portions of the work when such assignments will facilitate efficiency. Less experienced members of the firm should not be assigned duties solely for training purposes.
   b. Law Department attorneys are a part of the team and as such should be considered for performance of portions of the work either with or without direct participation by members of the firm.
   c. Duplication of effort, such as assigning more than one lawyer to attend a deposition, should be avoided.

C. **Contacts with the Corporation**
Unless specific exceptions have been made, contacts with the Corporation by outside counsel should be made through the managing attorney.

D. **Document Preparation**
When practical, significant documents prepared by outside counsel should be received, reviewed, and approved prior to distribution or filing with courts or other agencies. The Law Department should receive copies of all significant documents and work product such as briefs, pleadings, or legal memoranda.

E. **Decision Making**
Any decision that may have a significant impact on the matter assigned to outside counsel must be approved by the managing attorney.

F. **Cost Management**
The managing attorney should discuss with the outside counsel those methods necessary for ensuring that each matter is handled as efficiently as possible. It should be a consistent practice of both counsel to consider whether the potential benefit of a possible course of action is justified by its anticipated cost. In every case the managing attorney must complete a Cost Digest (either Litigation or General) at the time the matter is referred to outside counsel and update it on a quarterly basis [Appendix V(A) and V(B)]. In more significant matters, or when the managing attorney otherwise feels it appropriate, a Fee Projection Worksheet [Appendix VI(A) and (B)] should be prepared and maintained on a quarterly basis. Preparation of both the Cost Digest and the Fee Projection Worksheet should be accomplished in close consultation with the outside attorney.

III. Fee and Billing Procedures

A. General

1. At the time outside counsel is retained, there should be a clear understanding of how fees are to be determined, the frequency of billings, and the information to be contained in the billings.
2. The managing attorney should prepare a memorandum clearly describing the fee and billing arrangements that have been agreed upon.
3. The managing attorney is responsible for determining that the bill is consistent with the fee and billing procedures, that the work covered by the bill has been performed in a satisfactory manner, and that any unusual or unexpected charges are fully explained.

B. Fee Guidelines

1. The position of the Law Department is that the best protection against unreasonable fees is not any single fee arrangement (i.e., fixed hourly rate, lump sum for each project, contingent fee, etc.), but (a) the reputation of the firm, including its awareness that costs and efficiency are significant factors in the provision of legal services; (b) the knowledge of the firm that the Corporation is concerned about costs; and (c) the ability of in-house counsel to work with the firm to minimize costs by the efficient utilization of the time of in-house and outside counsel. Therefore, it is not the policy of the Law Department to require that any particular fee arrangement be agreed to in every instance. Instead, there should be an agreement on a fee arrangement that is appropriate for the work to be performed.
2. Arrangements for contingent fees or for additional fees to be paid at the end of a project for results obtained or any unique or unusual fee arrangement should be approved in advance by the General Counsel.

C. Billing Guidelines

1. The policy of the Law Department is to require certain minimum information on all statements for outside legal services. Only bills containing such information will be processed for payment. The bills should be rendered monthly and include the following:
   a. date and description of service;
   b. number of hours spent for each itemized service;
   c. identification of person performing work and billing rate;
   d. expenses and disbursements; and
   e. total legal expenses for each case or matter being handled.
2. Unless approved in advance, the Corporation is not to be billed for the following:
   a. computer legal research;
   b. other computer time;
   c. outside research service;
   d. overtime expense;

  e. word processing service;
  f. temporary help;
  g. transportation other than coach.

IV. Evaluation of Outside Counsel

In order to ensure the best available Counsel, it is essential to properly evaluate those outside firms that have provided services. It is the responsibility of each managing attorney to complete the Outside Counsel Evaluation Report (Appendix VII). Generally, the form should be completed at the conclusion of each matter. In protracted or routine matters, however, the form should be completed on an annual basis at the conclusion of the year in which service is provided. One copy is to be retained in the file and one sent to the Manager of Litigation.

V. Conclusion

The foregoing policy is to guide the managing attorney in his or her relations with outside counsel. Situations may arise that require flexibility in the administration of the policy. Where circumstances dictate the need for a change in policy, approval for required modifications should be sought from the General Counsel.

  Outside counsel make a critical contribution to the proper administration of the legal affairs of the Corporation. For this reason, all relations with outside counsel should be conducted in a manner that engenders mutual trust and respect. Implementation of this policy should be accomplished in a manner that is consistent with this objective.

Appendix I
Retention Letter

  RE:

Dear _____

  This will confirm our telephone conversation of _____ in which we agreed that your firm will represent us in the referenced matter. Enclosed is our file containing:

  As discussed, we have an established policy with regard to use of outside counsel, a copy of which is enclosed. This policy should be adhered to in the performance of your work on this matter. If you anticipate a need to deviate from the procedures established, please contact me in advance. With regard to the billing rates, this will confirm that we will be billed at $ _____ an hour for your time and $, $, and $ an hour for associates, paralegals and clerks, respectively.

The purpose of the policy is to ensure that we have a clear understanding of the working relationship between our outside counsel and the Law Department. While we highly value the contribution of our outside counsel, there is an increasing concern with the escalation in the costs for these services. Therefore, our goal is to encourage a continuous dialogue between our office and your firm so that the legal affairs of _____ are handled in a highly professional and cost-efficient manner. To this end, the policy has been carefully drawn to allow for the appropriate flexibility on the part of outside counsel while retaining the desired amount of accountability.

After you have become acquainted with the enclosed materials, please give me a call so that we may discuss the manner in which to proceed. At that time, we should be prepared to discuss the strategy to be employed and the estimated costs in pursuing this matter.

We look forward to a close association as this matter progresses.

Appendix II
Policy and Procedure for Outside Counsel

I. Purpose

The purpose of this policy is to establish a clear understanding with regard to the working relationship between the Law Department of _____ and the offices of outside counsel. While the value of the services provided by outside counsel is clearly recognized, there is an increasing concern with the escalation in costs for such services. Therefore, the intent of this policy is to encourage a continuous dialogue between the Law Department and outside counsel so that the legal affairs of _____ are handled in a highly professional and cost-efficient manner. To this end, the procedures that follow have been drawn carefully to allow for the appropriate flexibility on the part of outside counsel while retaining the desired amount of accountability.

II. Working Relationship Between Inside and Outside Counsel
A. Delegation of the Work
1. Selection of outside counsel is determined on the basis that specific attorneys in the firm have the skills necessary to accomplish a particular task. For this reason it is expected that the designated attorney will continue to be responsible for the matter through its completion and that such responsibility will not be delegated without the consent of the Law Department.
2. Should delegation of the work be required to accomplish greater efficiency, the following factors should be considered:
    a. Other members of the firm may be assigned portions of the work when such assignments will facilitate efficiency. Less experienced members of the firm should not be assigned duties solely for training purposes.

b. Law Department attorneys are a part of the team and as such should be considered for performance of portions of the work either with or without direct participation by members of the firm.
c. Duplication of effort, such as assigning more than one lawyer to attend a deposition, should be avoided.

B. **Contacts with the Corporation**
Unless specific exceptions have been made, contacts with the Corporation by outside counsel should be made through the managing attorney, who will be the attorney making the initial referral values otherwise specified.

C. **Document Preparation**
When practical, significant documents prepared by outside counsel should be received, reviewed, and approved prior to distribution or filing with courts or other agencies. The Law Department should receive copies of all significant documents and work product such as briefs, pleadings, or legal memoranda.

D. **Decision Making**
Any decision that may have a significant impact on the matter assigned to outside counsel must be approved by the managing attorney.

F. **Cost Management**
Outside counsel are to discuss with the managing attorney methods of ensuring that each matter is handled as efficiently as possible. Consideration should be given to whether the potential benefit of a possible course of action is justified by its expected cost. The outside counsel will be requested to provide cost estimates for the required work and in some instances may be asked to assist in the preparation of a budget.

III. **Fee and Billing Procedure**
A. **Fees**
Unless another basis for setting legal fees is agreed to in advance, charges for legal services shall be made on the basis of counsel's standard hourly rate. Changes in such rates must be disclosed to the managing attorney in advance.

B. **Billing Procedures**
1. The policy of the Law Department is to require certain minimum information on all statements for outside legal services. Only bills containing such information will be processed for payment. The bills should be rendered monthly and include the following:
   a. date and description of service;
   b. number of hours spent for each itemized service;

     c. identification of person performing work and billing rate;
     d. expenses and disbursements; and
     e. total legal expenses for each case or matter being handled.

2. Unless approved in advance, the Corporation is not to be billed for the following:
   a. computer legal research;
   b. other computer time;
   c. outside research service;
   d. overtime expense;
   e. word processing service;
   f. temporary help;
   g. transportation other than coach.

Appendix III
Case Digest

Title: _____
Counsel: _____
   Address: _____
                                             Phone: _____

In-house Staff: _____

    I. Statement of facts that gave rise to the dispute
   II. Disputed factual issues
  III. Legal issues involved
  IV. Legal issues to be researched
   V. Discovery schedule
      A. Production of personnel; where, when
      B. Production of documents

Appendix IV
Project Digest

Title: _____
Counsel: _____
   Address: _____
                                             Phone: _____

In-house Staff: _____

   I. Description of the project
  II. List of major tasks

A. To be performed by outside counsel
B. To be performed by in-house counsel
III. Timetable for completion

Appendix V(A)
Cost Digest (Litigation)

Date Originally Prepared _____
Most Recent Revision _____

I. Caption, venue, and description of claim
II. Status
III. Attorneys (House Counsel/Outside Counsel Law Firm)
IV. Prior expenses   Period   Amount
                       20
                       20
                       20
V. Expense projection ($000)   Date (Rev. or Prepared)
            20__   20__   19__   19__   20__
     Quarter   1st   2nd   3rd   4th   Total   20__
A. Current
B. Most Recent
C. Original
VI. Assumptions with respect to costs and case status

Appendix V(B)
Cost Digest (General)

Date Originally Prepared _____
Most Recent Revision _____

I. Caption, venue and description of claim
II. Status
III. Attorneys (House Counsel/Outside Counsel Law Firm)
IV. Prior expenses   Period   Amount
                       20
                       20
                       20
V. Expense projection ($000)   Date (Rev. or Prepared)
            20__   20__   19__   19__   20__
     Quarter   1st   2nd   3rd   4th   Total   20__
A. Current
B. Most Recent
C. Original
VI. Assumptions with respect to costs and case status

Appendix VI(A)
Fee Projection Worksheet (Litigation)

Case: _____
Firm: _____

<u>Work Assignments</u>

		Partner Hrs.	Associate Hrs.	Paralegal Hrs.	Other
I.	Retention-Rate agreement-Preliminary work assignments and strategy	____	____	____	____
II.	Factual investigation				
III.	Detailed strategy conference—Including fee projections for matter by calendar quarter	____	____	____	____
IV.	Initial legal research (if necessary) Issues				
	1. _____	____	____	____	____
	2. _____	____	____	____	____
	3. _____	____	____	____	____
V.	Answer to or preparation of possible counterclaim or complaint	____	____	____	____
VI.	Motions (nondiscovery)				
	A. _____	____	____	____	____
	B. _____	____	____	____	____
VII.	Witness interviews A. Number	____	____	____	____
VIII.	Discovery				
	A. Drafting interrogatories	____	____	____	____
	B. Answering interrogatories	____	____	____	____
	C. Drafting document request	____	____	____	____
	D. Reviewing documents produced	____	____	____	____
	E. Responding to document request				
	1. Search	____	____	____	____
	2. Review of documents	____	____	____	____
	F. Depositions				
	1. Preparation				
	a. defensive-number	____	____	____	____

	Work Assignments			
	Partner Hrs.	Associate Hrs.	Paralegal Hrs.	Other

        b. offensive-number
    2. Actual deposition
        a. defensive-number
        b. offensive-number
IX. Motions - Discovery
X. Additional legal research
    A. Issues
        1. _____
        2. _____
        3. _____
XI. Motions–Substantive
    A. _____
    B. _____
XII. Pretrial memoranda
XIII. Pretrial conferences
XIV. Settlement conferences
XV. Trial
    A. Preparation–days
    B. Trial–days
XVI. Strategy conferences
XVII. Miscellaneous telephone calls (Status reports, etc.)
XVIII. Contingencies (explain)
    1. _____
    2. _____
Total Hours
Hourly Charge   X$ X$ X$ X$
Projected Fees
Disbursements:
Travel
Copying
Telephone
Transcripts
Additional

Basic assumptions utilized in arriving at the above

Appendix VI(B)
Fee Projection Worksheet (General)

	Work Assignments			
	Partner Hrs.	Associate Hrs.	Paralegal Hrs.	Other

Subject Matter:
Firm: _____
1. Retention-Rate agreement-Work assignment
2. Legal research
   A. Issues
      1. _____   ____   ____   ____   ____
      2. _____   ____   ____   ____   ____
      3. _____   ____   ____   ____   ____
3. Conferences or meetings
   A. Purposes
      1. _____   ____   ____   ____   ____
      2. _____   ____   ____   ____   ____
4. Additional items
   A. Description
      1. _____   ____   ____   ____   ____
      2. _____   ____   ____   ____   ____
      3. _____   ____   ____   ____   ____
      4. _____   ____   ____   ____   ____

Total Hours
Hourly Charge   X$ X$ X$ X$
Projected Fees   ____   ____   ____   ____
Disbursements:
  Travel   ____   ____   ____   ____
  Copying   ____   ____   ____   ____
  Telephone   ____   ____   ____   ____
  Additional   ____   ____   ____   ____

Appendix VII
Outside Counsel Evaluation Report

City _____ Date Retained _____

Firm Name _____ Date Concluded _____

Address _____

	Rating 1*	Rating 2*	Hourly Charge
Partner _____	_____	_____	_____
Associate _____	_____	_____	_____
Associate _____	_____	_____	_____

Type of matter(s) handled: _____

Disposition:

Comments: _____

I (would) (would not) recommend this firm for use again.

                                  Attorney
                                  _____

Rating 1—Quality of legal advice, strategy
Rating 2—Efficiency of time, appreciation for costs
- One to Ten. Ten highest

To be filed at the conclusion of each matter or on an annual basis in the event of routine or protracted matters.

Exhibit 7

Agreement for Fixed-Fee Representation of a Bank for Major Collection Litigation with Bonus Clause

The innovative fee agreement in Exhibit 7 was used starting in 1989 with a large firm where the bank was instituting suits to recover unpaid indebtedness. This agreement may soon be used in cases where the bank is a defendant or is defending a counterclaim.

Initially, the bank entered into an agreement with the law firm to have a test period with 10 lawsuits where the bank was suing one or more entities legally liable for indebtedness. The law firm and the bank both kept detailed records of the amount of time spent in resolving those 10 cases, after which the parties mutually analyzed this information. During this initial experimental stage, it was agreed that for the legal services rendered in each of the 10 cases, the bank would pay the lesser of the fixed fee pursuant to the contract or the actual time value billing based on an hourly rate. No bonus amount would be involved for the 10 test cases, unless the bank felt that it was warranted.

Ten months after the beginning of these test cases, seven had been resolved to the bank's satisfaction. Of those seven cases, five resulted in the contractual fixed fee being less than the usual hourly rate calculation. The bank's analysis showed that these cases were resolved significantly faster than the cases handled by the same firm under the previous straight hourly fee system. Additionally, the law firm indicated that its revenues from the bank group significantly increased over this shorter time period. In short, both the bank and the law firm believed they had received value from this arrangement. The law firm and the bank plan to continue using this method to handle more cases.

From the law firm's standpoint, the most important element of this type of arrangement is a volume of cases. The law firm is willing to accept the risk of underestimating what it might actually take to resolve some of these disputes only if it is relatively assured that a number of other cases will be referred to the firm to serve as opportunities to compensate for any losses.

Internally, the bank's analysis of this arrangement indicated that using this method led to a proportionate reduction in the bank's overall outside litigation expense, as well as reducing the bank's person-hours and "time value" savings of money, since these matters were resolved faster than normal.

Note that the agreement specifies the characteristics of the cases that will be handled. There is a range stipulating a minimum and maximum amount in controversy. The law firm can reject a prescribed number of cases. The services to be performed are set forth, as are the services that are excluded, with the proviso that any excluded services under the fee agreement will be performed by the law firm for an hourly fee.

If an eligible claim is resolved quickly, the law firm is entitled to a bonus computed on an agreed-upon percentage of the amount in controversy.

If the services provided are satisfactory, the bank agrees to meaningfully consider engaging the firm for other legal representation, such as litigation of noneligible claims and business transactions. Under this agreement, the bank commits to providing a volume of business, with the prospect of more to come. The bank's interest in speedy resolution is met by the incentive for the bonus. Both the fixed-fee aspect and the bonus provision provide an incentive for the law firm to be efficient.

The innovation demonstrated by this corporate counsel in setting up this type of arrangement is admirable. The agreement certainly seems to be another win-win billing method.

Agreement for Fixed-Fee Representation

_____ agrees to represent _____ ("Client") and Client hereby engages _____ to represent Client in defense of Eligible Claims (defined herein) upon the following terms and conditions:

1. **Definitions.** As used herein, "Eligible Claims" means those claims (whether asserted by formal petition, complaint or application or pleading before any judicial or administrative entity) against Client which are frequently recurring and generally identified by common characteristics, such as the following:

    (a) All legal claims for relief by one plaintiff, or common claims by multiple (but not more than ___) plaintiffs acting in a community of interest, i.e., spouses, partners, etc., asserted in a separate proceeding identified by a case, cause or proceeding number;

    (b) Claims arising out of the same transaction or series of transactions between plaintiffs and Client;

    (c) Claims in which the amount of alleged unliquidated damages in controversy is not less than $_____ and does not exceed $_____; and

    (d) [Other common characteristics to be determined by Client and _____]

    "Client" means _____ and any related persons or entities named as defendant(s) in the proceedings who have or hold a common interest in defense of the Eligible Claims, such as parent or subsidiary corporations, directors, officers and employees, provided that representation of_____, its parent or subsidiary corporations, or its directors, officers or employees would or does not constitute an ethical conflict of interest.

2. **Term.** This agreement commences as of _____, 2002, and shall terminate on _____, 200__.

3. **Referral of Eligible Claims.** Client shall refer for legal representation all matters which are or may constitute Eligible Claims and which are served upon Client during the term of this agreement. In order to compensate for any disagreements as to whether a matter constitutes an Eligible Claim, _____ may decline to undertake representation of Client in as many as _____ such matters (exclusive of ethical conflicts), in which event Client is free to engage other legal counsel.

4. **Flat Fee.** Upon referral of each Eligible Claim matter, Client shall pay _____ $ _____ as a fee ("the Flat Fee") for the legal services, described herein, associated with the particular Eligible Claim.

5. **Legal Services.** Upon referral and undertaking of representation of Client with respect to Eligible Claims of a plaintiff, _____ shall represent Client with professional zeal and diligence and in a manner which, at a minimum, complies with the letter and spirit of the Texas Code of Professional Responsibility. Except as stated in paragraph 6 of this agreement, _____ shall provide all legal services reasonably necessary to resolve, settle and terminate the Eligible Claims and to defend Client from the date that the Eligible Claims are referred to _____ through the trial and any post-trial proceedings. Except as specified in paragraph II of this agreement or otherwise agreed, _____ representation of Client in each separate matter shall terminate on the day that is the earlier of the date that (1) the Eligible Claims are dismissed by mutual request of plaintiff(s) and Client or (2) an appeal bond, if any, is filed by plaintiff(s) or Client.

The legal services which _____ shall provide, as necessary, include but are not limited to the following:
  (a) Pleadings;
  (b) Motions and responses to plaintiff(s)'s motions, if any;
  (c) Fact investigation and discovery, including depositions, witness interviews, interrogatories, document production requests and requests for admissions;
  (d) Legal research;
  (e) Client consultation, including status reports, strategy formulation and advice;
  (f) Hearings upon pre-trial motions and applications;
  (g) Trial of the Eligible Claims;
  (h) Settlement negotiation and communication;
  (i) Simple settlement agreements (which contemplate full performance of all terms upon closing of the settlement); and
  (j) Termination of any litigation via order of dismissal or final judgment.

6. **Services Not Encompassed by Flat Fee.** The following services related to the Eligible Claims are expressly excluded from the scope of _____ representation pursuant to this agreement:
    (a) Prosecution of any counterclaim(s) by Client against plaintiff(s);
    (b) Negotiation, drafting and preparation of agreements which contemplate a continued relationship between Client and plaintiff(s) or future performance by either party (i.e., restructured loans, payout of settlement amounts, etc.);
    (c) Appeals by either Client or plaintiff(s) including interim appeals or requests for appellate court review of pretrial orders (such as by mandamus, etc.);
    (d) [other].

    If requested by Client, _____ will provide legal representation to Client with respect to any of such excluded matters. Unless agreed otherwise, _____ shall provide and Client will pay for such representation based upon normal hourly rates of the _____ attorneys providing such legal services.

7. **Client Cooperation.** Client recognizes, acknowledges, and approves of _____ intention, and authorizes _____ to cause prompt settlement and resolution of Eligible Claims and prompt termination of any litigation arising therefrom. Client shall provide all assistance necessary to accomplish prompt settlement and resolution of Eligible Claims and related litigation, including the following:
    (a) Provide factual information deemed relevant by _____;
    (b) Advance necessary expenses;
    (c) Participate in good faith in settlement discussions or events such as alternative dispute resolution methods (arbitrations, mediations, etc.) and informal settlement communication with plaintiff(s) or plaintiff(s)'s attorneys; and
    (d) Timely perform all obligations undertaken pursuant to a binding settlement agreement with plaintiff(s).

8. **Expenses.** Client shall pay _____ all reasonably necessary out-of-pocket expenses advanced in connection with the representation and legal services provided with respect to Eligible Claims. Such expenses shall be identified upon monthly statements by itemized description, such as photocopying, long-distance telephone charges, travel, secretarial overtime (including paralegals), supplies, expert witnesses, court costs, depositions, etc. Where any single expense item exceeds $200, such as a court reporter's statement for depositions, _____ may forward such statements to Client and same shall be promptly paid by Client directly to the vendor.

9. **Bonus.** _____ shall be entitled to add to the final statement related to any specific Eligible Claims and to be paid a bonus if the Eligible Claims are resolved to Client's satisfaction in no later than _____ months from the day of their referral to _____. Resolution of the Eligible Claims shall be evidenced by a written agreement signed by Client and plaintiff(s). The amount of the bonus shall be ____ % of the "amount in controversy" in the proceeding in which the Eligible Claims are asserted. The "amount in controversy" shall be established by agreement of Client and _____.

10. **Representation of Client in Other Legal Matters.** If Client is satisfied with _____ representation and legal services with respect to Eligible Claims, Client will meaningfully consider engaging to provide legal representation in other matters requiring such services, such as litigation of non-Eligible Claims, business transactions, etc.

11. **Termination of Representation.** Client may terminate _____ representation of Client with respect to any Eligible Claims upon reasonable notice. If ____ representation is terminated (by Client, disqualification or withdrawal necessary under the circumstances) before such representation would otherwise naturally terminate by resolution or disposition of the Eligible Claims, then _____ shall be paid the value of legal services performed and expenses incurred to the date of termination of such representation, but in no event more than the Flat Fee.

SIGNED this _____ day of _____, 200__.
"Client"

By:

Its _____

By:

Vice President

Fixed Fee Corporation Representation Service Election Form

Exhibit 8 is the election form for a corporate client to elect certain services to be provided at a fixed fee by a service agent company established by a law firm to act in that capacity. The service is discussed in Chapter 8, dealing with technology.

Corporate Representation Services, llc
Business Compliance Solutions

Corporate Representation Services, llc was established to provide business compliance solutions for private companies—ensuring that the necessary legal formalities are met and providing service agent, corporate meeting and stock transfer services to our clients. With special updates and reminders, we keep our clients abreast of new legal developments that might affect private businesses.

For a single annual fee of $150 for each legal entity, we provide corporations and limited liability companies with the following basic services:

- Prepare standard annual meeting minutes for shareholders and directors of corporations or members of limited liability companies.
- Act as the Oklahoma service agent for the company.
- Provide an annual company audit and compliance questionnaire used to identify compliance issues and keep the corporate records accurate and current.
- Prepare a company profile reflecting the current owners and management in addition to other key legal business items.
- Make available conference room facilities for meetings.

Additional services are provided at a reasonable cost to our clients, including private company stock transfer services, director and member packets and guidebooks, and special assistance in preparing shareholder agreements, dependent care assistance and medical reimbursement plans, stock option and other benefit programs.

ELECTION: [Organization]

❑ **Yes**—I elect to continue the Corporate Representation Service for [Organization] and wish you to prepare the necessary meeting minutes for [Years Due].

❑ Please check if there have been no changes since last year and the accompanying profile information is correct.

❑ **No**—I do not wish to continue the Corporate Representation Service for [Organization]; please remove this company from the service.

If you would like to receive your minutes and other corporate documents electronically, please check below and list your e-mail address.

❑ I would like to receive my information electronically. My e-mail address is:

MAIL OR FAX RESPONSE PLEASE: Fax Number 405-843-6707

Exhibit 9

Fixed Fee for First-Year Services to Emerging Businesses

Davis Wright Tremaine, Seattle, Washington, has successfully developed the Emerging Business Program described in the brochure reprinted as Exhibit 9. This program provides specified first-year corporate services for qualified start-up businesses for a flat fee of $10,000. Most of the clients accepted for the program are embryonic technology businesses. On the negative side, Peter Parsons reports that in some instances the flat fee covered services that would have produced three times that amount in the first year, if billed on an hourly basis. On the plus side, services not included within the scope of the defined services quite often generated five or six times the annual fee in the first year. The firm takes this discounted fee approach in the expectation of long-term relationships with businesses that prove successful.

Summary

Davis Wright Tremaine created its Emerging Business Program in 1988 to assist clients in establishing their new ventures on a solid legal footing without having to constantly worry about legal fees. For a fixed amount of $10,000, Davis Wright Tremaine will incorporate a new venture and provide basic corporate legal services (excluding some specialized services, as explained below) for 12 months. Under the Program, an entrepreneur can get the right start in structuring his or her corporation, have available the resources of a full-service law firm, and be able to predict basic legal fees.

Services Offered Under the Program

Under the Emerging Business Program, we will assist you in examining the following legal issues and in preparing and filing, where appropriate, documents that meet your corporation's needs:

Confirmation of Name Availability

Before you commit to a corporate name, we will confirm that it is available in the state in which you wish to incorporate. If the company plans to do business under another name, we will help register that "trade name."

Preliminary Trademark Search

Even if the corporate name you choose is available for incorporation, it may turn out later that it clashes with an established trademark or noncorporate business name owned by another company. Typically, this issue surfaces only after a company has invested considerable sums in marketing and product design (as well as stationery, cards, etc.). To help avoid this problem, one of our attorneys with experience in trademark and copyright matters will advise whether your chosen name is likely to infringe upon other marks. The Program covers preliminary trademark and advice, which is usually sufficient for basic business name clearance. However, if you plan to use your corporate name extensively in advertising, we strongly recommend more exhaustive research and trademark registration. General consulting on these options is covered, but the research and registration services themselves are outside of the Program.

Corporate Formation

To help structure your corporation, we will advise you of alternative means to attract outside financing or to protect your founding shareholders. When you select the features you wish, we will prepare and file, where appropriate:

- Articles of Incorporation
- Bylaws
- Consent of Directors in Lieu of Organizational Meeting
- Subscription Agreements
- Shareholders' Buy-Sell Agreement
- Stock Certificates

Whether to Elect S Corporation Status

Together with your accountants, one of our tax attorneys will advise you of the advantages and disadvantages of electing to do business as an "S Corporation." If you wish to make the election, we will help you prepare and file an "Election to Do Business as an S Corporation" within the time limits set by the Internal Revenue Service.

Business Licenses

We will assist the corporation in filing the necessary applications to do business with federal, state and city authorities. These can include:

- Washington State Master Business License Application
- Application for Internal Revenue Service Employer Identification Number
- Seattle/Bellevue/Redmond/ Kirkland/Bothell or other City Business License
- Applications to do business as a Foreign Corporation (if you wish to do business in other states)

Employment Matters

We will advise you of how similar companies structure employment arrangements and compensation and how they attract and provide incentives for employees. We can then assist you in preparing appropriate:

- Employment Agreements for Key Employees, perhaps with noncompetition provisions
- Consulting Agreements
- Confidentiality and Nondisclosure Agreements for Employees and Consultants
- Stock Repurchase Agreements
- Section 83(b) Elections

Our Employment Law and Employee Benefits attorneys also offer the following outside the scope of the Program:

- Periodic seminars on subjects of interest to employers
- A half-day or day-long program to train managers with employee evaluations
- A program to assist a client in preparing an Employee Policy and Procedure Manual, tailored to its particular needs
- Preparation and administration of Employee Stock Ownership Plans
- Preparation of and counsel relating to other employer-assisted health plans

Although these services are outside the Program, general legal discussion of their features is within it. Attorneys in those Departments will be happy to discuss these programs with you.

Employee Stock Option Plan

Frequently, emerging companies wish to offer stock options as an incentive for some or all of their employees. Under the Program we will advise you about the necessary steps to adopt a stock option plan, the advantages of such a plan, and what numbers of shares are routinely subject to plans. If the board of directors decides the corporations should grant stock options, for an additional $1,000, we will prepare a standard Stock Option Plan and Stock Option Agreement and help the corporation file for exemptions under federal and appropriate state securities laws.

Continued Corporate Maintenance

As the corporation's board of directors and shareholders take actions throughout the year, we will prepare the necessary Consents of Directors and/or Shareholders (or minutes of meetings). We will also attend directors' and shareholders' meetings if you wish.

Strategy and Advice

Most important, under the Emerging Business Program, the corporation's officers and directors can call or schedule meetings with us at any time to discuss corporate matters, upcoming strategic decisions or general business concerns. One goal of the Program is to educate entrepreneurs as to when they should seek legal advice. We encourage you to take advantage of the Program and call whenever you have a question. We will return your calls promptly.

Services Not Covered Under the Program

Services beyond basic corporate advice and documentation, such as advice in the area of securities (raising money from outside investors), trademark and copyright protection, litigation or bankruptcy, are not included within the Program. We will provide these services, but only after we have alerted you that they are not covered by the Program, provided you with an estimate of the costs involved, and received your instructions to proceed. For services outside the Program, you will be billed separately each month.

Fees and Disbursements

While the Emerging Business Program covers legal services, it does *not* include filing fees or out-of-pocket costs, such as long-distance telephone and copying costs. Each month you will receive an invoice describing the services provided and showing amounts owed. The invoice will bill for all out-of-pocket disbursements and costs. If you ever have questions regarding these amounts, you should call your principal attorney immediately.

Davis Wright Tremaine

By selecting Davis Wright Tremaine, with offices in Anchorage, Bellevue, Honolulu, Los Angeles, New York, Portland, San Francisco, Seattle, Washington, D.C., and Shanghai, China, you acquire the services of a law firm with broad resources and an international reputation. We proudly serve companies with one to several thousand employees.

An emerging company may immediately require the services of several legal disciplines. And, as the corporation grows and its legal needs become more complex, we will be there to serve you. We represent clients with specialized needs in securities, computer software and hardware, biotechnology, trademarks, licensing, strategic alliances, international transactions, communications, employment, employee benefits, tax, real estate, health care and other disciplines.

Eligibility

If you have not yet incorporated, you are eligible to apply for our Emerging Business Program. It is designed to help entrepreneurs who are starting with a clean slate to position themselves for success and growth.

If you would like to be considered for the Program, you should discuss enrollment with your attorney and deliver a $10,000 check made payable to "Davis Wright Tremaine" with a note indicating the check is to be applied to the Emerging Business Program. This fee is not refundable and must be paid at the beginning of the Program. (Unfortunately, no exceptions can be made to this rule.) When we receive your check, we will forward a letter confirming whether your venture has been accepted under the Emerging Business Program. If it is not accepted, of course, we return your check.

Offices

Anchorage
Suite 800
701 W Eighth Avenue
Anchorage, Alaska 99501-3468
(907) 257-5300

Bellevue
1800 Bellevue Place
10500 NE Eighth Street
Bellevue, Washington 98004-4300
(425) 646-6100

Honolulu
1360 Pauahi Tower
1001 Bishop Street
Honolulu, Hawaii 96813-3429
(808) 275-0100

Los Angeles
Suite 2400
865 South Figueroa Street
Los Angeles, California 90017-2566
(213) 633-6800

New York
1740 Broadway
New York, New York 10019-4315
(212) 489-8230

Portland
Suite 2300
1300 SW Fifth Avenue
Portland, Oregon 97201-5682
(503) 241-2300

San Francisco
Suite 600
One Embarcadero Center
San Francisco, California 94111-3611
(415) 276-6500

Seattle
2600 Century Square
1501 Fourth Avenue
Seattle, Washington 98101-1688
(206) 622-3150

Washington, D.C.
Suite 450
1500 K Street NW
Washington, D.C. 20005-1272
(202) 508-6600

Shanghai, China
Suite 450 East Tower
Shanghai Centre
1376 Nanjing Xi Lu
Shanghai, China 200040
011-86-21-6279-8560

CONTACT US
For more information about Davis Wright Tremaine and our attorneys, visit us at www.dwt.com, call us toll-free at (877) 398-8415, or email us at info@dwt.com <mailto:info@dwt.com>.

Exhibit 10

Fixed-Fee Retainer Agreement for Handling Insurance Defense Cases Based on a Prescribed Volume of Cases

The law firm and the insurance company that signed the retainer agreement in Exhibit 10 agreed that for a period of two years, based on a caseload of 180 cases, the law firm would defend all cases in four contiguous counties for a fixed annual fee payable in monthly installments. The duties of the law firm and the insurance company are set forth. If trials run more than 10 trial days, additional compensation would be paid on an hourly basis. If the caseload drops below the prescribed 180 cases, the agreement can be modified at prescribed times. Also, either party can terminate the agreement on giving 60 days' notice.

RETAINER AGREEMENT BETWEEN THE LAW FIRM OF _____ AND _____ INSURANCE CO.

This is a 2-year Retainer Agreement entered into between the _____ Insurance Co. (Company) and the law firm of _____ (Law Firm) to become effective on the 1st day of January, 20___, and to continue until the last day of December, 20___.

Whereas, the Company is desirous of having the Law Firm represent it in certain areas on a retainer basis and the Law Firm is desirous of representing the Company, the following terms will be applicable to this Agreement.

The following is a list of some of the major items that the Law Firm will obligate itself to perform pursuant to this Agreement:

1. To maintain in force during the life of this 2-year Retainer Agreement a policy of malpractice insurance, with limits of not less than One Million Dollars ($1,000,000.00).
2. To receive and handle lawsuits received from the Company in _____ Counties.
3. To provide opinions on coverage or cases not in suit.
4. To prepare and file declaratory judgment actions.
5. This Retainer Agreement does not include filing of subrogation suits in automobile or fire cases.
6. While not inclusive of all the handling of such suits, the following list will cover the major activities with respect to the handling of such suits:
    A. To send the Company a written acknowledgment of each suit file received;
    B. To prepare and timely file all responsive pleadings in the suits;

C. To take all necessary depositions and to provide a summary of the contents of the same to the Company;
D. To generally handle all the activities involved in defending suits including, but not limited to, all court calls, motions, hearings, pretrials, and such;
E. To conduct trial whenever requested by the Company. This Retainer covers a trial of 2 weeks (10 actual trial days) after which, if the trial continues, the Law Firm will be paid for the remainder of the trial time at its current hourly rate; except on cases tried by _____ the retainer covers 7 actual trial days after which, if the trial continues, the Law Firm will be paid for the remainder of the trial time at its current hourly rate;
F. To make written status reports to the Company regarding all such suits. The initial opinion letter is to be sent to the Company within 45 days of the assignment and written status reports shall be made at no less than 90-day intervals unless otherwise agreed;
G. To provide legal opinions and analysis to Company personnel upon request, both on cases in suit and on cases not yet in suit, but falling within the categories set forth above;
H. To handle any necessary post-trial motions;
I. To be available for consultation or conference with claims personnel of the Company;
J. To arrange for the proper termination of suits by filing of the necessary documents and making a final report to the Company; and
K. To negotiate settlement of claims in suits when requested by the Company but not to settle cases under any circumstances without prior approval from the Company.

In consideration for the services rendered by the Law Firm, the Company will pay the Law Firm the sum of _____ Dollars ($_____) per year in the following manner:

_____ Thousand Dollars ($_____) per month paid on the first day of each month this Agreement is in effect.

In addition to the amount listed above, the Company agrees to pay all of the expenses incurred in the handling of such suits including, but not limited to, the following:

1. Court reporter bills, court costs, appearance fees, subpoena fees, witness fees, photocopy expenses, reproduction of records expenses, and any other approved expenses incurred and allocated to the handling of the suit;
2. Long-distance telephone call expenses incurred in the course of handling such suits.

It is further agreed between the parties that the final decision to appeal a lawsuit will be made by the Company. If the Company decides that an appeal is to be taken, the Company will pay additional sums for the attorneys' fees for the handling of the appeal based either upon a flat dollar amount or upon an hourly rate to be agreed upon by the parties. The Company will bear all of the costs and expenses with respect to the appeal.

The Company further agrees that it will photostat its files and forward originals to the Law Firm for its use in the defense of suits.

This Agreement may be terminated by either party on 60 days' prior written notice of termination. If the 2-year Retainer Agreement is terminated by either party, the Law Firm agrees to immediately return all suit files in its possession, including attorneys' work product, to the Company and agrees to a substitution of Attorneys on such pending suits. The Law Firm further agrees to cooperate fully in an orderly transfer of such suits from its control and to protect the interests of the Company and the Company's insureds in doing so. Payment of the 2-year Retainer fees by the Company will cease as of the effective date of termination. The Law Firm agrees not to file any Attorney's Liens on suits transferred to other attorneys.

It is anticipated that, and this Retainer Agreement has been entered into with the belief of the parties that, it will involve approximately 180 files.

Executed this ___ day of _____, 20__.

"Company"   _____ INSURANCE COMPANY

                                             By: _____

"Law Firm"   _____

                                             By: _____

Exhibit 11

The fee letter attached as Exhibit 11 is for estate planning and quotes a fixed fee for the work outlined in the letter agreement. If the time required exceeds a set number of hours, additional work is charged at an hourly rate. One-half of the fixed fee is due prior to any work being performed, with the balance due when the estate planning documents are signed. The fee arrangement greatly reduces collection problems for the lawyer, permits the client to pay the fee in two installments, and covers those situations where an undue amount of time is spent in the representation due to numerous client meetings, calls, and changes.

Neal A. Kennedy
Attorney at Law

(830) 693-9911 (Marble Falls)
(830) 693-1908 (Fax)
neal@kennedylaw.com
404 Main Street
Marble Falls, Texas 78654
(512) 497-3835 (Austin)
(512) 597-1053 (Fax)
www.kennedylaw.com

[DATE]

Mr. and Mrs. [HUSBAND'S NAME]
[ADDRESS]
[CITY, STATE & ZIP CODE]

Re: [CLIENTS' LAST NAME] - Estate Planning Documents
Our File No. [CLIENT MATTER NO.]

Dear Mr. and Mrs. [CLIENTS' LAST NAME]:

Thank you for selecting my law office to represent you in connection with your estate plan. The purpose of this letter is to set forth the terms of my legal representation of you.

Scope of Representation

You have asked me to help you with planning your estate. This representation will include the following:

1. Drafting your estate planning documents based on the information you have provided to me. Your estate plan will include the following documents for each of you:

   - Last Will and Testament;
   - Statutory Durable Power of Attorney;
   - Medical Power of Attorney;
   - Declaration of Appointment of Guardian for Your Children;
   - Directive to Physicians and Family or Surrogates; and
   - Declaration of Guardian in the Event of Later Incapacity or Need of Guardian.

2. Sending these drafts to you and answering any questions that you may have.
3. Preparing final drafts of the documents for signing.
4. Supervising your execution of these final documents in my office.
5. Sending you the completed, signed documents for your records.

Excluded from Representation

My representation of you is limited to matters described above. My duties to you under this agreement will end when I have sent you your completed documents and you have had two weeks to review them for accuracy. After that time, my representation of you will cease, and I will owe you no duty to update your plan or to notify you of law changes which may affect you. Any future representation is not a part of this engagement and will be covered by a separate agreement.

Planning Objectives

In helping you with your estate plan, my objective will be planning for the death or disability of either or both of you. A husband and wife may have different interests in estate planning that concern their community and separate interests. Whenever a husband and wife partition community property or transfer community or separate property as part of an estate plan, the possibility of a subsequent divorce must be recognized.

As part of your estate plan, I will not be considering the effects of a possible divorce. Either or both of you may be adversely affected by your estate plan in the event your marriage ends in divorce. If you have any questions about how this plan may affect you in the event of a divorce, please consult with an attorney experienced in family law matters.

[In addition, you have indicated that you want your estate plan to include provisions designed to save your family estate and/or gift taxes. By including these provisions, you should recognize that (a) your estate planning documents are likely to be more complex than they would have been if tax savings was not an objective and (b) restrictions may be placed on your beneficiaries (including the surviving spouse) that may make it more difficult to fully utilize and enjoy the property free from interference by and/or liability to others. This will confirm that we have discussed these issues at some length and that you have decided that the potential tax savings to be gained from this plan take priority over these potential detriments.]

Fees and Expenses

I will perform the services described above for a fee of $_____, which fee includes up to _____ hours of attorney time. If this project takes more than this amount of time, you agree to pay for time in excess of _____ hours of attorney time at my regular hourly rate of $175.00 per hour. I will keep track of all time that I spend on this matter, and all of that time will count toward this limit. This will include the time that I have already spent discussing this matter with you; time that I spend talking to you on the telephone or in person; time that I spend doing research on your matter; time that I spend drafting, revising and reviewing your documents; time that I spend drafting and reading correspondence; and time that I spend supervising your execution of the estate planning documents.

I have been able to prepare estate plans like the one you have indicated you want for the majority of my clients within this time frame. Therefore, I have priced my services so that the majority of my clients can get a fair price for their plans and have a good idea of what those plans will cost. If I exceed the time limit in your case, I will charge you a larger fee based on the hourly rate stated above. Reasons why the time limit may be exceeded are: the need to make more revisions than usual; the need to spend more time than usual explaining provisions or answering questions; and delay in providing me with requested information. I mention these reasons not to discourage you from asking questions or having your documents prepared just the way you want, but to explain to you the effect this may have on the fee I charge so that you are in a position to control costs if you wish to do so.

In addition to the fee described above, you agree to pay any actual, out-of-pocket expenses incurred related to this matter. Expenses related to your estate plan may include, but are not limited to, postage, long distance telephone, photocopying, overnight messenger charges and filing fees.

As we discussed, payment for one half of the agreed fee, in the amount of $_____, will be required prior to the preparation of your estate-planning documents. The remainder of the fees and expenses will be due when you come in to sign your documents.

Multiparty Representation

My representation of you in this matter requires me to represent each of you as clients at the same time. Of course, you could each retain your own attorney to prepare your estate-planning documents, but you have indicated that you prefer to have me prepare estate-planning documents for both of you. I am happy to do this, subject to the following conditions regarding multi-party representation:

Since there are two of you, the possibility of a conflict between you exists. You acknowledge and understand that since I am representing both of you, no communication either of you has with me can be kept confidential from the other of you. If a conflict develops between the two of you, I may decline to continue to represent you.

Privacy Policy

Attorneys, like other professionals who advise on personal financial matters, are now required by a new federal law to inform their clients of their policies regarding privacy of client information. Attorneys have been and continue to be bound by professional standards of confidentiality that are even more stringent than those required by this new law; therefore, I have always protected your right to privacy.

In the course of providing my clients with income tax, estate tax, and gift tax advice, I receive significant personal financial information from my clients. If you are a client of this law firm, you should know that all information that I receive from you is held in confidence, and is not released to people outside the firm, except as agreed by you or as required under applicable law.

I retain records relating to professional services that I provide so that I am better able to assist you with your professional needs, and in some cases, to comply with professional guidelines. In order to guard your nonpublic personal information, I maintain physical, electronic and procedural safeguards that comply with my professional standards.

Termination of Representation

The terms of this engagement will be governed by Texas law, and you are free to terminate the engagement at any time, as am I. If the engagement is terminated, you will remain responsible for payment of fees (calculated at the hourly rate stated above) and expenses incurred through the date of termination.

I look forward to working with you on this matter. If you agree to the terms of my proposed engagement, as set out above, please confirm your agreement with these terms of engagement by signing one copy of this letter in the space provided below and returning it to me. (The other copy is for your records.)

I appreciate your trust in my law office. If you have any questions concerning my fees or this legal matter, please call me at (830) 693-9911.

Very truly yours,

Neal A. Kennedy
NAK/jh

Agreed to and accepted on the _____ day of June, 2002.

[HUSBAND'S NAME]

[WIFE'S NAME]

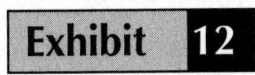

Fee Agreement Incorporating Hourly, Fixed and Unit Fees for a Real Estate Development Project

The following innovative fee proposal to a real estate developer covers several alternative billing methods – discounted hourly rates, maximum fees, fixed fees, and unit fees based upon an agreed unit rate per square foot.

A Sample Fee Proposal for Real Estate Development

We are pleased to present XYZ Limited Partnership (the "**Client**") with this fee proposal in connection with the Client's efforts to develop [retail center] and [office park] (together, the "**Project**") in the Village of Arcadia. Our understanding of the Project is based on the [dated site plan] prepared by Design Group.

Fee Structures Defined
In discussing our legal services fees, this proposal incorporates the terms "**Discounted Hourly Fee**," "**Maximum Fee**," "**Fixed Fee**," and "**Unit Fee**." What we mean by these terms is the following:

> **Discounted Hourly Fee** means a total fee calculated by multiplying an agreed hourly services rate by the total number of hours devoted to the applicable matter. Each of the lawyers on our practice team is assigned a standard hourly services rate, which we have set forth on the attached <u>Exhibit A</u>. The hourly services rates we propose for the Project, however, have been reduced from the standard rates we would expect to charge for such a development. These rates are also shown on <u>Exhibit A</u>.
>
> **Maximum Fee** means a total fee calculated by multiplying an agreed hourly services rate by the total number of hours devoted to the applicable matter, provided that the total fee shall not exceed a specified maximum amount. In this instance, the hourly service rate shall be the Discounted Hourly Rate set forth on <u>Exhibit A</u>.
>
> **Fixed Fee** means a specified fee payable by the Client without regard to the number of service hours devoted to the pertinent matter.
>
> **Unit Fee** means a total fee calculated by multiplying an agreed unit rate by the total number of units involved in the applicable matter. In this instance, Unit Fees are established for certain leasing matters based on the rentable square footage of the demised premises.

Fee Breakdown: [retail center]

We understand that the Client's plans for [retail center], the retail portion of the Project, call for development of three anchor pads (one each for a home improvement store, food center, and department store), eight outlots (including one each for a drug store, fast-food restaurant, and bank), and from 25,000 to 45,000 square feet of in-line retail space. We propose to provide legal services for this part of the Project on the following bases:

>   **REA and Project Planning—Discounted Hourly Fee.** *Team Members: Adams, Brown, and Carter.* A substantial effort will be required to lay the Project's groundwork. This effort obviously must include defining and establishing the Project's tax parcels, determining its common areas, and drafting and negotiating—and, as development goes forward, amending—the controlling reciprocal easement agreement. Laying the groundwork for the Project must also include preparing standard documentation (such as standard purchase and sale agreements, ground leases, in-line retail leases, and letters of intent) for use in connection with prospective buyers, tenants, and lenders.
>
>   We will provide services in connection with drafting the Reciprocal Easement Agreement (REA) and with addressing the general planning tasks we have identified, as well as others as they arise, at the Discounted Hourly Fee.
>
>   Adams will be the Client's principal contact for all REA and project planning matters. He will be assisted in REA matters and in preparing anchor tenant agreements by Brown. In the balance of the project planning matters (including establishing tax parcels, preparing other forms of agreement, and all other planning efforts), Adams will be assisted by Carter.
>
>   **Financing—Fixed Fee to be agreed based on the Client's determination of financing arrangements.** *Team Members: Adams, Brown, Davis, and Ellis.* Client plans to develop the Project in phases. This phased development will call for a number of different credit facilities. Right now, however, the outlines of the required credit transactions remain subject to a considerable number of variables, including the number and location of the Project's tax parcels, the identity of the retail anchor tenants and the nature of their realty interest in the Project, and the Client's specific plans for phasing the projected retail and office portions of the development.
>
>   We are confident that our services in connection with the required financings can be provided on a Fixed Fee basis for each such financing transaction. We are also confident that we can reach agreement with the Client on the terms of such Fixed Fee arrangements as the key details of the Project emerge with greater clarity. Alternatively, such services—whether uniformly or on a financing-by-financing basis—could also be provided at the Discounted Hourly Rate.

In any event, Adams will be the Client's principal contact for all financing matters. We expect that he will be regularly assisted by Davis, a partner in our real estate practice group who specializes in lending matters—especially in construction lending. Carter and Legal Assistant would assist Adams and Davis as required, particularly in addressing title, title insurance, and survey matters.

Anchor Pad Sales and Ground Leasing—Maximum Fee. *Team Members: Brown, Carter, and Legal Assistant.* For anchor pad sales and ground leases ultimately consummated with a purchaser or ground lessee, services will be charged per transaction based on the Discounted Hourly Fee, up to a maximum total fee of $[_] per sale and $[_] per ground lease. Services rendered in transactions not ultimately consummated will also be billed at the Discounted Hourly Rate, but the total invoice for any unconsummated transaction will not exceed the specified Maximum Fee.

Brown will be the Client's principal contact for all anchor pad ground leases and Carter will be the Client's principal contact for all anchor pad sales. Legal Assistant will help prepare sale and, where practical, leasing documentation.

Anchor Tenant Build-to-Suit Leases—Unit Fee. *Team members: Brown and Carter.* For original build-to-suit leases ultimately executed by an anchor tenant, services will be provided at a Unit Fee per transaction of [_]¢ per rentable square foot of the leased space. Rentable square footage will be determined according to the rentable area figure (calculated by the prevailing Building Owners and Managers Association (BOMA) standard) specified in the controlling lease.

Services rendered in preparing lease amendments, lease renewals, lease assignments, and subleases will be billed at the Discounted Hourly Rate. Services rendered in transactions not ultimately consummated will also be billed at the Discounted Hourly Rate, but the total invoice will not exceed the Unit Fee that would have been owing had the lease been executed.

Brown will be the Client's principal contact for all anchor build-to-suit leasing. Brown and Carter together will be responsible for preparing lease documentation.

Outparcel Sales and Ground Leasing—Maximum Fee. *Team Members: Brown, Carter, and Legal Assistant.* For outparcel sales and ground leases ultimately consummated with a purchaser or ground lessee, services will be charged per transaction based on the Discounted Hourly Fee, up to a maximum total fee of $[_] per sale or ground lease to a local tenant and $[_] per ground lease to a national tenant. (National tenants include all chain and franchise entities and their affiliates; local tenants include all other entities.) Services rendered in transactions not ultimately consummated will also be billed at the Discounted Hourly Rate, but the total invoice for any unconsummated transaction will not exceed the specified Maximum Fee.

Brown will be the Client's principal contact for all outparcel ground leases and Carter will be the Client's principal contact for all outparcel sales. Legal Assistant will help prepare sale and, where practical, leasing documentation.

In-line Retail Leasing—Unit Fee. *Team Members: Carter and Legal Assistant.* For original leases ultimately executed by both landlord and tenant, services will be provided based on a Unit Fee calculated per transaction based on the rentable square footage of each leased space. Unit Fees will be [ ]¢ per rentable square foot for national tenants and [ ]¢ per rentable square foot for local tenants. Rentable square footage will be determined according to the rentable area figure (calculated by the prevailing BOMA method) specified in the controlling lease.

Services rendered in preparing lease amendments, lease renewals, lease assignments, and subleases will be billed at the Discounted Hourly Rate. Services rendered in transactions not ultimately consummated will also be billed at the Discounted Hourly Rate, but the total invoice will not exceed the Unit Fee that would have been owing had the lease been executed.

Carter will be the Client's principal contact for all in-line leasing. Carter and Legal Assistant together will be responsible for preparing lease documentation

Fee Breakdown: [office park]
We understand that the Client's plans for [office park], the office park portion of the Project, call for the development of six sites suitable to accommodate Class A office uses. We propose to provide legal services for this part of the Project on the following bases:

REA and Project Planning—Discounted Hourly Fee. *Team Members: Adams and Carter.* As noted in our remarks on the REA and project planning for the retail portion of the Project, we will provide services in connection with the office park REA (including, in addition to the same issues arising with the retail spaces, organizing and documenting an owners association) and general office park planning on the basis of the Discounted Hourly Fee. Again, Adams will be the Client's principal contact for all REA and project planning matters. He will be assisted in office park REA and project planning matters by Carter.

Financing—Fixed Fee to be agreed based on the Client's determination of financing arrangements. *Team Members: Adams, Davis, Carter, and Legal Assistant.* Servicing in connection with financing transactions required for the office portion of the Project will be provided on the same basis as with the retail portion of the Project—that is, on the basis of a Fixed Fee to be negotiated as the Client's plans solidify or on the basis of a Discounted Hourly Fee. Again, Adams and Davis will be the Client's principal contacts for all financing matters, with Carter and Legal Assistant assisting in title, title insurance, and survey matters.

Parcel Sales and Ground Leasing—Fixed Fee. *Team Members: Carter and Legal Assistant.* For office parcel sales and ground leases ultimately consummated with a purchaser or ground lessee, services will be charged per transaction based on a Fixed Fee of $[_] per sale or ground lease. Services rendered in any transaction not ultimately consummated will be billed at the Discounted Hourly Rate, but the total invoice for an unconsummated transaction will not exceed the specified Fixed Fee.

Carter will be the Client's principal contact for all office parcel ground leases and sales. Legal Assistant will help prepare sale and, where practical, leasing documentation.

Office Build-to-Suit Leases. *Team Member: Carter.* For original build-to-suit leases ultimately executed by an office park tenant, services will be provided at a Unit Fee per transaction of [ ]¢ per rentable square foot of the leased space. Rentable square footage will be determined according to the rentable area figure (calculated by the prevailing BOMA method) specified in the controlling lease.

Services rendered in preparing lease amendments, lease renewals, lease assignments, and subleases will be billed at the Discounted Hourly Rate. Services rendered in transactions not ultimately consummated will also be billed at the Discounted Hourly Rate, but the total invoice will not exceed the Unit Fee that would have been owing had the lease been executed.

Carter will be the Client's contact for all office park build-to-suit leasing.

Construction Contracting

As indicated in our original presentation to the Client, Ellis of our office will be the project team member responsible for all construction contracting matters. This includes review of all AIA and AGC agreements and handling of all lien, contracting, and subcontracting matters. Charges for services rendered in connection with construction contracting matters will be billed at the Discounted Hourly Fee.

Other Matters

Matters not outlined in this proposal will be handled by project team members where appropriate. In other instances—for example, environmental matters, state regulatory matters, and *ad valorem* tax assessment contests arising in connection with the Project—we will propose other members of the firm whose experience may be more appropriate. Charges for services rendered in connection with such matters will be billed at the Discounted Hourly Rate. (In the case of lawyers other than project team members, the Discounted Hourly Rate will be a reduced hourly rate proportionately comparable to the discounts reflected on the attached Exhibit A.)

Assumptions on Which This Proposal Is Based

The proposal we have set forth rests on several assumptions. These assumptions reflect our collective experience with alternative fee structures. The pertinent assumptions are as follows:

1. The quoted structures are based on our mutual agreement that [law firm] will represent the Client throughout the Project's development. The fee structures we have outlined depend on our having confidence that our project team will be able to devote significant time to Project matters.
2. The quoted structures also depend on our ability to work together to lay the groundwork for the Client's systematic representation. Specifically, we believe that cost-effective representation in developing the Project will require (i) that we have a regular chance to review sales and leasing strategy with the Client and to assemble some objective guidance to direct us as we go forward, and (ii) that we work together with the Client—and with any brokers involved on the Client's behalf—to establish a uniform approach to the contemplated sales and leasing transactions. We should work together, for example, to establish objective criteria on some of the most important legal and business points (cost pass-throughs, indemnities, and environmental provisions, for example) that we will face in every sale and lease transaction. As for point (ii), our experience recommends that we spend some time putting together a form of term sheet that proactively seeks to resolve key legal and business points in every deal even before lawyers become involved.
3. We must have regular, personal contact with you and your business people. Communication is important; personal contact and personal relationships help cultivate good communication. Accordingly, we should commit ourselves together at the outset to regular, face-to-face meetings with a specified core of Project team members.
4. Availability of individual lawyers will occasionally require that we staff matters with other firm members of comparable experience and repute. From time to time, circumstances will dictate that a Project team member be unavailable. In these unusual instances, we may—subject to your approving our selection—temporarily substitute another firm member of comparable experience and repute. If the particular matter is subject to billing on a Fixed Fee or Unit Fee basis, the substitution will not affect the total fee. If the particular matter is subject to billing on a Discounted Hourly Fee or Maximum Fee basis, the services of the replacement lawyer will be billed at a reduced hourly rate proportionately comparable to the discounts reflected on the attached <u>Exhibit A</u>. In no instance will a substitution affect the specified fee cap under a Maximum Fee.
5. No matter what the governing fee structure, statements of account will include an additional charge for disbursements made for photocopying, outgoing telecopies, local and overnight delivery charges, travel outside Grace County, and charges for computerized legal research on outside databases

for which we are charged access fees. We constantly strive to keep these charges at or below market rates. The Client will not be billed for a number of other items that, in our experience, other law firms routinely charge for—including library services, administrative computer time, domestic long-distance telephone calls, ordinary postage, secretarial straight time, or equipment overhead.

Some Final Thoughts on Risk
Finally, experience has taught us that our efforts in transactional matters like this depend in large part on the tendencies and negotiating posture of our Client. The rates quoted in this proposal are based on data from many different transactions we have handled, as well as on the contact we have had with the Client over the past several months. Nonetheless, unforeseen situations will arise.

We expect to assume the risk of many of these situations. If truly unusual circumstances were to arise, though, we would notify you of those circumstances in writing as soon as possible, and would then trust that such instances would be handled in good faith and in a spirit of fairness both by the Client and by [law firm].

<u>**Exhibit A**</u>
Project Team Hourly Services Rates

Team Member	Standard Hourly Rate	Discounted Hourly Rate
Adams		
Brown		
Carter		
Davis		
Ellis		
Fox		
Legal Assistant		

NOTE: Hourly services rates are subject to change annually as of ____.

Exhibit 13

Uniform Task-Based Management System*

Overview

The Uniform Task-Based Management System is a budgeting and billing system designed to provide clients and law firms with meaningful cost information on legal services. The first major area of legal work addressed by the System is litigation. This document presents the Litigation Code Set and definitions developed by a tripartite effort of the American Bar Association Section of Litigation, the American Corporate Counsel Association, and a group of major corporate clients and law firms coordinated and supported by Price Waterhouse LLP. The System enables lawyers to budget and bill by litigation task, aiding client and counsel in understanding, managing and conducting litigations. It is intended to cover all contested matters, including judicial litigation, binding arbitration and regulatory/administrative proceedings.

The goals of the Litigation Code Set are to:

1. Enable client and counsel to plan and maintain an efficient and effective litigation.
2. Facilitate effective communication of the tasks and costs of litigation and any variations from the expected or the norm.
3. Provide each client and law firm with a means to individually understand and compare the cost of litigation, for greater efficiency and as a foundation for use of alternative billing arrangements.
4. Harmonize the various task-based efforts to ease widespread adoption of a simple, concise and flexible task-based management approach.

The Litigation Code Set is grouped into five basic phases or aspects of a litigation, plus expenses:

- Case Assessment, Development and Administration
- Pre-Trial Pleadings and Motions
- Discovery

---

* This document has not been approved by either the Council of the Section of Litigation or the ABA House of Delegates and, therefore, does not constitute official Section or ABA policy. This book and any forms and agreements herein are intended for educational and informational purposes only.

- Trial Preparation and Trial
- Appeal

Each phase consists of a number of tasks, such as Written Discovery, Document Production and Depositions. In total, 29 tasks comprise the Litigation Code Set.

All work associated with a task should be included in that category. For example, Depositions (L330) encompasses all time spent on depositions including deposition notices and subpoenas, deposition scheduling and logistics, planning for and preparing to take the depositions, and any deposition summaries. The intent is to provide a true picture of the labor cost of each task. (Out-of-pocket expenses, such as witness fees and transcripts, are treated under Expenses.)

For each billing period, the time charges by attorney or other professional are recorded by task. The System also allows for accumulation of the time charges, providing a comparison at a glance of the cost of each phase and each task for the month, for a specified budget period, and cumulatively for the litigation. Expenses can also be reported on a period and cumulative basis on request.

For those desiring, a budget can be prepared for each phase, and within that, each task for the whole case and/or by quarter (or other time period). The monthly bills would then compare that month's bill and the cumulative total with the budget.

The System also provides a long form for those wishing to capture the task-based work by specific activity. The activity identifies how the work is being performed (e.g., communicating in firm, researching, drafting, and reviewing). For this purpose, any or all of eleven activities can be used with any or all of the tasks of the System.

The intention of the Litigation Code Set is to minimize multiple interpretation and options for coding time. It is recognized that not all litigation work will fit neatly in a particular category. Work can overlap tasks, categories may be imprecise, or time may be expended on the truly unusual. Users should categorize the work to its primary purpose. Definitions are provided for guidance. Where uncertainty envelops substantial or repeating work, it is best for client and counsel to agree in advance on the category to be used.

It is important to understand the considerations that went into the development of consensus around a single standard. Therefore, following the definitions is a discussion of the background of this initiative, and the guiding principles and assumptions that informed the development of the Litigation Code Set.

Background, Definitions, Principles, and Assumptions

A. Background: The Need

Until the past decade, law firm billing was relatively straightforward. Firms billed their clients in greater or lesser detail, typically providing in-depth narrative descriptions of the tasks and processes underlying their hourly charges. In issuing bills and providing the underlying detail, each firm followed its own approach. In recent years, however, clients have become more focused in requesting additional billing information of their outside law firms, or asking that billing data be presented in specific formats. In some instances companies have wanted to analyze their costs along various dimensions to provide benchmarks for the more systematic evaluation of legal costs. In others, there has been a desire to develop a database of costs on discrete legal activities. Most of these efforts have been part of an overriding effort to manage corporate legal expenses more effectively by considering inside/outside mix, comparative performance by attorneys and firms of discrete activities, and other aspects of cost.

As a consequence of these trends, many law firms' administrative organizations are faced with the challenge of complying with a broad range of specialized billing requirements —each unique to one client. This situation already poses a substantial burden to a number of firms. As law departments expand their use of "task-based billing" and broaden their efforts to manage outside legal costs more effectively, firms face the prospect of overwhelming complexity as they strive to comply with the various requests of dozens of clients. Ultimately, law departments will be burdened by different law firm coding structures and billing systems.

Aside from "need" narrowly defined, there are significant benefits to both law firms and law departments in terms of administrative simplicity and cost reduction to be gained from standardization. In addition, the development of standard billing categories will permit introduction of billing based on Electronic Data Interchange (EDI). This technology is already widely employed in other areas of commercial activity. By linking the suppliers and consumers of legal services, EDI offers the prospect of "paperless billing" and a new level of administrative and cost efficiency.

The need, therefore, is for a uniform set of billing and task categories - detailed describers of legal work that would be acceptable to both law departments and firms, and that could prevail across American industry, financial services, and commerce. Analogous to the role of standards in other industries and functions, standard billing categories would make it possible for law firms to standardize their billing systems and for corporate law departments to work with their law firms in a far more efficient manner than prevails today.

B. Definitions

Following is a glossary of terms that will be helpful in understanding the Litigation Code Set.

Coding set/coding scheme. A list of alphanumeric codes and corresponding terms and definitions that describe the universe of legal work in a given area.

Field. A specific, defined category of information that is entered into an information management system or database.

Area of law. A label describing a discrete area of legal practice or specialization. Examples include real estate, intellectual property, and environmental. The group envisions that each department and firm would define these as appropriate.

Matter type. This designation describes or categorizes a specific legal services project for purposes of analysis and reporting. In most cases, matter types are more detailed than areas of law, though for some specialized areas of law there may not be a more detailed listing of matter types. For example, a litigation case might be categorized as an antitrust, environmental, international trade, etc., matter.

Phase. This is the highest-level category in the coding hierarchy. For litigation, examples are Pre-Trial Pleadings and Motions, and Discovery. Phases represent collections of tasks and activities that occur largely in a sequence during the course of a case or matter. Typically, timekeepers will enter time at the task level, but phase-level time entry will also be permitted. This might be useful in smaller cases in which task-level detail is not needed.

Task. This represents more detail under the phase level in the coding hierarchy. All tasks roll up to a phase. Tasks are intended to capture tangible work product produced or business results achieved. Tasks (or phases) are one of two fields to be recorded by timekeepers.

Activity. This is a code intended to describe how work is accomplished (e.g., communicating, drafting). Activities represent the second field to be recorded (optionally) by timekeepers.

C. Principles

The following list of guiding principles has informed the development of the Litigation Code Set. These principles emerged throughout a number of meetings held during 1994 and early 1995 and discussions of the various options under consideration.

Support of business objectives and processes. A primary, recurring consideration has been to focus on the purposes and uses of standardized coding. A number of business objectives and administrative processes that should be supported by the coding scheme were identified. These include planning and budgeting, time entry, status monitoring and reporting, bill preparation, electronic transmission of bills and payments, bill review and analysis, development of alternative financial arrangements, and practice and profitability analysis. Consistently, the group returned to the question: How are we going to use the data to be tracked?

Simplicity. The Litigation Code Set must be simple and straightforward to ensure widespread use. This includes limiting the total number of codes to a manageable level. The team consistently returned to this fundamental principle as it explored a wide range of alternatives, which frequently suggested more detailed coding schemes than we developed.

Ease of use. In practice, the Litigation Code Set should be easy for attorneys and other staff to use. The codes should be intuitive and capture an attorney's logical work processes.

Suitability for all size offices. Currently-available technology will be an important asset in the efficient implementation of the coding scheme. Still, the group has assumed that not all law offices will have advanced technology solutions at their disposal to facilitate the capture and analysis of time. For the coding scheme to be used widely, law offices and attorneys must be able to use the codes in a manual fashion.

Avoidance of multiple interpretation. A primary concern with some existing code sets is the multitude of ways in which a single time entry can be coded, depending on individual interpretation. The codes should minimize opportunity for multiple interpretation.

Flexibility to track both tasks and activities. Some team members value the ability to analyze work according to categories of activity (e.g., communication, drafting) in addition to task (e.g., deposition). Others emphasize the importance of tracking and analyzing the level of effort expended to complete tangible work product, segments of a case, or defined business objectives. For this group, simply using task codes is sufficient. As an option for those seeking activity detail, the System permits firms and departments to code activities separately from tasks.

D. Assumptions

Following is a list of assumptions that guided the development of the Litigation Code Set. These assumptions were drawn from discussions during initiative meetings.

The fundamental coding structure has two fields: tasks (embedded within phases) and activities. Whereas task codes track time associated with tangible work product accomplished (e.g., motion, deposition), activity codes describe how the work was performed (e.g., communicating, drafting). Not every law office will wish to use activity codes, but the coding scheme is flexible to accommodate those who value activity analysis. The team discussed the desirability of coding at a lower level below task. In the interest of simplicity, though, this additional detail may be captured using narrative rather than adding more levels. This experience was borne out by those team members with direct experience coding time.

Narrative time entries will be retained. The Litigation Code Set does not envision the elimination of narrative descriptions of time entries. However, the need for this level of detail may be reduced in smaller, less complex cases with successful adoption and implementation of the coding scheme.

For purposes of tracking and analysis, a matter type code distinguishes among various types of matters. A matter type designation can be used to distinguish among various types of litigation and to identify alternative dispute resolution matters.

The Litigation Code Set focuses on meeting the requirements of most matters. The Litigation Code Set has been designed to be suitable for use with most matters. However, there may exist cases of such size, complexity, or other unique characteristics that the codes are not sufficiently detailed. The objective was to develop a code set for the vast majority of cases and to provide a framework in which more detailed codes can be developed for extraordinary cases.

Litigation Code Set and Definitions

The Litigation Code Set is intended for use in all adversarial matters including litigation, binding arbitrations, and regulatory/administrative proceedings. The following definitions elaborate on the intended scope of each phase and task and should guide attorneys in coding time.

L100 **Case Assessment, Development and Administration.** Focuses on the case as a whole, the "forest" rather than the "trees."

L110 **Fact Investigation/Development.** All actions to investigate and understand the facts of a matter. Covers interviews of client personnel and potential witnesses, review of documents to learn the facts of the case (but not for document production, L320), work with an investigator, and all related communications and correspondence.

L120 **Analysis/Strategy.** The thinking, strategizing, and planning for a case, including discussions, writing, and meetings on case strategy. Also includes initial legal research for case assessment purposes and legal research for developing a basic case strategy. Most legal research will be under the primary task for which the research is conducted, such as research for a summary judgment motion (L240). Once concrete trial preparation begins, use L440 for trial strategy and planning.

L130 **Experts/Consultants.** Identifying and interviewing experts and consultants (testifying or non-testifying), working with them, and developing expert reports. Does not include preparing for expert depositions (L340) or trial (L420).

L140 **Document/File Management.** A narrowly defined task that comprises only the processes of creating and populating document and other databases or filing systems. Includes the planning, design, and overall management of this process. Work of outside vendors in building litigation support databases should be an Expense.

L150 **Budgeting.** Covers developing, negotiating, and revising the budget for a matter.

L160 **Settlement/Non-Binding ADR.** All activities directed specifically to settlement. Encompasses planning for and participating in settlement discussions, conferences, and hearings and implementing a settlement. Covers pursuing and participating in mediation and other non-binding Alternative Dispute Resolution (ADR) procedures. Also includes pre-litigation demand letters and ensuing discussions.

B170 Fee/Employment Objections. Review of and objections to the employment and fee applications of others.

B180 Avoidance Action Analysis. Review of potential avoiding actions under Sections 544-549 of the Code to determine whether adversary proceedings are warranted.

L190 Other Case Assessment, Development and Administration. Time not attributable to any other overall task. Specific use in a given matter often may be predetermined jointly by the client and law firm.

L200 Pre-Trial Pleadings and Motions. Covers all pleadings and all pretrial motions and procedures other than discovery.

L210 Pleadings. Developing (researching, drafting, editing, filing) and reviewing complaints, answers, counterclaims and third-party complaints. Also embraces motions directed at pleadings such as motions to dismiss, motions to strike, and jurisdictional motions.

L220 Preliminary Injunctions/Provisional Remedies. Developing and discussing strategy for these remedies, preparing motions, affidavits and briefs, reviewing opponent's papers, preparing for and attending court hearing, preparing witnesses for the hearing, and effectuating the remedy.

L230 Court-Mandated Conferences. Preparing for and attending hearings and conferences required by court order or procedural rules (including Rule 16 sessions) other than settlement conferences (L160).

L240 Dispositive Motions. Developing and discussing strategy for or opposing motions for judgment on the pleadings and motions for complete or partial summary judgment, preparing papers, reviewing opponent's papers, defensive motions (e.g., motion to strike affidavit testimony, Rule 56(f) motion), and preparing for and attending the hearing.

L250 Other Written Motions/Submissions. Developing, responding to, and arguing all motions other than dispositive (L240), pleadings (L210), and discovery (L350), such as motions to consolidate, to bifurcate, to remand, to stay, to compel arbitration, for MDL treatment and for change of venue.

L260 Class-Action Certification and Notice. Proceedings unique to class-action litigation and derivative suits such as class certification and notice.

L300 Discovery. Includes all work pertaining to discovery according to court or agency rules.

L310 Written Discovery. Developing, responding to, objecting to, and negotiating interrogatories and requests to admit. Includes mandatory meet-and-confer sessions. Also covers mandatory written disclosures as under Rule 26(a).

L320 Document Production. Developing, responding to, objecting to, and negotiating document requests, including the mandatory meet-and-confer sessions to resolve objections. Includes identifying documents for production, reviewing documents for privilege, effecting production, and preparing requested privilege lists. (While a general review of documents produced by other parties falls under this task, coding and entering produced documents into a data base is Task L140 and reviewing documents primarily to understand the facts is Task L110.)

L330 Depositions. All work concerning depositions, including determining the deponents and the timing and sequence of depositions, preparing deposition notices and subpoenas, communicating with opposing or other party's counsel on scheduling and logistics, planning for and preparing to take the depositions, discussing deposition strategy, preparing witnesses, reviewing documents for deposition preparation, attending depositions, and drafting any deposition summaries.

L340 Expert Discovery. Same as L330, but for expert witnesses.

L350 **Discovery Motions.** Developing, responding to, and arguing all motions that arise out of the discovery process. Includes the protective order process.

L390 **Other Discovery.** Less frequently used forms of discovery, such as medical examinations and on-site inspections.

L400 **Trial Preparation and Trial.** Commences when lawyer and client determine that trial is sufficiently likely and imminent so that the process of actually preparing for trial begins. It continues through the trial and post-trial proceedings in the trial court. Once trial begins, lawyers who appear in court presumptively should bill their court time to L450 Trial and Hearing Attendance. Litigation work outside the courtroom during this phase (e.g., evenings, weekends and the time of other attorneys and support personnel) should continue to be classified using other L400 Tasks.

L410 **Fact Witnesses.** Preparing for examination and cross-examination of non-expert witnesses.

L420 **Expert Witnesses.** Preparing for examination and cross-examination of expert witnesses.

L430 **Written Motions/Submissions.** Developing, responding to and arguing written motions during preparation for trial and trial, such as motions in limine and motions to strike proposed evidence. Also includes developing other written pre-trial and trial filings, such as jury instructions, witness lists, proposed findings of fact and conclusions of law, and trial briefs.

L440 **Other Trial Preparation and Support.** All other time spent in preparing for and supporting a trial, including developing overall trial strategy, preparing opening and closing arguments, establishing an off-site support office, identifying documents for use at trial, preparing demonstrative materials, etc.

L450 **Trial and Hearing Attendance.** Appearing at trial, at hearings and at court-mandated conferences, including the pre-trial conferences to prepare for trial. For scheduling conferences that are denominated as "Pre-Trial

Conferences" but not directed toward conduct of the trial, use Task L230.

L460 **Post-Trial Motions and Submissions.** Developing, responding to and arguing all post-verdict matters in the trial court, such as motions for new trial or j.n.o.v., for stay pending appeal, bills of costs, and requests for attorney's fees.

L470 **Enforcement.** All work performed in enforcing and collecting judgments and asserting or addressing defenses thereto.

L500 **Appeal.** Covers all work on appeal or before a reviewing body.

L510 **Appellate Motions and Submissions.** Developing, responding to and arguing motions and other filings before a reviewing body, such as motions and other filings for stay pending appeal.

L520 **Appellate Briefs.** Preparing and reviewing appellate briefs.

L530 **Oral Argument.** Preparing for and arguing an appeal before a reviewing body.

Bankruptcy Code Set and Definitions This code set is intended for use on bankruptcy matters. Tasks relating to adversarial matters, such as preference actions, must be captured using the Litigation Code Set. The Bankruptcy Code Set is derived from the code set published by the U.S. Department of Justice, Executive Office for the United States Trustee.

B100 Administration

B110 **Case Administration.** Coordination and compliance matters, including preparation of statement of financial affairs; schedules; list of contracts; United States Trustee interim statements and operating reports; contacts with the United States Trustee; general creditor inquiries.

B120 **Asset Analysis and Recovery.** Identification and review of potential assets including causes of action and non-litigation recoveries.

B130 Asset Disposition. Sales, abandonment and transaction work related to asset disposition.

B140 Relief from Stay/Adequate Protection Proceedings. Matters relating to termination or continuation of automatic stay under 362 and motions for adequate protection.

B150 Meetings of and Communications with Creditors. Preparing for and attending the conference of creditors, the 341(a) meeting and other creditors' committee meetings.

B160 Fee/Employment Applications. Preparations of employment and fee applications for self or others; motions to establish interim procedures.

B170 Fee/Employment Objections. Review of and objections to the employment and fee applications of others.

B180 Avoidance Action Analysis. Review of potential avoiding actions under Sections 544-549 of the Code to determine whether adversary proceedings are warranted.

B185 Assumption/Rejection of Leases and Contracts. Analysis of leases and executory contracts and preparation of motions specifically to assume or reject.

B190 Other Contested Matters (excluding assumption/rejection motions). Analysis and preparation of all other motions, opposition to motions and reply memoranda in support of motions.

B195 Non-Working Travel. Non-working travel where the court reimburses at less than full hourly rates.

B200 Operations

B210 Business Operations. Issues related to debtor-in-possession operating in Chapter 11 such as employee, vendor, tenant issues and other similar problems.

B220 Employee Benefits/Pensions. Review issues such as severance, retention, 401K coverage and continuance of pension plan.

Fee Letters, Agreements, and Other Resources **263**

B230 **Financing/Cash Collections.** Matters under 361, 363 and 364 including cash collateral and secured claims; loan document analysis.

B240 **Tax Issues.** Analyses and advice regarding tax-related issues, including the preservation of net operating loss carry-forwards.

B250 **Real Estate.** Review and analysis of real estate-related matters, including purchase agreements and lease provisions (e.g., common area maintenance clauses).

B260 **Board of Directors Matters.** Preparation of materials for and attendance at Board of Directors meetings; analysis and advice regarding corporate governance issues and review and preparation of corporate documents (e.g., Articles, Bylaws, employment agreements, compensation plans, etc.).

B300 **Claims and Plan**

B310 **Claims Administration and Objections.** Specific claim inquiries; bar date motions; analyses, objections and allowances of claims.

B320 **Plan and Disclosure Statement (including Business Plan).** Formulation, presentation and confirmation; compliance with the plan confirmation order, related orders and rules; disbursement and case-closing activities, except those related to the allowance and objections to allowance of claims.

B400 **Bankruptcy-Related Advice**

B410 **General Bankruptcy Advice/Opinions.** Analysis, advice and/or opinions regarding potential bankruptcy-related issues, where no bankruptcy case has been filed.

B420 **Restructurings.** Analysis, consultation and drafting in connection with the restructuring of agreements, including financing agreements, where no bankruptcy case has been filed.

Counseling Code Set and Definitions

The Counseling Code Set is part of the broader Uniform Task-Based Management System, which also includes codes for litigation, bankruptcy and projects (including transactions and administrative filings). The Counseling Code Set provides flexibility in the Uniform Task-Based Management System. It is intended to capture time spent by attorneys in preparing and delivering general legal advice for all areas of law (e.g., tax, labor, corporate, regulatory, lobbying). The Counseling Code Set may also be used to capture time over a monthly billing period that is not otherwise attributable to a discrete matter, transaction, project or litigation. Communication between client and counsel about which code set to use at the onset of any matter is advisable.

The following definitions elaborate on the intended scope of each task and should guide attorneys in coding time.

Counseling Code Set

C100 **Fact Gathering.** This phase includes all initial inquiries, meetings and instructions, and the identification and collection of information relevant to the assignment.

C200 **Researching Law.** This phase includes all legal research tasks, including internal meetings and consultations with those with special expertise, and computer and online research.

C300 **Analysis and Advice.** This phase includes all tasks associated with analysis of both the facts and research performed (under C100 and C200) and communicating related opinions or advice to clients. Written communication, meetings, and telephone conversations during which advice is conveyed would all be captured by this phase.

C400 **Third-Party Communication.** This phase includes all discussions with third parties not otherwise covered above, such as communications with regulators or parties to contracts with the client.

Expense Code Set E100 Expenses

E101 Copying

E102 Outside printing

E103 Word processing

E104 Facsimile

E105 Telephone

E106 Online research

E107 Delivery services/messengers

E108 Postage

E109 Local travel

E110 Out-of-town travel

E111 Meals

E112 Court fees

E113 Subpoena fees

E114 Witness fees

E115 Deposition transcripts

E116 Trial transcripts

E117 Trial exhibits

E118 Litigation support vendors

E119 Experts

E120 Private investigators

E121 Arbitrators/mediators

E122 Local counsel

E123 Other professionals

E124 Other

Project Code Set   The Project Code Set includes all legal tasks performed for non-litigation matters of a similar task pattern described below. This code set can be used for transactions (e.g., real estate, securities, financings, restructurings, mergers and acquisitions), for administrative filings with federal and state agencies, and for stand-alone projects (e.g., establishing an environmental compliance program). All of these assignments share, to a large extent, the same underlying process steps.

    The Project Code Set is part of the broader Uniform Task-Based Management System, which also includes codes for litigation, bankruptcy, and counseling. The Project Code Set applies to all areas of law.

    The following definitions elaborate on the intended scope of each phase and task and should guide attorneys in coding time.

P100 **Project Administration.** Focuses on administrative aspects of the assignment, including planning, budgeting, and maintenance of documents. Covers developing, negotiating, and revising the administrative plan and the budget for a matter. Also includes developing and communicating project status reports. Time coded here is to be distinguished from strategizing about the project, which is included in the P300 code.

P200 **Fact Gathering/Due Diligence.** Includes all time spent investigating facts, obtaining documents and completing due diligence, and the preparation of related reports and reviews with clients.

Also includes coordination with third parties (including other counsel) in connection with fact investigation, interviews of client and non-client personnel, document review performed for purposes of identifying, understanding and analyzing facts and issues, and all related communications and correspondence.

P210 **Corporate Review.** This task includes all fact investigation/due diligence from a corporate perspective, such as structural reviews, material contract reviews, SEC filing reviews, financing document reviews, and industry information reviews.

P220 **Tax.** This task includes all steps involved in conducting fact investigation/due diligence from a tax perspective.

P230 **Environmental.** This task includes all fact investigation/due diligence from an environmental perspective.

P240 **Real and Personal Property.** This task includes all fact investigation/due diligence from a real and personal property perspective.

P250 **Employee/Labor.** This task includes all fact investigation/due diligence from an employee benefits and labor perspective.

P260 **Intellectual Property.** This task includes all fact investigation/due diligence from an intellectual property (patent, trademarks, copyrights) perspective.

P270 **Regulatory Reviews.** This task includes fact investigation/due diligence from a regulatory perspective not covered elsewhere. Includes review of agency filings (e.g., FCC, FTC, and State analogues) by a party to or the subject of the transaction or project. Also includes consumer credit reviews.

P280 Other. This task includes all fact investigation/due diligence not captured more specifically in the P200 codes set forth above.

P300 Structure/Strategy/Analysis. Includes time spent in planning the approach to the deal or project. Tasks include all analysis performed for purposes of developing and reassessing the strategy for the project or transaction, and all steps taken to develop a written outline or description of the structure of a transaction or the strategy for a matter (e.g., term sheets) throughout the life of the matter.

P400 Initial Document Preparation/Filing. This phase includes all tasks undertaken to prepare transaction documents and opinions prior to their being sent to non-client third parties. Also includes all tasks undertaken to file documents (including regulatory filings). All related communications with the client and review of client-generated transaction documentation should be coded here.

P500 Negotiation/Revision/Responses. This phase includes conducting negotiations, revising the initial (P400) transaction documentation as a result of such negotiations, attendance at meetings, and responses thereto (including communications with clients with respect thereto). The review of documents received from non-client third parties should also be coded here.

P600 Completion/Closing. This phase includes all tasks related to transaction pre-closing and closing, project completion or filing acceptance, such as attendance at closing.

P700 Post-Completion/Post-Closing. This phase includes all post-completion or post-closing tasks such as amendments to final documentation and resolution of post-closing issues. Also includes all implementation tasks (e.g., funds held in escrow) and preparation of closing binders (i.e., primarily clerical actions). Would not typically include total or significant restructuring, which should be considered a new assignment.

P800 Maintenance and Renewal. This phase includes all tasks related to subsequent maintenance and renewal requirements under the terms of the transaction or project such as monitoring of lease agreements, routine waivers and coordination of UCC requirements.

Disclaimer & Copyright

NOTE: This document contains the Counseling Code Set, the Project Code Set, and the Bankruptcy Code Set developed by a sponsoring group of major corporate law departments and law firms coordinated and supported by Price Waterhouse LLP.

The authors hereby grant permission to use the codes and related definitions, in whole or in part, on a non-exclusive, royalty-free basis. In addition, this document may be freely reproduced and distributed in any electronic or hardcopy medium, on a non-exclusive, royalty-free basis, provided that this reproduction and distribution are not for profit, and that this title page is included in its entirety.

November 30, 1995

A copy of this document may be received by calling the ABA Membership Services Department at (312) 988-5522 and asking for Product Code #: 5310202 or by using the online order form. An $8.00 fee will be charged to cover copying and postage, plus $2.00 for handling ($10.00 for non-ABA members, plus $3.95 for handling).

Exhibit 14

Probate Case Plan for Joe Bereaved

Overview

Probate is a legal proceeding that is at its heart very simple. Someone has died, and his or her property has to be transferred according to the established legal procedures. If the person left a will, then the property will generally be distributed and transferred to survivors according to its terms. This is called a testate probate proceeding. If no will is found, then the laws of Oklahoma provide how the property is to be distributed and transferred. This is called an intestate probate proceeding.

Probate is often misunderstood and often mischaracterized. One term you will hear is *estate*. Since the deceased cannot now own property, all of the property is now owned by the estate. Debts, too, are now owed by the estate. The estate can act only through a court-appointed individual, known as the Personal Representative or Executor, in the same way that a corporation can only through one of its officers.

Sometimes only a few family members are interested in a probate proceeding. In other cases, others may have an interest in the proceeding. These could include people who claim the deceased owes them money (creditors), business partners of the deceased, or people who are not family members but who have been named to receive something under the will. If a certain amount of money is involved, then estate taxes may be owed to the state or federal taxing authorities. Estate tax returns must be prepared and filed whether or not estate taxes are owed. There will usually be income tax returns required for both the state and federal taxing authorities.

It is helpful to view the probate case as a series of steps that must be taken in proper order so that the probate judge can be assured that everyone who might have an interest has either been heard or at least has been given an opportunity to be heard. Then the judge will issue a Final Decree distributing all of the property to those entitled to it. Those people are called the heirs.

This case plan outlines these steps and the estimated charges if everything proceeds normally and there are no contested matters. If, however, someone makes a claim and we (or in some cases others) do not agree, the judge may have to make a determination as to who is correct. This is called a contested matter and will both increase the expenses of probate and extend the length of time that the probate takes to be completed. A contested matter might occur over many things, such as whether a creditor's claim is valid, whether a will itself is validly executed, the value of certain property, or even the identity of the heirs. Fortunately, most probate proceedings are uncontested, and many minor disagreements can be ultimately resolved by simple investigation and agreement without having to have a contested hearing before the judge.

**Time Line for Joe Bereaved's
Testate Case (with a Last Will and Testament)**

Probate Activity	Approximate time frame	Attorney fees paid from trust account at this stage
Get all information required from the client, perform initial legal analysis, prepare petition, orders, notices and other documents required for initial filings.	Within 15-30 days after being retained *and* receiving all required information from client.	
Client reviews and executes all documents to complete preparation for filing.		
Attorney appears in court to file pleadings, obtain hearing date from judge and arrange for publication. Notices are mailed and copies sent to client.	Hearing date will be scheduled not less than 10 days nor more than 30 from filing of petition	$500 (Court Costs approximately $____)
Attorney prepares Affidavit of Mailing Notices, Order Admitting Will to Probate, Letters Testamentary, Oath of Executor, and Notice to Creditors and obtains Publisher's Affidavit.		
Attorney appears at court with Executor for hearing on admission of Will to Probate and Appointment of Executor. Judge makes determination on Executor's Bond. Signed documents are filed with the court clerk and certified copies are obtained. Arrangements are made for publication of Notice to Creditors.		$350

Probate Activity	Approximate time frame	Attorney fees paid from trust account at this stage
	Deadline for Presentment Date of Claims by Creditors is two months from the Notice Date. The notice must be published for two consecutive weeks.	
Lawyer mails notice to all known creditors, obtains publisher's affidavit, files with Internal Revenue Service to obtain Tax I.D. Number.		$125, plus mailing costs
Executor works with lawyer to prepare a complete inventory of the estate, with the value of all assets of the estate.	The final General Inventory is due to the lawyer's office one month after the Executor's appointment and due to the court two months after the appointment.	
General Inventory filed with the court.		$500, plus $ _____ filing fee
Up to six tax returns must be prepared, including Federal Estate Tax Return, Oklahoma Estate Tax Return, Oklahoma Estate Income Tax Return, Federal Estate Income Tax Return, Oklahoma Personal Income Tax Return, and Federal Personal Income Tax Return.	The time to complete this may vary depending on the complexity of the estate and the ease or difficulty of obtaining all records, but generally should be completed within 30-45 days.	Attorney to prepare returns for fee of $_____ or Third Party to prepare and bill for returns.
Executor meets with lawyer to approve and sign all tax returns, which are then submitted to the proper authorities.		

Probate Activity	Approximate time frame	Attorney fees paid from trust account at this stage
Taxing authorities must approve returns and prepare documents.	This stage is out of our hands once we file the returns. But generally we can expect an Oklahoma Tax Release within ___ to ___ days and a Federal Estate Tax Closing Letter within ___ to ___ days.	
Lawyer prepares Final Account, the Petition for Hearing Final Account, Determination of Heirs, and Distribution Order Setting Hearing and Notice of Hearing.	5-10 days after tax releases are received.	
Executor meets with lawyer to approve and sign Final Account and Petition for Hearing Final Account.		
Lawyer appears at court to file Final Account, Petition, and Notice, and to obtain judge's signature on Order. Arrangements are made for publication of Notice of Hearing Final Account.		$375
Lawyer mails the Notices of Hearing the Final Account.	The Notice must be mailed at least 10 days before hearing and published for two consecutive weeks. The hearing should take place not less than 20 days after filing Petition for Final Account.	
Lawyer prepares Affidavit of Mailing Notices and Order Allowing Final Account. Attorney obtains Publisher's Affidavit.		

Probate Activity	Approximate time frame	Attorney fees paid from trust account at this stage
Lawyer and Executor appear in Court for Hearing on Final Account. After hearing, lawyer files the Order Allowing Final Account and other pleadings.		$175
Certified copy of Final Order is filed in each county where real property interests exist.		$___ for each additional county, plus $___ filing fees
Receipts prepared for distribution of personal property, final informational letter goes out to all heirs.		
Executor returns receipts.		
Lawyer presents receipts to the court and obtains Final Discharge approval from the judge.		$125

Other Matters

You acknowledge that we have made no promises or guarantees regarding the outcome of your case.

Contested matters will be charged at our hourly rate. Hourly charges may also be made for excessive telephone calls or office visits.

The case plan is acceptable by both lawyer and client.

_____
Lawyer

_____
Client

_____
Date

Index

A

The ABA Guide to Lawyer Trust Accounts, 26
Accounting. *See* Cost accounting
Accounting firms, legal services offered by, 18
Accounting software, 108–109
Advanced fee payments, 24, 26, 144
The Advance Fee Payment Dilemma: Should Payments Be Deposited to the Client Trust Account or to the General Office Account?, 26
Advertising by lawyers, 13, 59
Agreements. *See* Fee agreements; Legal representation agreements
American Bar Association (ABA), 13. *See also* Model Rules of Professional Conduct
   Ethics 2000 Commission, 27, 28
   Law Practice Management Section, 20, 21
   Section of Legal Education and Admissions to the Bar, 13
American Corporate Counsel Association, 113
Amicus, 114
Arbitration, 25, 27
Are Advance Fee Payments Clients' Funds?, 26
The Art of Talking So That People Will Listen, 86
Assurance, 95, 98

Attorney-client relationship, 11, 86, 87
Audits, client, 170–172
Availability-only retainer, 143–144

B

Backward integration, 17
Bates & O'Steen v. State Bar of Arizona, impact of, 32–33
Billing, 53. *See also* Billing methods; Hourly billing; Value billing
   accounting systems, 108–109
   charge recording, 106–108
   collection policy, 111–112
   communication with, 85–104
   disputed bills, 110
   processes, 105–112
   profitability and, 82–83
   relative-value method of billing, 140–141
   statement preparation, 109
   statement transmittal, 110
   technology and, 33, 105–117
Billing adjustments, 73
Billing lawyer level, accounting for costs at, 77
Billing methods. *See also* specific methods
   arguments in favor of change, 156–161
   changing, 153–154
   corporate counsel concerns about change, 162–163

evaluating results of, 169–174
impediments to change, 161–162
Billing software, 107
Blended hourly rate, 47, 130–132
Brand name services, 39, 56, 59–60
Brand names in legal profession, 16
Budgeting, technology and, 112–113

C

Case management software, 108
Case plan, 64–65
    client goals and expectations, 122–124
    development of, 119–124
    elements of, 121–122
    preparation of, 122
    probate (sample), 269–273
    reasons for, 119–121
Client audits, 170–172
Client level, accounting for costs at, 77
Clients. *See also* Client satisfaction; Communication with client
    attitudes of, 11–12
    intake, 45
    interviewing, 43, 44
    key, 46
    management of, 45
    objectives of, 122–124
    perceptions of value, 1–3, 34, 37, 152
    questionnaires to, 172, 173
    relationship with, 94
    sophistication of, 17–18, 61–64
    technology perceptions, 9–11
Client satisfaction, 94, 172
    price and, 99–100
    value and, 100
    worksheet, 102

Cobb, William C., 20, 37
Collection policy, 111–112
Commodity services, 39, 56, 57–59
Communication with client
    barriers to, 89–90
    billing and, 85–104
    of billing changes, 154
    effective, 85–87
    elements of, 87–89
    of fee agreement, 27, 93, 165
    feedback, 93
    improving, 93–95
    setting for, 90
    substance of, 91–95
    of value, 103
Competitive position, and value curve, 41–42
Competitive position profile, 37, 38
Computer systems. *See* Technology
Conflicts of interest, 16, 28, 29
Consolidation in legal profession, 13, 15–16
Contingency fee
    hourly rate plus contingency, 133–134
    hourly rates with, if business is acquired (sample), 199–203
    if litigation required (sample), 195–197
    use of, 48, 63
Contingent fee, 127–128
    advantages of, 127
    disadvantages of, 127
    fee agreements for, 24, 27
    formal agreement (sample), 185–193
    incentive for efficiency, 128
    total fee predictability, 128
    use of, 34, 82, 127–128
    value to client recognition, 128

Corporate counsel, 162–163
Corporate Representation Service, 114
Cost accounting, 72–77
   at billing lawyer level, 77
   at client level, 77
   costs determined through, 72–74
   issues in, 74
   at matter level, 77
   at practice group level, 76
Cost curve, 72
Cost pricing, 80
Costs
   closed files review and, 80–81
   cost accounting, determining through, 72–74
   event, 74, 76, 77
   hourly billing and, 33, 50–51
   money, 74, 76, 77
   overhead, 74, 76, 77
   of partners, 74
   reducing, 150
   revenue adjustment, 73, 76, 77
   service package determined by, 77–78
   task-based analysis, 78–79
   timekeeper, 73–74, 76, 77
   types of, 70, 73–74
   value and, 71
Counsel
   corporate, 162–163
   outside, 205–217
Cowles Estate Planning System, 113, 115
Criminal defense, 24, 34, 60
Critical path, 48
Critical Path Method (CPM), 79
Curran, Barbara A., 91, 95, 96

D

Demographics of legal profession, 13–14
Document assembly systems, 113–115, 116
Drucker, Peter F., 88, 89

E

The Effective Estate Planning Practice: Procedures and Strategies for a Client-Focused Business, 115
Empathy, 95, 97–98
Engagement letter. *See* Legal representation agreements
Environmental consulting firms, legal services offered by, 18
Ethical rules, 23–29
Evaluation of billing method, 169–174
Event costs, 74, 76, 77
Expectations of client, 122–124
Experiential services, 39, 56, 60–61

F

Fee agreements. *See also* Legal representation agreements
   elements of, 165–168
   ethics check on, 29
   mandatory arbitration of, 27
   negotiating, 62, 165
   written, 24, 27, 165
Fees. *See also* Contingent fee; Fee agreements; Fixed fee; Pricing; Task-based fee; Unit fee
   advance payment of, 24
   arbitration of disputes, 25
   competition in, 21
   conflict of interest and, 28, 29
   contingency, 48, 63

decreasing, 65–66
discounted, 62
golden rule of, 25–26
lodestar method of setting fees, 141–142
percentage, 135–136
predicting from closed files, 80–81
prepaid, 26
property in payment of, 24, 27–28
reasonableness of, 23–24, 25, 34
retrospective fee based on value, 137–139
setting, 112–113, 141–142
splitting, 24, 29
statutory, 142–143
transaction, 116
Fee-shifting, 34
Files
checklist for closing, 171
review of closed, 80–81, 169–170
Financial institutions, legal services offered by, 18–19
Firms. *See* Law firms
Fixed fee, 125–126
advantages of, 125–126
corporate representation service election form (sample), 225–226
disadvantages of, 126
in first-year services to emerging business (sample), 227–231
fixed fee plus hourly rate, 132–133
incentive for efficiency in, 126
in real estate development project (sample), 243–249
in representation of a bank for major collection litigation with bonus clause (sample), 219–223
retainer agreement for insurance defense cases (sample), 233–235
total fee predictability, 126
use of, 48, 60, 62, 82, 126
value to client recognition, 126
Fixed fee plus hourly rate, 132–133
Flat fee. *See* Fixed fee
Ford, Henry, 99
Free agency, 19

G

Goals of client, 122–124
Guarantees of performance, 152–153

H

Harvard Project Management, 48
HotDocs, 113
Hourly billing. *See also* Hourly rate
cost of services and, 33
costs and, 50–51
evolution of, 32–33
productivity paradox, 8–9
value and, 85
Hourly rate, 128–130. *See also* Hourly rate plus contingency
advantages of, 129
blended hourly rate, 47, 130–132
cost and, 70–71
disadvantages of, 129–130
fixed fee plus hourly rate, 132–133
formal agreement (sample), 185–193
incentive for efficiency, 130

increased for negotiations (sample), 195–197
in real estate development project (sample), 243–249
total fee predictability, 130
use of, 47, 82, 130
value to client recognition, 130
variable, 49
variations of, 51–52
Hourly rate plus contingency, 133–134
advantages of, 134
disadvantages of, 134
fee agreement if business acquired (sample), 199–203
incentive for efficiency, 134
total fee predictability, 134
use of, 134
value to client recognition, 134
How Organizations Manage What They Know, 115
How to Draft Bills Clients Rush to Pay, 94, 108

I

Inc. magazine, 96
Income compression, 14
Independent paralegals, 58
Insurance, legal, 13
International Bar Association, 13

K

Katz, Roberta, 20
Knowledge management, 115–116

L

Labor consulting firms, legal services offered by, 18
Law firms

external positioning of, 44–45
small, 32, 55–66
structure of, 43–44
Lawyer as communicator, 86–87
Legal clinics, 13, 17
Legal Fees and Representation Agreements, 165, 167
The Legal Needs of the Public, 91
Legal profession
backward integration in, 17
brand names in, 16
changes in, 7–22
client sophistication and, 17–18
consolidation in, 13, 15–16
demographics of, 13–14
free agency in, 19
future of, 20–21
income compression in, 14
incursion by other service providers, 18–19, 58
marketing and, 18
price competition in, 17
profit squeeze in, 14
Legal representation agreements, 177–249
alternative billing if business acquired (sample), 199–203
alternative fee options (sample), 181–184
corporate representation service election form (sample), 225–226
elements of, 165–168
for estate planning (sample), 237–241
fixed-fee for collection litigation (sample), 219–223
fixed-fee retainer for insurance defense cases (sample), 233–235

formal agreement (sample), 185–193
increased hourly rate for negotiations (sample), 195–197
for real estate development (sample), 243–249
standard fee letter (sample), 177–179
Legal research, 9, 116
Legal services. *See also* Service package; Value of services
accounting firms offering, 18
bargaining power of buyers of, 20
classifications of, 39, 56–61
financial institutions offering, 18–19
gross domestic product, 15
labor and environmental consulting firms offering, 18
maturing marketplace for, 15–20
model for, 95–99
pricing, 31–53, 55–66
unbundling, 11–12
Leveraging, 43–44
LEXIS/NEXIS, 116
Life, quality of, 172–174
Listening to clients, 94, 97–98
Lodestar method of setting fees, 141–142

M

Management: Tasks, Responsibilities, Practices, 88
Marketing, 18, 59
The Marketing Imagination, 98
Marketing Warfare, 1
Marketplace for legal profession
constraints on, 34
consumer clients, 61

maturing, 15–20
Maslow, Herbert, 37
Matter level, accounting for costs at, 77
Meaning, transfer of, 89
Message, 88
receiver of, 88
sender of, 87–88
Minimum-fee schedules, abolition of, 12, 32
Mobar-Pren-Hall Survey, 92
Model Rules of Professional Conduct, 97
Rule 1.5, 23–24, 25, 27, 29, 165
Rule 1.7, 28
Rule 1.8, 24, 28, 29, 167
Rule 2.1, 28
Rule 5.4, 29
Money costs, 74, 76, 77

N

Noncompetition agreements, 19
Non-refundable Retainers: Impermissible under Fiduciary Statutory and Contract Law, 26

O

Office automation. *See* Technology
Outside counsel, 205–217
Overhead costs, 74, 76, 77

P

Paralegals, 12, 58
Payment of bill, 110
Percentage fee, 135–136
Performance evaluation, 172
Peters, Dr. Tom, 20
Positioning of firm, 44–45, 151
Practice group level, accounting for costs at, 76

Prepaid fees, 26
Prepaid legal services plans, 13
Price
    client satisfaction and, 99–100
    competition in, 17, 61
Pricing
    Bates, impact of, 32–33
    historical influences on, 31–37
    internal determination of, 45–46
    legal services, 31–53, 55–66
    limits on, 36–37
    marketplace constraints on, 34
    structure, 64–65
    value curve and, 42–43
Probate case plan (sample), 269–273
Productivity paradox, 8
Professional discount, 62
Profitability, 14
    analysis of, 172
    billing and, 82–83
    market forces and, 66
    raising value of service enhancing, 149–150
    reducing cost per unit of service enhancing, 150
    value billing and, 148–149
Profitability pyramid, 75
Program Evaluation and Review Technique (PERT), 79
Project management, 46–48
Project plan, 48
ProLaw, 114
Property, received in payment of fees, 24, 27–28
Pro se representation, 11, 20
Pure retainer, 143–144

Q

Questionnaire to client, 172, 173

R

Rate adjustments, 73
Realization, 43, 148, 149
Realization rate, 148
Reasonableness of fees, 34
    ethics codes requirements, 23–24, 25
    factors determining, 23–24
Receiver of message, 88
Relative-value method of billing, 140–141
Reliability, 95, 97
Representation agreements. *See* Legal representation agreements
Research, legal, 9, 116
Retainer
    availability-only, 143–144
    as deposit against future services, 145–146
    fixed-fee agreement for insurance defense (sample), 233–235
Retrospective fee based on value, 137–139
Revenue adjustment costs, 73, 76, 77
Reverse contingency fee, 48
Right-to-call retainer, 143–144
Robinson, Charles F., 20, 21

S

Satisfaction. *See* Client satisfaction
Securities and Exchange Commission Rule 10b-5, 28
Seize the Future: Forecasting and Influencing the Future of the Legal Profession, 21
Self-assessment checklist, 67–70
Sender of message, 87–88
Service Management, 98

Service package, 100
  adding value to, 101–103
  costs in, 77–78
  perception of, 101
  preparing and pricing, 101–103
Should Prepaid Fees Be Put in a Trust Account?, 26
Small-firms, pricing legal services by, 32, 55–66
Solo practitioners, pricing legal services by, 32, 55–66
Statements
  preparation of, 109
  transmittal of, 110
Statutory fee system, 142–143
Substantive systems, 113–115

T

Tangibility, 95, 98–99
Task-based fee, 113, 136–137
  advantages of, 136
  disadvantages of, 136–137
  incentive for efficiency, 137
  total fee predictability, 137
  use of, 137
  UTBMC billing codes, 113, 251–268
  value to client recognition, 137
Technology, 151
  billing and, 105–117
  budgeting and, 112–113
  clients' understandings about, 9–11
  collaborative, 116–117
  cost sharing, 116
  document assembly systems, 113–115, 116
  fee-setting and, 112–113
  knowledge management, 115–116
  legal profession changes with, 8–9, 12
  substantive systems, 113–115
Texas Unauthorized Practice of Law Committee, 19
Timekeeper costs, 73–74, 76, 77
Timeline, 48
Timeliness, 95, 96–97
TimeMatters, 114
Time-rate billing. *See* Hourly rate
Time records
  determination of costs and, 70
  recording, 106–108
Transaction fees, 116
Transaction plan
  client goals and expectations, 122–124
  development of, 119–124
  elements of, 121–122
  preparation of, 122
  reasons for, 119–121
Transforming the Law: Essays on Technology, Justice and the Legal Marketplace, 21
TREAT, 95
Trust account, fees prepaid to, 26

U

Unauthorized practice of law, 19
Unbundling Legal Services: A Guide to Delivering Services à la Carte, 11
Uncertainties, 80, 81
Uniform Task-Based Management System (UTBMS) billing codes, 113, 251–268
Unique services, 39, 56, 60–61
Unit fee, 139–140
  advantages of, 139
  disadvantages of, 139

incentive for efficiency, 140
in real estate development project (sample), 243–249
total fee predictability, 140
use of, 139
value to client recognition, 140

V

Value billing, 22
  implementing, 147–164
  objective of, 148
  profitability and, 148–149
  strategies for profitable, 149–151
Value curve, 37–50, 72
  applications of, 40–41
  client management and intake, 45
  competitive position and, 41–42
  external positioning of firm and, 44–45
  implications of, 41–44
  importance of, 48–49
  internal determination of pricing and, 45–46
  interpreting, 39
  law firm structure and, 43–44
  legal services classifications, 39, 56–61
  multiple curves, 49–50
  position on, 151–153
  by practice area, 50
  price and, 42–43
  project management and, 46–48
  using, 44–48
Value of services. *See also* Value billing
  adding to service package, 101–103
  client satisfaction and, 100
  clients' perceptions of, 1–3, 34, 37, 152
  communicating to clients, 103
  cost and, 71
  focus on, 35–37
  increasing, 149–150
  retrospective fee based on, 137–139
  sources of, 3–5
Variables, 80, 81

W

Westlaw, 116
Word, 113
WordPerfect, 113
Work product, quality of, 150, 172–174
Write-off adjustments, 73

About the Editors

JIM CALLOWAY
Jim Calloway is a lawyer who currently serves as the director of the Oklahoma Bar Association Management Assistance Program. He received his J.D. from the University of Oklahoma, where he was named to the Oklahoma Law Review.

Mr. Calloway is a member of the American Bar Association, where he serves on the ABA TECHSHOW® Board. He is an active member of the ABA Law Practice Management Section and is on its Practice Management Advisors Committee. He is also an active member of the ABA's General Practice, Solo and Small Firm Section, where he serves as Technology Chair for the Solo and Small Firm Division and serves on the Web site committee for the National Association of Bar Executives. As a part of his duties with the OBA, he manages the OBA-NET, the official online service of the Oklahoma Bar. He has made numerous presentations on law office management, legal technology, ethics, and legal business operations. He also manages the annual OBA Solo and Small Firm Conference. Before taking his present position with the OBA, he was in private practice for approximately sixteen years in south Oklahoma City and Norman. He is a former president of the Cleveland County, Oklahoma Bar Association. He is a member of the Oklahoma City PC Users Group and, back in the pre-Internet era, ran a computer bulletin board for lawyers and those wishing to discuss legal issues called the Barrister's Club BBS.

Mr. Calloway has been a featured speaker at many prominent legal technology and legal management conferences. He has also spoken at bar association meetings in several states. His articles have been published in *Lawyers Weekly USA*, *Law Practice Management*, *LLRX.com* and *GPSolo*, as well as the *Oklahoma Bar Association Journal*.

MARK A. ROBERTSON
Mark A. Robertson is a lawyer with the law firm of Robertson & Williams in Oklahoma City. His practice is focused on corporate and securities law. He received his B.A. degree from DePauw University and his J.D. from the University of Oklahoma College of Law. He also attended the University of Edinburgh, where he studied international law.

Mr. Robertson is a member of the Oklahoma County, Oklahoma, and American Bar Associations. He is currently Vice Chair of the ABA Law Practice Management Section and a Fellow of the College of Law Practice Management. He has been on the Editorial Board and served as the articles editor and the columns editor for *Law Practice Management,* published by the ABA Law Practice Management

Section, and presently serves on the Publishing Board for the Law Practice Management Section.

Mr. Robertson is a frequent lecturer (preferably in warm climates) on small and mid-sized law firm marketing and management issues and is a contributing author on law firm management topics to various national, state, and local bar association publications.

About the Diskette

The accompanying diskette contains the text of each of the exhibits in the Appendix, as well as Exhibits 7-1, 7-2, 7-4, 13-1, and 13-2 from *Winning Alternatives to the Billable Hour: Strategies That Work*, Second Edition. The file are in Microsoft® Word 97 format.

For additional information about the files on the diskette, please open and read the "readme.doc" on the diskette.

NOTE: The set of files on the disk may only be used on a single computer or moved and used on another computer. Under no circumstance may the set of files be used on more than one computer at one time. If you are interested in obtaining a license to use the set of files on a local network, please contact: Director, Copyrights and Contracts, American Bar Association, 750 N. Lake Shore Drive, Chicago, IL 60611, (312) 988-6101.

CUSTOMER COMMENT FORM

Title of Book: _____

We've tried to make this publication as useful, accurate, and readable as possible. Please take 5 minutes to tell us if we succeeded. Your comments and suggestions will help us improve our publications. Thank you!

1. How did you acquire this publication:

- ☐ by mail order
- ☐ by phone order
- ☐ other: (describe) _____
- ☐ at a meeting/convention
- ☐ at a bookstore
- ☐ as a gift
- ☐ don't know

Please rate this publication as follows:

	Excellent	Good	Fair	Poor	Not Applicable
Readability: Was the book easy to read and understand?	☐	☐	☐	☐	☐
Examples/Cases: Were they helpful, practical? Were there enough?	☐	☐	☐	☐	☐
Content: Did the book meet your expectations? Did it cover the subject adequately?	☐	☐	☐	☐	☐
Organization and clarity: Was the sequence of text logical? Was it easy to find what you wanted to know?	☐	☐	☐	☐	☐
Illustrations/forms/checklists: Were they clear and useful? Were there enough?	☐	☐	☐	☐	☐
Physical attractiveness: What did you think of the appearance of the publication (typesetting, printing, etc.)?	☐	☐	☐	☐	☐

Would you recommend this book to another attorney/administrator? ☐ Yes ☐ No

How could this publication be improved? What else would you like to see in it?
_____
_____
_____

Do you have other comments or suggestions? _____
_____
_____

Name _____
Firm/Company _____
Address _____
City/State/Zip _____
Phone _____
Firm Size: _____ Area of specialization: _____

We appreciate your time and help.

Fold

BUSINESS REPLY MAIL
FIRST CLASS   PERMIT NO. 16471   CHICAGO, ILLINOIS

POSTAGE WILL BE PAID BY ADDRESSEE

NO POSTAGE
NECESSARY
IF MAILED
IN THE
UNITED STATES

AMERICAN BAR ASSOCIATION
PPM, 8th FLOOR
750 N. LAKE SHORE DRIVE
CHICAGO, ILLINOIS 60611-9851

Fold

ABA Law Practice Management Section

Membership Application

Access to all these information resources and discounts – for just $3.33 a month!

Membership dues are just $40 a year – just $3.33 a month.
You probably spend more on your general business magazines and newspapers.
But they can't help you succeed in building and managing your practice
like a membership in the ABA Law Practice Management Section.
Make a small investment in success. Join today!

☑ **Yes!** I want to join the **ABA Section of Law Practice Management Section** and gain access to information helping me add more clients, retain and expand business with current clients, and run my law practice more efficiently and competitively!

Check the dues that apply to you:
❏ $40 for ABA members ❏ $5 for ABA Law Student Division members

Choose your method of payment:
❏ Check enclosed (make payable to American Bar Association)
❏ Bill me
❏ Charge to my: ❏ VISA® ❏ MASTERCARD® ❏ AMEX®

Card No.: _____ Exp. Date: _____

Signature: _____ Date: _____

ABA I.D.*: _____
(* *Please note: Membership in ABA is a prerequisite to enroll in ABA Sections.*)

Name: _____

Firm/Organization: _____

Address: _____

City/State/ZIP: _____

Telephone No.: _____ Fax No.: _____

Primary Email Address: _____

Get Ahead.

Save time by Faxing or Phoning!
▶ Fax your application to: (312) 988-5820
▶ Join by phone if using a credit card: (800) 285-2221 (ABA1)
▶ Email us for more information at: lpm@abanet.org
▶ Check us out on the Internet: http://www.abanet.org/lpm

750 N. LAKE SHORE DRIVE
CHICAGO, IL 60611
PHONE: (312) 988-5619
FAX: (312) 988-5820
Email: lpm@abanet.org

I understand that Section dues include a $24 basic subscription to *Law Practice Management*; this subscription charge is not deductible from the dues and additional subscriptions are not available at this rate. Membership dues in the American Bar Association are not deductible as charitable contributions for income tax purposes. However, such dues may be deductible as a business expense.